Doing Basic Math with Manipulatives

ideal school supply

Gr. 1-3
ID3091

BASED ON NCTM STANDARDS

Make MATH Make SENSE!

- Counting
- Addition
- Subtraction
- Multiplication
- Division
- Time & Money
- Measurement
- Geometry & Spatial Sense
- Data, Probability, & Graphing
- Patterns & Algebra Thinking
- Problem Solving

Judy Goodnow
Shirley Hoogeboom

GRADES
1 - 3

with Manipulatives

By
Judy Goodnow & Shirley Hoogeboom

Art Director: Sara Mordecai
Cover Illustration & Page Design: Sara Mordecai
Production Design: Piper Brown
Text Illustrations: George Riemann
Project Coordinator: Judy Crum

ISBN: 1-56451-323-8
Doing Basic Math with Manipulatives, Grades 1 - 3
©2000 Ideal School Supply
A Division of Instructional Fair Group, Inc.
A Tribune Education Company
3195 Wilson Drive NW, Grand Rapids, MI 49544 • USA
Duke Street, Wisbech, Cambs, PE13 2AE • UK

All Rights Reserved • Printed in USA

Limited Reproduction Permission: Permission to duplicate these materials is limited to the teacher or parent for whom they are purchased. Reproduction for an entire school or school district is unlawful and strictly prohibited.

Table of Contents

Chart of Math Skills and Manipulatives	iv
Notes to the Teacher	v
Solutions	ix
Blackline Master: Tangrams	xiv
Blackline Master: Hundred Number Chart	xv
Blackline Master: Geoboard Arrays	xvi
Counters: Introduction	1
Counters: Explorations 1-12	5
Linking Cubes: Introduction	17
Linking Cubes: Explorations 1-12	21
Dominoes: Introduction	33
Dominoes: Explorations 1-12	37
Learning Clocks: Introduction	49
Learning Clocks: Explorations 1-12	53
Play Money: Introduction	65
Play Money: Explorations 1-12	69
Colored Cubes: Introduction	81
Colored Cubes: Explorations 1-12	85
Base Ten Blocks: Introduction	97
Base Ten Blocks: Explorations 1-12	101
Hundred Number Chart: Introduction	113
Hundred Number Chart: Explorations 1-12	117
Fraction Pieces: Introduction	129
Fraction Pieces: Explorations 1-12	133
Attribute Blocks: Introduction	145
Attribute Blocks: Explorations 1-12	149
Pattern Blocks: Introduction	161
Pattern Blocks: Explorations 1-12	165
Tangrams: Introduction	177
Tangrams: Explorations 1-12	181
Geoboards: Introduction	193
Geoboards: Explorations 1-12	197
3-D Shapes: Introduction	209
3-D Shapes: Explorations 1-12	213

Math Skills & Manipulatives

	Counters	Linking Cubes	Dominoes	Learning Clocks	Play Money	Colored Cubes	Base Ten Blocks	Fraction Pieces	Attribute Pieces	Pattern Blocks	Tangrams	Geoboards	Hundred Number Chart	3-D Shapes
Sorting & Classifying									X	X				X
Counting & Numbers	X	X	X	X	X	X	X	X					X	
Operations	X	X	X		X	X	X						X	
Place Value		X			X		X						X	
Fractions						X		X		X	X	X		
Patterns & Algebra Thinking	X	X	X			X			X	X		X		
Geometry & Spatial Sense									X	X	X	X		X
Data, Probability, & Graphing			X		X			X						
Measurement		X		X	X					X	X	X		X
Problem Solving & Reasoning	X	X	X	X	X	X	X	X	X	X	X	X	X	X

Notes to the Teacher

What Is *Doing Basic Math With Manipulatives?*

This series of teacher resource books is designed to show how children can develop basic math skills, using a variety of the most versatile and valuable math manipulatives. The series consists of two books:

Doing Basic Math With Manipulatives, Grades 1-3
Doing Basic Math With Manipulatives, Grades 4-6

Each book is a resource of math explorations for 14 different manipulatives. The 168 explorations contained in each book can be integrated into any existing math curriculum.

What Are Manipulatives?

Manipulatives are materials that children can touch, hold, and move around. These materials are concrete models that represent powerful mathematical ideas. As the students interact with the materials, they begin to develop an understanding of these mathematical ideas and build basic skills. The materials may be objects from the students' environment, such as money or clocks; or the materials may have been designed to teach concepts, such as fraction pieces or base ten blocks. It is important that the materials represent mathematical concepts in a clear and simple way.

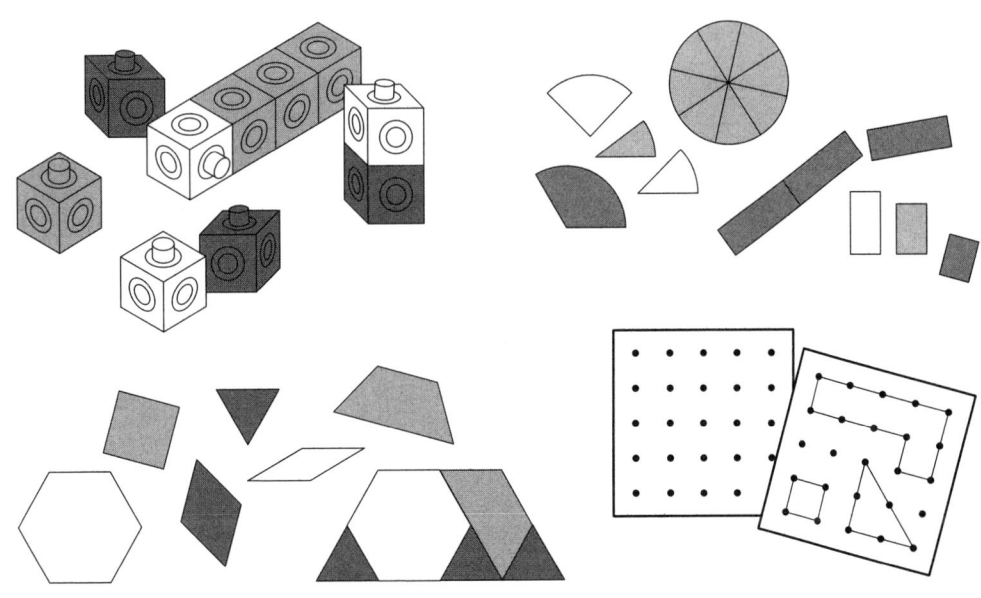

Why Use Manipulatives to Teach Basic Math?

A great deal of research has been carried out to determine the effect of manipulatives in the mathematics classroom. This research has shown a definite improvement in scores of students who used manipulatives, as opposed to those who did not. There is a strong belief among many teachers that these materials help to build a firm foundation of mathematical concepts.

Learning theorists suggest that using manipulatives helps students make the connection between the math in their daily lives and the abstract world of math symbols and concepts. But it is crucial that teachers help students bridge the gap between the concrete objects and the abstract mathematical symbols.

One important way of bridging the gap is by talking about what is happening as the children work with the manipulatives. Children clarify their thinking as they describe what they are doing and why they are doing it. It is useful for the children to hear what other children are thinking as they use the concrete objects. It gives them new ways to think about the process, and it may just help them define their own thinking. You can think of this process of moving from concrete to abstract in four stages:

1. Using concrete materials, such as base ten blocks
2. Drawing pictures of the blocks
3. Talking about what they are doing
4. Making an alphanumeric representation, such as: 3 tens and 5 ones, 30 + 5 = 35

An added benefit for the teacher whose students use manipulatives is that you gain immediate feedback on how your students are grasping a lesson. You can circulate and see what an individual student or small group is doing, and get a picture of what they are thinking.

Who Should Use Manipulatives?

People often ask who benefits most from using manipulatives. It turns out that everyone does. Those students who are more able will need fewer concrete examples, but according to learning theorists, they still need this concrete stage to solidify many concepts.

You will find that students will need different amounts of time with the manipulative materials. Different children will make that connection between the concrete and the abstract at different times. It's important to allow students to proceed at their own pace. If the materials are rich, they will be beneficial for children of all ability levels. They will allow the more able students to discover patterns and relationships, expand their vocabulary, and explore new ideas.

What Are the Contents of *Doing Basic Math With Manipulatives, Grades 1-3?*

The chart on page iv shows the basic math concepts and skills, and shows which manipulatives help children develop those concepts and skills. This book is organized into 14 sections. Each section begins with an introduction to a manipulative. It lists the math concepts and skills children can develop by using the manipulative, then gives an overview of 12 explorations children can do with the manipulative. It includes suggestions for organizing materials to be used in the explorations, and also provides ideas for introducing the manipulative to the children. The introduction is followed by reproducible masters for the 12 explorations. The explorations are chosen as examples of the different kinds of activities children can do with this particular manipulative. You and the students can extend the learning of each exploration by designing similar kinds of activities.

Suggestions for Using *Doing Basic Math With Manipulatives* in Your Classroom

Select the explorations that you want to use with your students. The 12 explorations in each section are arranged according to level of difficulty, from level 1 through level 3. If you find an exploration too challenging or not challenging enough for your students, you can modify it. You can also repeat many of the explorations, by varying the content. The students may also enjoy designing extension explorations.

At the beginning of each section you will find suggestions about materials and the amount that a class or group will need for the explorations. Most of the explorations work well with an entire class, a small group, pairs of students, or individual children. They also work well in a learning center or math lab situation.

Manipulative Resources

The manipulatives used in the book can be found in the latest Ideal School Supply catalog or at your nearest educational store.

Solutions

Many problems have more than one possible answer. Some of these solutions are just samples, and children may find other correct solutions. Their answers may also be in a different order.

Counters Explorations 1-12

1   A. red   B. green   C. red
2   Answers will vary.
3   A. 4 green; 4 yellow; 8 in all   B. 6 blue; 6 red; 12 in all
4-6 Answers will vary.
7   A. 5 + 7 = 12   B. 4 + 10 + 6 = 20
8   A. 9 - 5 = 4   B. 10 - 6 = 4
9   A. 3 + 3 + 3 + 3 = 12; 4 x 3 = 12   B. 5 + 5 + 5 + 5 + 5 = 25; 5 x 5 = 25
10 A. 8, 2, 4; 8 ÷ 2 = 4   B. 8, 4, 2; 8 ÷ 4 = 2
    Extra Challenge: Answers could be 12 ÷ 2 = 6, 12 ÷ 6 = 2, 12 ÷ 3 = 4, or 12 ÷ 4 = 3
11 A. red, blue, yellow, red, yellow   B. Y R B
                                           G R Y
12 A. 4 red, 7 blue   B. 6 green, 6 yellow, 3 red
    C. 5 red, 5 blue, 2 green, 6 yellow

Linking Cubes Explorations 1-12

1   A. red, yellow   B. green, green   C. brown, white
2   1: R; 2: Y Y or G G; 3: Y Y R or G G R; 4: Y Y G G; 5: R Y Y G G
    Extra Challenge: 1, 2, 3, 4, and 5: Y Y B B B or G G B B B;
    6: B B B Y Y R or B B B G G R; 7: B B B Y Y G G; 8: B B B Y Y G G R
3   B P P P P P; B B P P P P; B B B P P P; B B B B P P; B B B B B P
    Explore Some More: B P P P P P; B B P P P P;
    B B B P P P; B B B B P P; B B B B B P; B B B B B B
4   A. 2 + 3 = 5   B. 2 + 6 = 8; 3 + 6 = 9; 2 + 3 + 6 = 11
    Mystery Train Puzzle: 3 red + 5 blue = 8 cars
5   A. 7; 2 + 5 = 7   B. 5; 7 - 2 = 5   C. 2; 7 - 5 = 2
    Mystery Train Puzzle: 4 green, 4 white; 8 - 4 = 4
6   A. 5 + 3 + 8 = 16   B.-D. 16 - 5 = 11; 16 - 3 = 13; 16 - 8 = 8
    Mystery Train Puzzle: 6 blue, 8 pink, 6 green, 6 + 8 + 6 = 20
7   A. 2; 20; 2; 22   B. 2; 20; 5; 25   C. 3; 30; 0; 30
    Mystery Puzzle: 46
8   nose = 1 cube; horns = 2 cubes; arm = 3 cubes;
    Monster is 7 cubes long; friend is 3 cubes high
9   A. 5 + 5 + 5 + 5 = 20; 4; 5; 20; 4 x 5 = 20
    B. 4 + 4 + 4 + 4 + 4 = 20; 5; 4; 20; 5 x 4 = 20
10 A. perimeter = 12 units
    Mystery Shape Puzzle: Answers will vary.
11 A. G B Y or Y G B   B. O P Bl
       Y W G   G Y W   R Y R
12 A. 12; 3; 4; 12 ÷ 3 = 4
    B. Possible answers: 12 ÷ 2 = 6; 12 ÷ 4 = 3; 12 ÷ 6 = 2
    Mystery Train Puzzle: 24-car train

Dominoes Explorations 1-12

1   A. 4-1, 5-0   B. 4-2, 3-3
    Extra Challenge: 2-6, 4-4, 3-5
2   A. 1-6   B. 2-6
3   Answers will vary.
    Mystery Domino Puzzle: 4-3
4   Examples for A/B: A. 0-2, 3-3, 2-2   B. 6-1, 3-2, 3-0
                          1-2, 1-4, 1-3   4-4, 3-1, 2-1
5   Answers will vary.
    Mystery Dominoes Puzzle: 4-6
6   Answers will vary.
    Mystery Dominoes Puzzle: 6-5
7   Other Doubles: 1-1, 3-3, 4-4, 5-5, 6-6
    Mystery Dominoes Puzzle: 2-2 + 4-4 or 1-1 + 5-5
8   1-2, 3-4, 4-5, 5-6
    Mystery Dominoes Puzzle: 3-4 + 2-3 or 1-2 + 4-5
9   A. 1-6   B. 2-5   C. 4-6   D. 1-4
10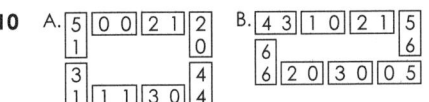
11 A. 1-6, 3-4, 3-6, 4-5, 5-6   B. 0-2, 0-4, 2-2
    C. 0-6, 1-5, 2-4, 2-6, 3-3, 3-5, 4-4, 5-5, 6-6
12 A. Rule: 4 fewer total dots; 6-2, 4-4, or 5-3
    B. Double the total number of dots; 5-5, or 6-4

Learning Clocks Explorations 1 - 12

1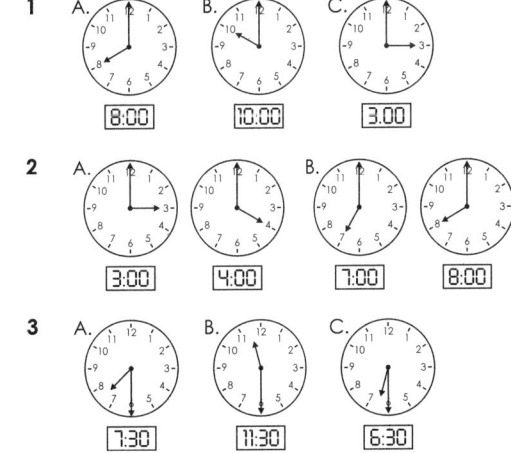

2   (see above)

3   (see above)
    Mystery Time Puzzle: 1:30 or half past one

4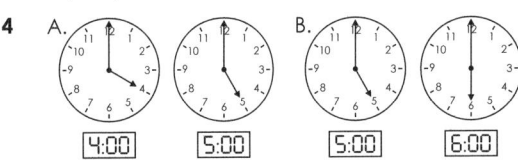
    Mystery Time Puzzle: 8:30

5   A. a. Go to Lisa's house 1:00   b. Go swimming 2:00
       c. Stop swimming 3:00
    B. a. Meet at park 10:30   b. Stop riding bikes 11:30
       c. Get to Pete's house 12:00
    Extra Challenge: 11:00

6 A. Begins 7:00, Stops 7:45   B. Begins 5:30, Stops 5:45
   C. Begins 12:30, Over 1:15
   Extra Challenge: 11:00

7 A. Get mail 4:00, Get back 4:05   B. Make pie 6:00,
   Finish pie 6:50   C. Start planting 9:30, Stop planting 10:10
   Mystery Time Puzzle: 11:15

8 Times will vary.

9 A. Get to lake 3:00   B. Go fishing 4:00   C. Stop fishing 6:00
   D. Eat dinner 7:00
   Extra Challenge: 4 hours

10 A. 8:30   B. 12:50   C. 10:25   D. 3:45

11 A. Get on tram 9:30   B. Get off at Rodeo Roundup 9:40
   C. Get on tram again 10:40   D. Get off at Ghost Town 10:45
   E. Stop at Old Mine 11:15
   They had been at the park for 1 hour and 45 minutes.

12 A. 11:00   B. 5:30   C. 5:30   D. 2:30

Play Money Explorations 1-12

1 A. 10, 15, 20, 21, 22; 22 cents
   B. 25, 35, 40, 45, 46, 47, 48; 48 cents
   Explore Some More: rhino bank; 26 cents

2 A. 1 nickel, 5 pennies   B. 1 dime, 2 nickels, 5 pennies or
   1 dime, 1 nickel, 10 pennies
   Mystery Puzzle: 1 dime, 3 nickels

3 A. Coins left: 1 dime, 4 nickels, 8 pennies; Money left:
   38 cents   B. Coins left: 4 nickels, 8 pennies; Money left:
   28 cents
   Mystery Puzzle: 2 dimes, 2 nickels

4 A. Way 1: 1 quarter, 1 dime, 1 nickel; Way 2: 3 dimes,
   2 nickels   B. Way 1: 1 half-dollar; Way 2: 2 quarters;
   Way 3: 1 quarter, 2 dimes, 1 nickel
   Mystery Coins Puzzle: 1 quarter, 1 dime, 2 nickels

5 Answers will vary.
   Mystery Puzzle: 1 dime, 1 nickel, 1 penny

6 A. 2, 6, 10, 11, and 15 cents
   B. 3, 7, 11, 12, 15, 16, and 20 cents
   Mystery Money Puzzle: 2 quarters, 1 nickel, 2 pennies
   (other solutions possible)

7 A. 85 cents; 14 cents; 85 + 14 = 99 cents; 1 dime and 4
   pennies   B. $1.27; 23 cents; $1.27 + 0.23 = $1.50; 2 dimes,
   3 pennies
   Mystery Puzzle: 66 cents (65+1), 70 cents (65+5),
   75 cents (65+10), 90 cents (65+25), $1.15 (65+50)

8 A. pizza and fruit bar or milk and cookie and fruit bar
   (total = $1.50)   B. pizza and orange and fruit drink
   or cookie and milk and fruit drink and orange
   (total = $1.80)
   Extra Challenge: orange and cookie (total = $1.10)

9 A. 1 $1, 3 quarters; total = 4   B. 1 $1, 3 quarters, 2 dimes;
   total = 6   C. 2 $1, 2 quarters; total = 4

10 A. 4 pennies, 1 nickel, 1 dime; 19 cents   B. 2 dimes; 20 cents
   Extra Challenge: $1.13

11 A. 1 quarter, 4 nickels or 4 dimes, 1 nickel
   B. 1 quarter, 3 dimes, 3 nickels, 1 penny
   C. 1 half-dollar, 5 nickels or 2 quarters, 1 dime, 3 nickels
   (other solutions possible)

12 A. $5.45   B. first person: 2 $1, 1 dime; second person:
   1 $1, 3 quarters, 3 dimes, 3 nickels

Colored Cubes Explorations 1-12

1 A. 6 yellow, 6 green; 12 total   B. 4 blue, 6 orange; 10 total
   C. 5 white, 2 brown; 7 total

2 Answers will vary.

3 A. 13; 8 + 5 = 13   B. 8 + 6 = 14; 5 + 6 = 11; 8 + 5 + 6 = 19
   Mystery Cubes Puzzle: 4 yellow, 4 blue, 8 red

4 A. 5 cubes; 9 - 4 = 5   B. 3 cubes; 10 - 7 = 3
   Mystery Cubes Puzzle: 5 cubes taken away

5 A. 8; 4 + 4 = 8; 2 x 4 = 8   B. 12; 4 + 4 + 4 = 12; 3 x 4 = 12
   Extra Challenge: 20

6 A. $\frac{2}{4}$ yellow; $\frac{2}{4}$ green   B. $\frac{1}{3}$ red; $\frac{2}{3}$ blue   C. $\frac{3}{4}$ black; $\frac{1}{4}$ orange
   Extra Challenge: $\frac{2}{6}$ cats, $\frac{4}{6}$ dogs

7 A. 14 cubes around the pool

8 A. 11 square inches

9 A. 15 cubes for 3 robots
   B. 8 robots = 40 cubes; 10 robots = 50 cubes
   Extra Challenge: 20 robots = 100 cubes

10 A. 6 rooms in first floor; 12 rooms in two floors; 18 rooms
   in three floors; volume is 18 cubic units
   B. 30 rooms in five floors; 30 cubic units
   Extra Challenge: 4 rooms

11 green/yellow is the same as yellow/green
   A. green/yellow, green/white, yellow/white
   B. BGGG, BBGG, BBBG, BBBB, GGGG
   Extra Challenge: yellow/green, yellow/red, yellow/blue,
   green/green, red/red, blue/blue (other solutions possible)

12 A. Equal chance for each color   B. Twice as likely for
   blue, but sometimes 20 trials won't show this. It may take
   many more trials.

Base Ten Blocks Explorations 1-12

1 A. 16   B. 9   C. 18

2 A. Way 1: 2 tens, 3 ones; Way 2: 1 ten, 13 ones; Way 3:
   23 ones; 23   B. Way 1: 3 tens, 4 ones; Way 2: 2 tens,
   14 ones; Way 3: 1 ten, 24 ones or 34 ones; 34

3 A. ▫ = 1, ▯ = 11, ▯▫ = 21, ▯▯ = 20, ▯ = 10,
   B. ▯ = 10, ▯▫ = 11, ▯▫▫ = 12, ▯▯ = 20, ▯▯▫ = 21, ▯▯▫▫ = 22,
   ▯▯▯ = 30, ▯▯▯▫ = 31, ▯▯▯▫▫ = 32, ▫ = 1, ▫▫ = 2
   Mystery Puzzle: 2 tens-blocks, 3 ones-blocks; 23

4 A. Before trade: 24 ones; After trade: 2 tens, 4 ones; 24
   B. Before trade: 3 tens, 2 ones; After trade: 32 ones; 32
   Mystery Puzzle: 4 tens-blocks, 4 ones-blocks; 44

5 A. 23   B. 65   C. 126

6 A. a and c; a and b   B. 33 + 25 = 58; 33 + 111 = 144;
   25 + 111 = 136; 33 + 25 + 111 = 169
   Mystery Puzzle: 1 hundreds-block, 1 tens-block, 7 ones-blocks

7 Answers will vary.
   Mystery Puzzle: 1 hundreds-block, 1 tens-block, 2 ones blocks

8 A. 12, 24, 36; 48   B. 24, 48, 72; 96

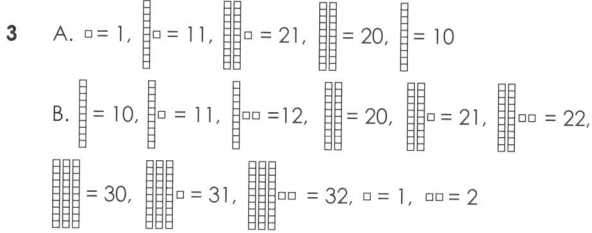

x   © Ideal School Supply • A Division of Instructional Fair Group, Inc. • Doing Basic Math with Manipulatives, Grades 1-3

9 Answers will vary.
Mystery Blocks Puzzle: 4 tens-blocks, 1 ones-block

10 12, 48; 12 + 12 + 12 + 12 = 48; 4, 12, 48; 4 x 12 = 48
Mystery Puzzle: 2 tens, 2 ones, 4 x 22 = 88

11 The blocks show 12. Division sentences may show:
12 ÷ 2; 12 ÷ 3; 12 ÷ 4
Mystery Puzzle: 2 tens, 14 ones

12 A. 1 ten, 13 ones   B. 3 tens, 21 ones   C. 1 ten, 10 ones

Hundred Number Chart Explorations 1-12

1 A. 7, 19, 30, 11, 44, 32   B. 2, 16, 40, 49, 25, 34
Mystery Number Puzzle: 10

2 A. 11, 20, 36, 55, 99   B. 65, 42, 28, 9, 90
Mystery Number Puzzle: 19

3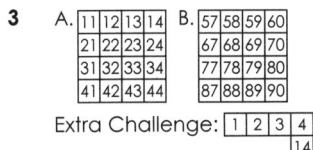
Extra Challenge:
```
1 2 3 4
    14 15 16
          26 27 28
                38 39 40
```

4 A. 27, 29, 31, 33, 35, 37, 39, 41, 43, 45, 47   B. The last digits repeat: 1, 3, 5, 7, 9, 1, 3, 5, 7, 9   C. 65, 87, 91, 93, 95, 99

5 A. 22, 24, 26, 28, 30, 32, 34, 36, 38, 40, 42, 44, 46, 48
B. The last digits repeat: 2, 4, 6, 8, 0, 2, 4, 6, 8, 0
Mystery Number Puzzle: 54

6 A. 5, 10, 15, 20, 25, 30, 35, 40, 45, 50, 55, 60, 65, 70, 75, 80, 85, 90, 95, 100   B. The last digits repeat: 5, 0, 5, 0, 5, 0, and so on.   C. 105, 110, 115, 120
Mystery Number Puzzle: 45

7 A. 8, 8, 6, 6, 10, 10   B. 1, 5, 4, 8, 2, 3
Mystery Number Puzzle: 8

8 A. 56, 64, 66, 60, 62, 100   B. 11, 53, 37, 75, 25, 26
Mystery Number Puzzle: 25

9 A. The sums of the diagonal number neighbors are the same. This pattern is true for the groups of 4 numbers and 5 numbers.

10 A. 18, 21, 24, 27, 30, 33; 48, 56, 64, 72, 80, 88; 60, 50, 40, 30, 20, 10; 66, 55, 44, 33, 22, 11; 60, 55, 50, 45, 40, 35
B. 37, 46, 56, 67, 79, 92

11 A. 25, 14, 49, 31   B. 70, 99, 7, 60
Mystery Number Puzzle: 54

12 skip-count by 3's   skip-count by 5's
(Venn diagram with numbers: 93, 96, 51, 57, 54, 99, 63, 66, 72, 69, 78, 81, 84, 87 / 15, 30, 75, 45, 90, 60 / 55, 65, 70, 80, 85, 95, 100)

Fraction Pieces Explorations 1-12

1 B. 3 equal parts of 1 whole
Mystery Fractions Puzzle: $\frac{5}{5}$

2 A. 4 equal parts of 1 whole   B. 6 equal parts of 1 whole
Mystery Fractions Puzzle: $\frac{8}{8}$

3 A. 1 of 4 equal parts   B. 1 of 3 equal parts
Explore Some More: 2 of the 3 bugs should be colored.

4 A. 2 of 5 equal parts   B. 3 of 6 equal parts
Explore Some More: 2 of the 6 spiders should be colored.

5 A. 1 of 2 equal parts   B. 2 fourths; 2 of 4 equal parts; $\frac{1}{2}$ is the same size as $\frac{2}{4}$
Explore Some More: 2 of the 4 fish should be colored.

6 A. 1 of 3 equal parts   B. 2 sixths; 2 of 6 equal parts; $\frac{1}{3}$ is the same size as $\frac{2}{6}$
Mystery Fractions Puzzle: $\frac{3}{6}$

7 A. 8 of 8 equal pieces   B. 3 fifths, 3 of 5 equal parts
C. 4 tenths, 4 of 10 equal parts
Extra Challenge: 3 of 4 robots should be colored.

8 A. 1 of 4 equal parts   B. and C. should be $\frac{2}{8}$ and $\frac{3}{12}$
Explore Some More: 2 of 8 birds should be colored.

9 A. one half, 1 of 2 equal parts   B. and C. Answers will vary.
Mystery Fractions Puzzle: $\frac{9}{12}$

10 A. 1 of 6 equal parts
B. 1 of 4 equal parts; $\frac{1}{4}$ is greater than $\frac{1}{6}$
Explore Some More: 3-7 mice should be colored.

11 A. $\frac{2}{4}$, $\frac{3}{4}$; $\frac{2}{4} + \frac{1}{4} = \frac{3}{4}$ B. $\frac{2}{5}$, $\frac{5}{5}$; $\frac{2}{5} + \frac{3}{5} = \frac{5}{5}$
C. $\frac{4}{10}$, $\frac{9}{10}$; $\frac{4}{10} + \frac{5}{10} = \frac{9}{10}$
Mystery Fractions Puzzle: $\frac{1}{4}$ and $\frac{2}{4}$

12 A. $\frac{4}{8}$; $\frac{7}{8} - \frac{3}{8} = \frac{4}{8}$ B. $\frac{3}{10}$; $\frac{8}{10} - \frac{5}{10} = \frac{3}{10}$
C. $\frac{6}{12}$; $\frac{9}{12} - \frac{3}{12} = \frac{6}{12}$
Mystery Fractions Puzzle: $\frac{8}{8}$

Attribute Blocks Explorations 1-12

1 A. 3; 10 red, 10 yellow, 10 blue   B. 5; 6 squares, 6 circles, 6 rectangles, 6 triangles, 6 hexagons   C. 15 large, 15 small

2 A. 5 large and yellow, 5 small and yellow
B. 5 large and red, 5 small and red
C. 5 large and blue, 5 small and blue
Mystery Puzzle: 5 small yellow blocks

3 Different color: large yellow and red triangles;
Different shape: large blue square, circle, hexagon, and rectangle; Different size: small blue triangle
Mystery Puzzle: large blue circle

4 Different color and shape: large yellow and blue squares, rectangles, hexagons, and triangles; Different color and size: small yellow and blue circles; Different size and shape: small red rectangle, square, triangle, and hexagon
Mystery Puzzle: small yellow circle

5 Different color, shape, and size: large red and blue circles, triangles, rectangles, and squares
Mystery Puzzle: large blue rectangle

6 The pattern is: shape, color

7 A. large thick red and blue squares, large thin yellow square, small thick yellow square, large thick yellow triangle, hexagon, circle, and rectangle
B. Color & shape: large red and blue thick circle, triangle, hexagon, rectangle; shape & thickness: large yellow thin circle, triangle, hexagon, rectangle; size & shape: small yellow thick triangle, hexagon, rectangle, circle; color & thickness: large red and blue thin square; color & size: small blue and red thick square; size & thickness: small yellow thin square
Mystery Puzzle: small thick blue square

8 A. Different size, color, and thickness: large thin red and yellow rectangles; Different color, size, and shape: large thick red and yellow circle, triangle, square, and hexagon; Different size, shape, and thickness: large thin blue circle, triangle, square, and hexagon; Different color, shape, and thickness: small thin red and yellow circle, triangle, square, and hexagon

B. Different in 4 ways: large red and yellow thin circle, hexagon, square, and triangle Mystery Puzzle: small thin yellow hexagon

9. A. large thick red triangle and large thick blue circle
B. large thick red triangle; large thin red rectangle; large thick yellow circle, square, and hexagon; large thin blue circle, square and hexagon
Mystery Puzzle: large thick red hexagon

10. A. The pattern is 2, 4

11. Rule for rows is 1 difference, rule for columns is 3 differences

12. Rule for circle A: blue, thick; rule for circle B: circles. Missing for a: small blue thick square, hexagon, triangle; large thick blue rectangle, triangle, and hexagon; Missing for b: all these circles: large yellow thick, large red thick and thin, large blue thin, small yellow thick and thin, small red thick and thin, small blue thin; Missing for c: large blue thick circle

Pattern Blocks Explorations 1-12

1. A.  B.

2. Answers will vary.
Mystery Pattern Blocks Puzzle: blue rhombus

3. A. most = 7, fewest = 2 B. most = 8, fewest = 3
Mystery Pattern Blocks Puzzle: hexagon

4. A. 4 sides and 4 corners B. 3 sides and 3 corners
C. 6 sides and 6 corners

5. A.
Mystery Pattern Blocks Puzzle: 2 yellow hexagons, 10 sides

6. A. 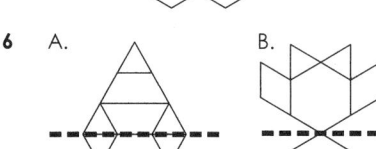 B.

7. A. green triangle B. Rule: Shapes that have 4 sides; orange square, tan rhombus, blue rhombus, and red trapezoid all fit in the circle

8. Examples:
Extra Challenge:

9. A.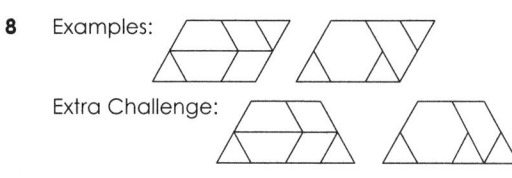

10. A. 1 bird = 4 blocks, 2 birds = 8 blocks, 3 birds = 12 blocks
B. 10 birds = 40 blocks
Extra Challenge: 20 birds = 80 blocks

11. A. 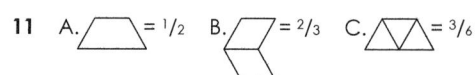 = $1/2$ B. = $2/3$ C. = $3/6$
Mystery Pattern Blocks Puzzle: 3 orange squares = $3/4$ of the whole square

12. A. 1 puff = 5 blocks, 2 puffs = 7 blocks, 3 puffs = 9 blocks
B. 10 puffs = 23 blocks
You can find the answer by multiplying the number of puffs by 2 and adding 3; $B = 2n + 3$ (B = number of blocks, n = number of puffs)

Tangram Explorations 1-12

2. Mystery Tangrams Puzzle: medium triangle

3. A. 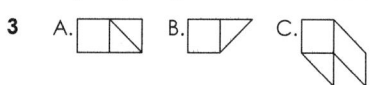 B. C.
Mystery Tangrams Puzzle: parallelogram

4. A. 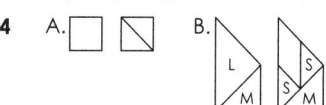 B.
Mystery Tangrams Puzzle: 2 large triangles

5. A. sides = 4, corners = 4 B.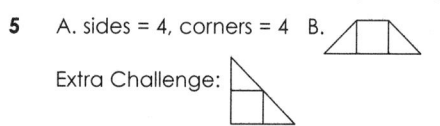
Extra Challenge:

6. A. square B. parallelogram
Mystery Tangrams Puzzle: large triangle

7. A. 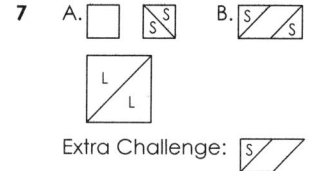 B.
Extra Challenge:

8. The shapes are reflected in the mirror, making the other half of a shape, or repeating a whole shape.

9. A. 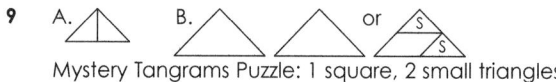 B. or
Mystery Tangrams Puzzle: 1 square, 2 small triangles

10. A. $\frac{1}{2}$ left B. $\frac{3}{4}$ left
Mystery Tangrams Puzzle: 2 small triangles

11. A. 2 units of area B. 2 units of area C. 4 units of area

12. A. 2 units of area B. 5 units of area

Geoboard Explorations 1-12

2. A. 3, 3 B. 4, 4
Extra Challenge: 5

3. A. 4, 4; 8, 8 B. 3, 3; 5, 5

4. A. 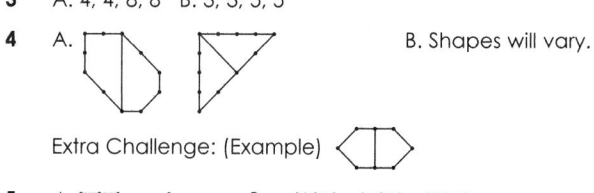 B. Shapes will vary.
Extra Challenge: (Example)

5. A. 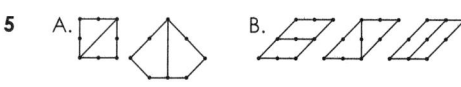 B.

6. A. 4; 2 B. 8; 4
Extra Challenge: 8

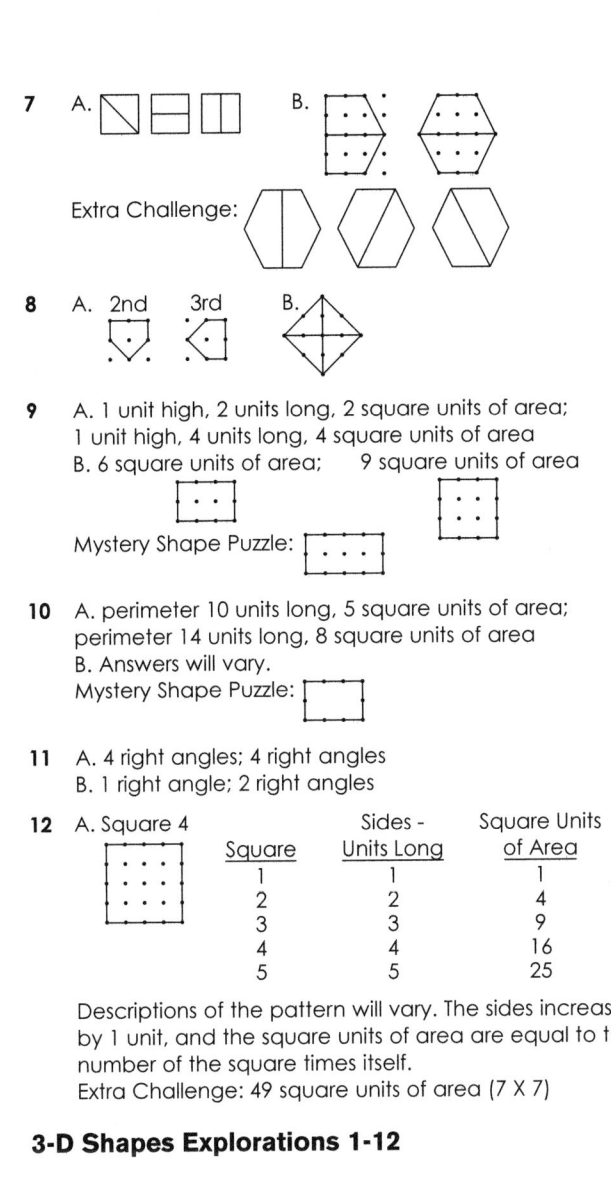

7 A. B.
Extra Challenge:

8 A. 2nd 3rd B.

9 A. 1 unit high, 2 units long, 2 square units of area;
1 unit high, 4 units long, 4 square units of area
B. 6 square units of area;   9 square units of area
Mystery Shape Puzzle:

10 A. perimeter 10 units long, 5 square units of area;
perimeter 14 units long, 8 square units of area
B. Answers will vary.
Mystery Shape Puzzle:

11 A. 4 right angles; 4 right angles
B. 1 right angle; 2 right angles

12 A. Square 4

Square	Sides - Units Long	Square Units of Area
1	1	1
2	2	4
3	3	9
4	4	16
5	5	25

Descriptions of the pattern will vary. The sides increase by 1 unit, and the square units of area are equal to the number of the square times itself.
Extra Challenge: 49 square units of area (7 X 7)

3-D Shapes Explorations 1-12

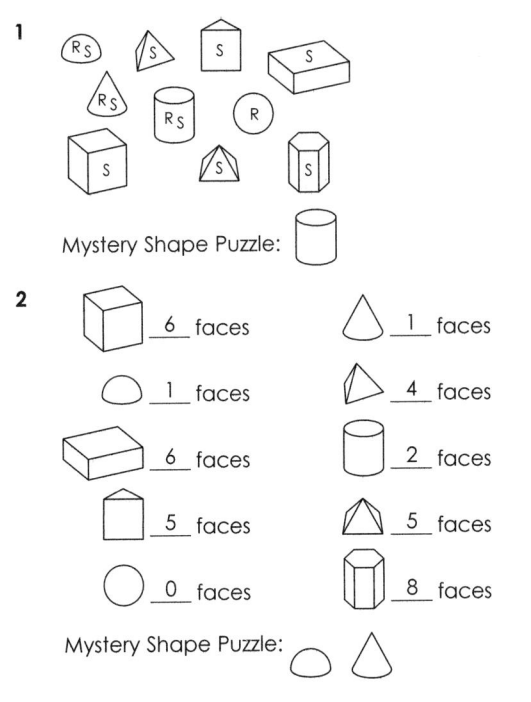

1 Mystery Shape Puzzle: cylinder

2 cube 6 faces, cone 1 faces, dome 1 faces, triangular pyramid 4 faces, rectangular prism 6 faces, cylinder 2 faces, square pyramid 5 faces, square pyramid 5 faces, sphere 0 faces, hexagonal prism 8 faces
Mystery Shape Puzzle: dome, cone

3 A.  B. 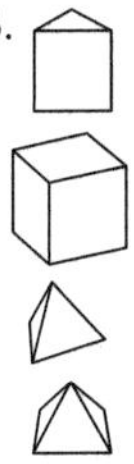 = square and tri
 = square
 = triangle
 = square

4 A. 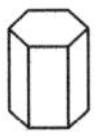 B. 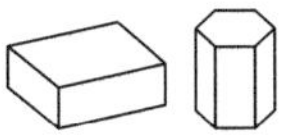
Mystery Shape Puzzle:

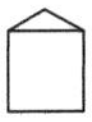

5 3-D shape left = E
Extra Challenge: B

6 Rule: □ face 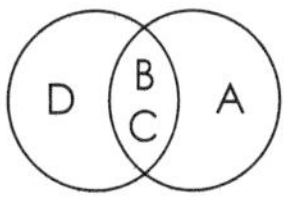   Rule: △ face
D B A / C
Mystery Shape Puzzle:

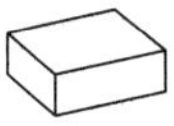

7 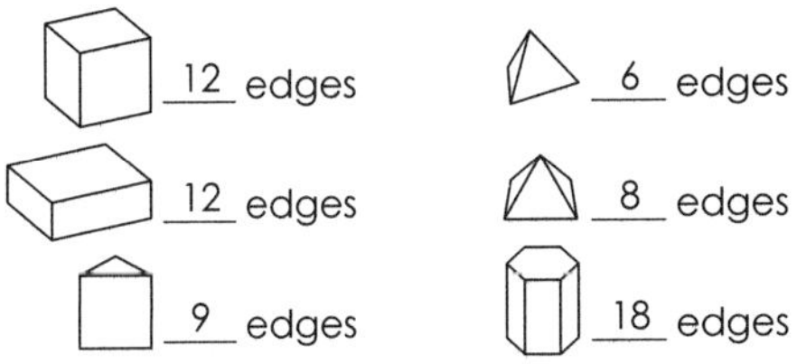 12 edges, 6 edges
12 edges, 8 edges
9 edges, 18 edges
Mystery Shape Puzzle:

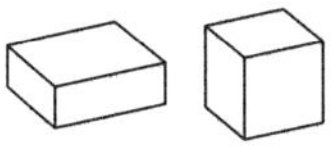

8 square pyramid

9 A. triangular pyramid B. cube

10 triangular prism 6 corners, rectangular prism 8 corners
cube 8 corners, hexagonal prism 12 corners
triangular pyramid 4 corners, square pyramid 5 corners
Mystery Shape Puzzle: square pyramid

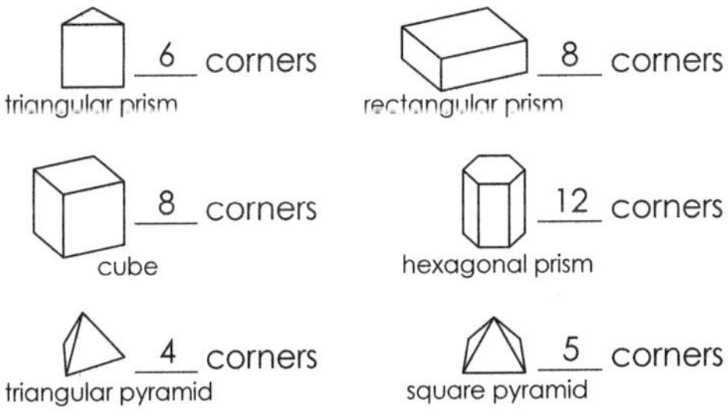

11 A. cylinder B. cone C. cube D. triangular prism and square pyramid

12 3-D shape left = H
Extra Challenge: E

xiii

Tangram Shapes

xiv

Hundred Number Chart

1	2	3	4	5	6	7	8	9	10
11	12	13	14	15	16	17	18	19	20
21	22	23	24	25	26	27	28	29	30
31	32	33	34	35	36	37	38	39	40
41	42	43	44	45	46	47	48	49	50
51	52	53	54	55	56	57	58	59	60
61	62	63	64	65	66	67	68	69	70
71	72	73	74	75	76	77	78	79	80
81	82	83	84	85	86	87	88	89	90
91	92	93	94	95	96	97	98	99	100

Geoboards

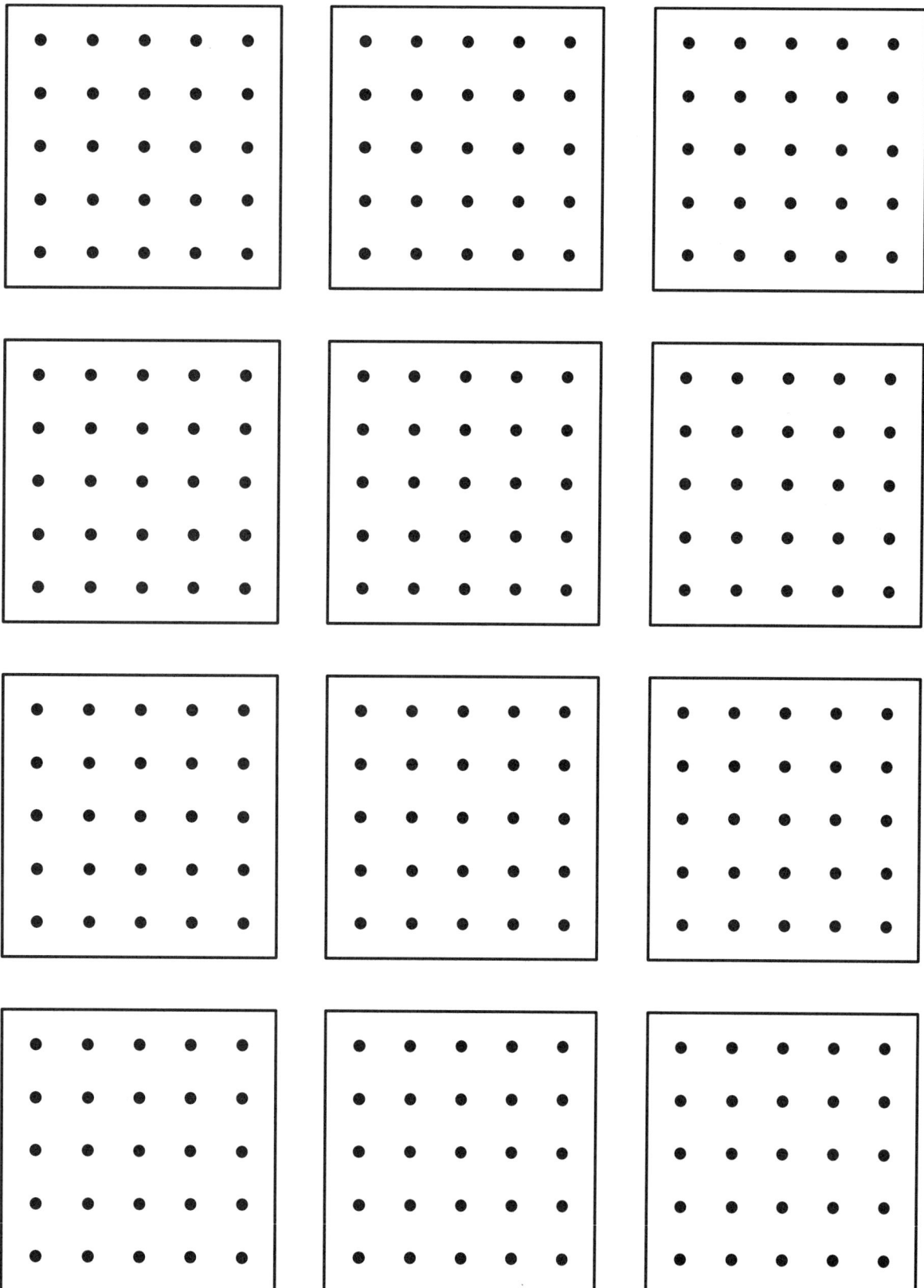

xvi © Ideal School Supply • A Division of Instructional Fair Group, Inc. • Doing Basic Math with Manipulatives, Grades 1-3

Counters

Counters help students develop these concepts and skills:

Patterns and Algebra Thinking
- Identify and extend color patterns
- Use algebra thinking to solve problems

Numbers and Operations
- Count and show numbers
- Build mental pictures of numbers
- Compare numbers: the same as, different than, more than, fewer than
- Find how many more than, fewer than
- Act out addition stories; write addition sentences
- Act out subtraction stories; write subtraction sentences
- Use repeated addition to show multiplication
- Use equal groups to show division

Problem Solving
- Use logical reasoning to solve problems
- Act out story problems with counters

What Are Counters?

You can use a variety of materials as counters. Some of the most commonly used counters are small plastic animals such as bears, cats, and frogs. These animals usually come in at least the four primary colors: green, blue, yellow, and red. We have used these four colors in the explorations. You can extend the activities if you have additional colors.

Why Use Counters?

For young children, counters can provide a concrete model for counting and showing numbers in a way that creates important mental pictures for them. Many children need these concrete experiences to help them link number meaning to numerals and to the operations of addition, subtraction, multiplication, and division. Using counters such as animal counters also allows these experiences to be put into story settings that are fun and enjoyable. Solving story problems with the counters also encourages children to create their own stories that involve numbers. It is important to help them make the link between numbers of animal counters and the abstract symbols we use to represent those numbers and operations.

Exploring Math With Counters

Following are descriptions of 12 explorations that children can do with the counters, and the concepts and skills they will be developing. Reproducible masters for the explorations are given on pages 5-16. Many of these explorations end by having the children create their own patterns or stories.

1 Identify and extend color patterns
The children line up counters to match the colors shown. They look for a pattern and show the color that comes next.

2 Count and show numbers
The children put a given number of counters on the picture of a house. Then they put more counters on the house, count their counters, and write the number.

3 Show the same number as a given number; count how many in all
The children put a given number of counters on the picture of a bus. Then they put the same number of counters of a second color on the bus. They count to see how many they have in all.

4 Show a different number than a given number; count how many in all
The children put a given number of counters on the picture of a pool. Then they put a different number of counters of a second color in the pool. They count to see how many there are in all.

5 Compare groups; find how many more there are of one color than the other
The children put a given number of counters on the picture of a beach. Then they put more counters of a second color on the beach. They compare the groups and find how many more there are of one color than the other.

6 Compare groups; find how many fewer there are of one color than the other
The children put a given number of counters on the picture of a boat. Then they put fewer counters of a second color on the boat. They compare the groups and find how many fewer there are of one color than the other.

7 Act out addition stories; write addition sentences
The children put together two groups of counters, and then three groups of counters. They write an addition sentence to show each story.

8 Act out subtraction stories; write subtraction sentences
The children count out a group of counters. Then they take away some of the counters and find how many are left. They write a subtraction sentence to show each story.

9 Use repeated addition to show multiplication
The children make groups of counters. Each group has the same number of counters in it. They add up the groups and write an addition sentence. Then they write a multiplication sentence to show the same story.

10 Use equal groups to show division
The children begin with a number of counters. Then they put the counters into groups, with each group having the same number of counters in it. They write a division sentence to show their work.

11 Use logical reasoning to solve problems
The children read stories about animals waiting in line and sitting in rows. They use clues and logical thinking to figure out where each animal is standing or sitting. They can move the counters around as they use the information from each clue.

12 Use algebra thinking to solve problems
The children are given a total number of animals in a group. Then they use clues and algebra thinking to figure out how many animals there are of each color in the group.

Organizing for Counters Explorations

Counters explorations can be used effectively with the whole class. Have students work in groups of two to three sharing materials. Give each group 40 counters – 10 each of 4 colors. Working in pairs or small groups will encourage children to discuss their thinking and develop problem-solving skills together.

Counters explorations can also be used effectively in centers. Each student or pair of students will need 10 counters of each of 4 colors, or 40 counters. Package each set of counters separately in a plastic bag or container.

Introducing Counters

Let the children begin by just exploring the counters–sorting them by color, putting them into groups, and making up stories about the animals. When the children are ready, have them act out a story with the counters.

Camping Trip

The animals are going camping. Six yellow animals get into a car, 4 red animals get into a van, and 8 green animals get into another van.

Then ask these questions:

How many yellow animals are there?
How many red animals are there?
How many green animals are there?
Are there more yellow or green animals?
Are there fewer red or yellow animals?
How many animals are there in all?
How many yellow and red animals are there in all?
What is another way we can count the animals?

Name: _____

Time for a Parade!

Counters
1

Use: counters

- The animals are lining up for the parade!
  Match the color of each bear with a counter.
  Look for a pattern.

A. (red) (blue) (red) (blue) (red) (blue) (red)

What color comes next? _____

B. (green) (yellow) (green) (yellow) (green) (yellow) (green)

What color comes next? _____

C. (red) (green) (green) (red) (green) (green) (red)

What color comes next? _____

- **Explore Some More**
  Make your own patterns. Use 4 red counters,
  4 yellow counters, and 4 green counters.

Animals at Home

Name: _____

Counters

Use: counters

- Act out each story with the counters.

A. There are 2 yellow animals at home.
Then more yellow animals come home.

How many yellow animals are at home? ____

B. There are 3 red animals at home.
Then more red animals come home.

How many red animals are at home? ____

- **Explore Some More**
Use green counters. Make up a story about green animals at home.

On the Bus

Name: _____

Counters

3

Use: counters

• Act out each story with the counters.

A. There are 4 green animals on the bus. Then the same number of yellow animals get on the bus.

How many green animals? _____

How many yellow animals? _____

How many animals in all? _____

B. There are 6 blue animals on the bus. Then the same number of red animals get on the bus.

How many blue animals? _____

How many red animals? _____

How many animals in all? _____

• **Explore Some More**
Use red, blue, and green counters. Make up your own story about animals on the bus.

At the Pool

Name: _____

Counters

4

Use: counters

• Act out each story with the counters.

A. There are 5 blue animals in the pool.
Then a different number of green animals
jump into the pool.

How many blue animals are in the pool? _____

How many green animals get in the pool? _____

How many animals in all are in the pool? _____

B. There are 8 yellow animals in the pool.
Then a different number of red animals
jump into the pool.

How many yellow animals are in the pool? _____

How many red animals get in the pool? _____

How many animals in all are in the pool? _____

• **Explore Some More**
Use the counters. Make up your own
story about animals in the pool.

At the Beach

Name: _____

Counters

5

Use: counters

• Act out each story with the counters.

A. There are 4 blue animals on the beach.
There are more red animals than blue animals on the beach.

How many blue animals are on the beach? ____

How many red animals are on the beach? ____

There are ____ more ____ animals than ____ animals.

B. There are 7 yellow animals on the beach.
There are more green animals than yellow animals on the beach.

How many yellow animals are on the beach? ____

How many green animals are on the beach? ____

There are ____ more ____ animals than ____ animals.

• **Explore Some More**
Use the counters. Make up your own story about animals on the beach.

On the Boat

Name: _____

Counters
6

Use: counters

• Act out each story with the counters.

A. There are 8 blue animals on the boat.
There are fewer red animals than blue animals on the boat.

How many blue animals are on the boat? ____

How many red animals are on the boat? ____

There are ____ fewer ____ animals than ____ animals.

B. There are 9 green animals on the boat.
There are fewer yellow animals than green animals on the boat.

How many green animals are on the boat? ____

How many yellow animals are on the boat? ____

There are ____ fewer ____ animals than ____ animals.

• **Explore Some More**
Use the counters. Make up your own story about animals on the boat.

Parties

Name: _____

Counters
7

Use: counters

• Act out each story with the counters.

A. There are 5 yellow animals and
7 red animals at Dog's party.

How many yellow animals? _____ How many red? _____

How many animals are there in all? _____

Write an addition sentence to show the story.

_____ + _____ = _____

B. There are 4 blue animals, 10 green animals,
and 6 yellow animals at Owl's party.

How many blue animals? _____ green? _____ yellow? _____

How many animals are there in all? _____

Write an addition sentence to show the story.

_____ + _____ + _____ = _____

• **Explore Some More**
Make up your own story about Dog's party.
Write an addition sentence to show your story.

Raccoon's Picnic

Name: _____

Counters
8

Use: counters

• Act out each story with the counters.

A. There are 9 green animals at Raccoon's picnic. Then 5 green animals leave. How many green animals are left? _____

How many green animals? _____

How many green animals go away? _____

How many green animals are left? _____

Write a subtraction sentence to show the story.

_____ – _____ = _____

B. There are 10 blue animals at Raccoon's picnic. Then 6 of the blue animals go home. How many blue animals are left? _____

How many blue animals? _____

How many blue animals go home? _____

How many blue animals are left? _____

Write a subtraction sentence to show the story.

_____ – _____ = _____

• **Explore Some More**
Make up your own story about Raccoon's picnic. Write a subtraction sentence to show your story.

Bear's WonderPark

Name: _____

Counters
9

Use: counters

- Act out each story with the counters.

A. At the Whippy Do Ride 3 animals got into each car.
There were 4 cars.
Write an addition sentence to show the story.

____ + ____ + ____ + ____ = ____

How many cars? ____

How many animals in each car? ____

How many animals in all? ____

Write a multiplication sentence to show the story.

____ x ____ = ____
cars   animals in   animals
       each car   in all

B. At the Windy Road Ride 5 animals got into each car.
There were 5 cars.
Write an addition sentence to show the story.

____ + ____ + ____ + ____ + ____ = ____

How many cars? ____

How many animals in each car? ____

How many animals in all? ____

Write a multiplication sentence to show the story.

____ x ____ = ____
cars   animals in   animals
       each car   in all

- **Explore Some More**
  Make up a story about Bear's WonderPark.

Frog's Game

Counters
10

Use: counters

- Act out each story with the counters.

A. Frog is making up a game. He tells 8 animals to get into a circle. Then he has them get into groups. There are 2 animals in each group.

How many animals in all? ____

How many animals in each group? ____

How many groups? ____

Write a division sentence to show the story.

_____ ÷ _____ = _____
animals   animals in   groups
in all   each group

B. Find another way that Frog can get the 8 animals into groups. Each group must have the same number of animals.

How many animals in all? ____

How many animals in each group? ____

How many groups? ____

Write a division sentence to show the story.

_____ ÷ _____ = _____
animals   animals in   groups
in all   each group

- **Extra Challenge**
  Make up a story about Frog's game.
  This time Frog has 12 animals get into a circle.
  Write a division sentence to show your story.

The Croaking Frogs

Name: _____

Counters

Use: counters

- Act out each story with the counters.

A. On Saturday morning there were 2 red animals, 2 yellow animals, and 1 blue animal in line for tickets. Use the clues to find out how they lined up.

CLUES
- The first animal in line was not yellow.
- A red animal was between 2 yellow animals.
- A blue animal was behind a red animal.

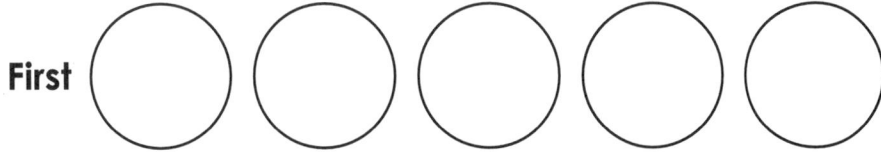

First

B. On Saturday night there were 2 yellow animals, 2 red animals, 1 green animal, and 1 blue animal watching the movie. The animals were sitting in 2 rows. Use the clues to see where each one was sitting.

CLUES
- No red animal was sitting at the end of a row.
- There was a yellow animal in each row.
- A blue animal sat to the right of a red animal and in front of a yellow animal.

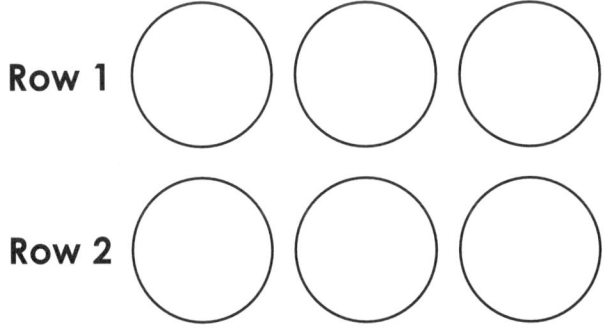

Row 1

Row 2

© Ideal School Supply • A Division of Instructional Fair Group, Inc. • Doing Basic Math with Manipulatives, Grades 1-3 - **Skill: Problem solving**

A Bug's Tale

Name: _____

Counters

12

Use: counters

- Act out each story with the counters.

A. On Friday, 11 animals came to see Bug's play. There were 3 more blue animals than red animals. How many animals of each color came to the play?

red ____   blue ____

B. On Saturday, 15 animals came to see Bug's play. There was the same number of green animals as yellow animals. There were 3 fewer red animals than yellow animals. How many animals of each color came to see Bug's play?

green ____   yellow ____   red ____

C. On Sunday, 18 animals came to see Bug's play. There was the same number of red animals as blue animals. There were 4 more yellow animals than green animals. There were 3 fewer green animals than red animals. How many animals of each color came to see Bug's play?

red ____   blue ____   yellow ____   green ____

- **Extra Challenge**
  Make up your own story about animals at the play.

Linking Cubes

Linking cubes help children develop these concepts and skills:

Patterns and Algebra Thinking
- Identify and extend color patterns

Numbers and Operations
- Show numbers
- Show addition
- Show subtraction
- Show the inverse relationship between addition and subtraction
- Explore beginning place value
- Explore beginning multiplication
- Explore beginning division

Measurement
- Measure with nonstandard units

Problem solving
- Use clues and logical reasoning to solve problems

What Are Linking Cubes?

Linking cubes are $\frac{3}{4}$ inch plastic cubes that link on all six sides. The cubes come in 10 bright colors. The cubes can be linked together or used individually.

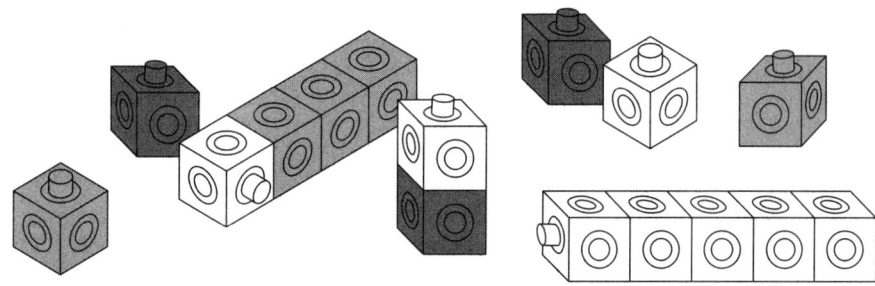

Why Use Linking Cubes?

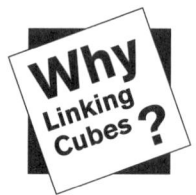

These cubes are a versatile math manipulative, because they can be used in many ways. They come in 10 bright colors, which allows the children to make a wide variety of patterns and color combinations. The linking attribute makes the cubes ideal for showing numbers in various ways. The children can also show all the operations easily by putting together colors and taking them apart. Linking materials have a natural appeal for children.

Exploring Math With Linking Cubes

Following are descriptions of 12 explorations that children can do with the linking cubes, and the concepts and skills they will be developing. Reproducible masters for the explorations are given on pages 21-32. Many of the explorations end with a challenging puzzle to extend the learning.

1 Identify and extend patterns
A key is given, showing the letters used for the colors of the cubes. The children match the cubes to the letters on the squares. They identify the color pattern and show what cubes come next.

2 Count and show numbers
The children first link cubes to make these colored trains: 1 red cube, 2 yellow cubes, 2 green cubes. Then they find the trains, or combine trains, to show the numbers 1, 2, 3, and 4. They can show 2 and 3 in two different ways.

3 Show a number in different ways
The children look for all the ways to show 6, using brown and purple cubes. They record all the ways in a table.

4 Show addition; write addition sentences
The children make three trains of different lengths. Then they combine the trains in different ways to show addition. They write addition sentences to show the combinations.

5 Show the inverse relationship between addition and subtraction
The children make two trains and put them together to show addition. They take away 1 train to show subtraction. They write the subtraction sentence. Then they put the trains back together, take away the other train, and write the subtraction sentence.

6 Show subtraction; write subtraction sentences
The children explore putting together 3 snakes (trains) and taking them apart in different ways. They will discover that they can show 3 different subtraction sentences with the snakes.

7 Show tens and ones; explore place value
The children make ten-sticks from a given number of cubes. They count by tens and then find the number of cubes left over. They record the number of tens, the number of cubes left over, and the number that the cubes show.

8 Measure length with nonstandard units
The children link cubes to measure the length of Monster and his friend. Then they use the cubes to measure things around their classroom.

9 Use repeated addition to show multiplication
The children make towers that all have the same number of cubes. First they write an addition sentence and then a multiplication sentence to show their work.

10 Measure perimeter, using nonstandard units
The children use the side of a cube as one unit of length. They cover a given shape with cubes to measure its perimeter. Then they use the same cubes to make a shape that has a different perimeter.

11 Use logical reasoning to solve puzzles
The children take a group of cubes, then follow clues to find where each cube belongs in a 2-by-3 grid.

12 Show division; write division sentences
The children make a train 12 cubes long. Then they take it apart so that each piece has the same number of cubes. They write a division sentence to show their work. Next they explore taking the train apart in different ways.

Organizing for Linking Cubes Explorations

Linking Cubes explorations can be used effectively with the whole class. Have students work in groups of two to three sharing materials. Give every group 9 each of 10 different colors, or 90 cubes. Working in pairs or small groups will encourage children to discuss their thinking and develop problem-solving skills together.

Linking Cubes explorations can also be used effectively in centers. Each student or pair of students will need 9 each of 10 different colors, or 90 cubes. Package each set of cubes separately in a plastic bag or container.

Introducing Linking Cubes

Let the children begin by just exploring the cubes–putting them together and taking them apart. When the children are ready, use some of these questions for discussion:

> Sort the cubes by color. How many different colors do you have?
> Look at the red cubes and estimate how many there are. Now count them. How many red cubes do you have?
> Do the same thing with the blue cubes. How many blue cubes do you have?
> Put the red cubes and the blue cubes together and count them. How many do you have in all?

Have the children explore different ways of putting the cubes together.

Patterns

Name: _____

Linking Cubes

1

Use: linking cubes

- Match the cubes to the squares.
  Look for a pattern.
  What color cubes come next?

R = red	Y = yellow
G = green	P = purple
B = blue	Br = brown
W = white	O = orange

A. | R | Y | R | Y | R | Y | | |

B. | G | G | P | G | G | P | | |

C. | Br | W | G | Br | W | G | | |

- **Extra Challenge**
  Use 7 orange and 7 white cubes.
  How many different patterns can you make?

Trains

Name: _____

Linking Cubes
2

Use: linking cubes and crayons

R	= red
Y	= yellow
G	= green
B	= blue

- Use the cubes to make these trains.

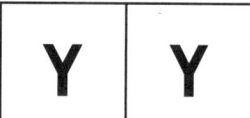 

[R] [Y][Y] [G][G]

- Use the trains to show these numbers.
  You may put trains together.
  Color to show each number.

1

2 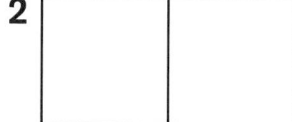   2 ☐☐

3 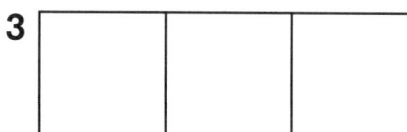   3 ☐☐☐

4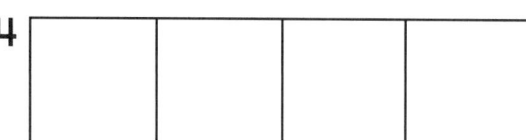

5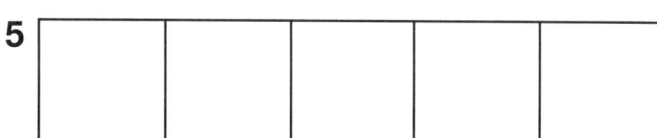

- **Extra Challenge**
  Make this train: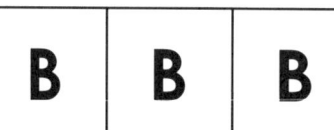

[B][B][B]

Use this train with the other trains.
Now what other numbers can you show?

Train Number Six

Name: _____

Linking Cubes
3

Use: linking cubes

- Use brown and purple cubes for train cars. Cover the train in different ways.

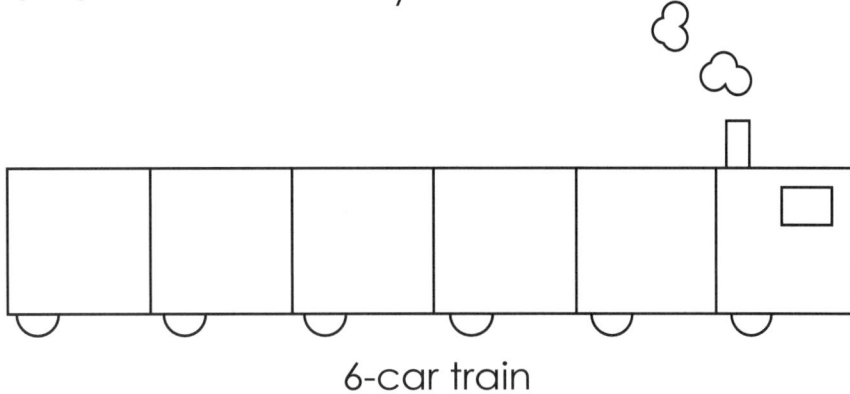

6-car train

- Show how many brown and purple cubes you use for each way.

Color	Way 1	Way 2	Way 3	Way 4	Way 5
brown					
purple					

- **Explore Some More**
  Add another car to the train. How many ways can you cover a train with this number of cars?

23

Putting Trains Together

Name: _____

Linking Cubes
4

Use: linking cubes

- Use cubes to make these trains.
  Write the number each train shows.

R = red
Y = yellow
G = green

G	G

_____
number

Y	Y	Y

_____
number

R	R	R	R	R	R

_____
number

A. Put the green train and the yellow train together.
What sum do they show? _____
Write an addition sentence to show your work.

____ + ____ = ____

B. Put the trains together to show other sums.
Write an addition sentence for each sum.

____ + ____ = ____

____ + ____ = ____

____ + ____ + ____ = ____

- **Mystery Train Puzzle**
  I have 3 red cars. I have 2 more blue cars
  than red cars. What do I look like?

24

Name: _____

Together and Apart

Linking Cubes

Use: linking cubes

- Use the cubes to make these trains.
  Write the number each train shows.

W = white
Y = yellow

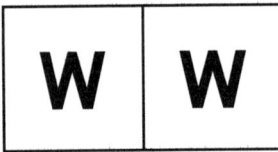

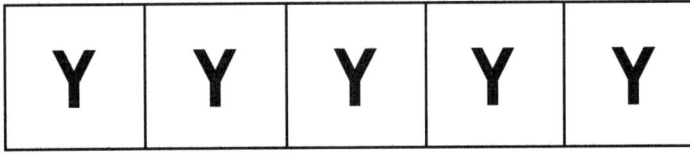

____
number

____
number

A. Put the white train and the yellow train together.
What sum do they show? ____
Write an addition sentence to show your work.

____ + ____ = ____

B. Take away the white train.
How many cubes are left? ____
Write a subtraction sentence to show your work.

____ − ____ = ____

C. Put the white train and the yellow train back together.
Take away the yellow train.
How many cubes are left? ____
Write a subtraction sentence to show your work.

____ − ____ = ____

- **Mystery Train Puzzle**
  I have 8 cars in all. If you take away my
  4 white cars, I have only green cars left.
  What do I look like?

Snakes

Name: _____

Linking Cubes
6

Use: linking cubes

W = white
B = black
P = purple

• Use the cubes to make these snakes.

W	W	W	W	W

B	B	B

_____ number   _____ number

P	P	P	P	P	P	P	P

_____ number

A. Put the snakes together to make one long snake.
What sum do they show? _____

B. Take away all the cubes of one color.
How many cubes are left? _____
Write a subtraction sentence to show your work.

____ – ____ = ____

C. Put the cubes together to make one long snake.
Take away all the cubes of a different color.
How many cubes are left? _____
Write a subtraction sentence to show your work.

____ – ____ = ____

D. How many other subtraction sentences can you show?

• **Mystery train puzzle**
I have 20 cars. If you take away the 6 blue cars, there are 2 more pink cars than green cars left. What do I look like?

Ten-Sticks

Name: _____

Linking Cubes

7

Use: linking cubes

A. Take 6 green, 8 orange, and 8 white cubes.
Make sticks of 10 with the cubes.
Write the numbers.

How many 10-sticks do you have? _____
What number do they show? _____
How many cubes are left over? _____
What number do the cubes show in all? _____

Tens	Cubes left over

B. Take 9 red, 7 green, and 9 yellow cubes.
Make sticks of 10 with the cubes.

How many 10-sticks do you have? _____
What number do they show? _____
How many cubes are left over? _____
What number do the cubes show in all? _____

Tens	Cubes left over

C. Take 7 purple, 6 black, 9 orange, and 8 white cubes. Make sticks of 10 with the cubes.

How many 10-sticks do you have? _____
What number do they show? _____
How many cubes are left over? _____
What number do the cubes show in all? _____

Tens	Cubes left over

- **Mystery Number Puzzle**
  I am 4 ten-sticks and 6 cubes left over.
  What number do I show?

Monster and His Friend

Name: _____

Linking Cubes
8

Use: linking cubes

- Link cubes together to measure Monster and his friend.

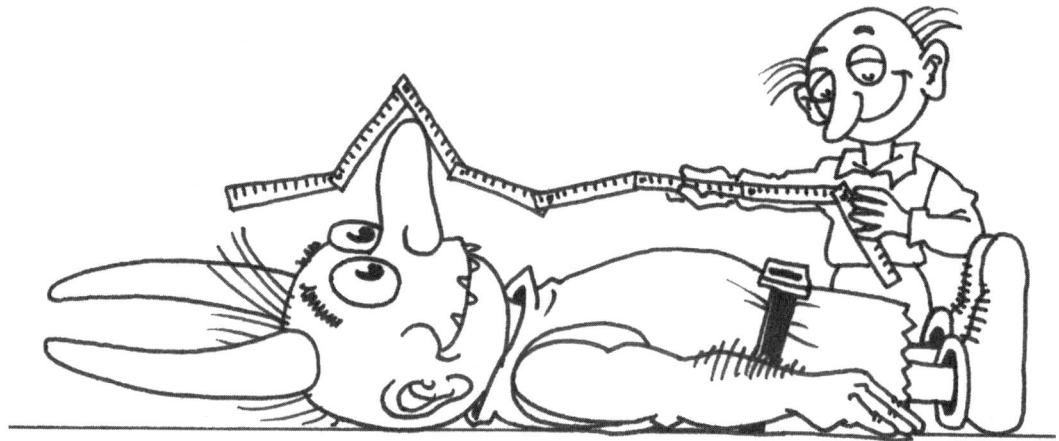

A. How long is Monster's nose? _____ cubes long

How long are Monster's horns? _____ cubes long

How long is Monster's arm? _____ cubes long

How long is Monster? _____ cubes long

How high is Monster's friend? _____ cubes high

B. Find things around your room to measure with cubes. Make a list of what you measure and how long each thing is.

- **Explore Some More**
  Make a 10-stick. Find big things to measure with your 10-stick.

Towers

Name: _____

Linking Cubes
9

Use: linking cubes

A. Build 4 towers with the cubes.
Put 5 cubes in each tower.
Write an addition sentence to show your work.

____ + ____ + ____ + ____ = ____

How many towers? ____

How many cubes in each tower? ____

How many cubes in all? ____

Write a multiplication sentence to show your work.

____ X ____ = ____
number   cubes in   cubes in all
of towers each tower

B. Build 5 towers. Put 4 cubes in each tower.
Write an addition sentence to show your work.

____ + ____ + ____ + ____ + ____ = ____

How many towers? ____

How many cubes in each tower? ____

How many cubes in all? ____

Write a multiplication sentence to show your work.

____ X ____ = ____
number   cubes in   cubes in all
of towers each tower

- **Explore Some More**
  Make up your own tower problem.

Around the Edge

Name: _____

Linking Cubes

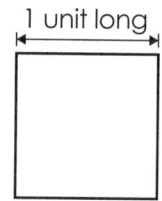

Use: linking cubes

- Use the side of a cube as 1 unit of length.

- **Perimeter** is the distance around the outside of a shape.

The perimeter of this square is 4 units long.

A. Cover this shape with cubes.

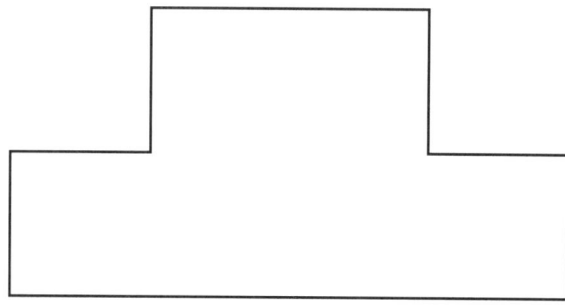

Count the units of length around the outside of the shape.

How long is the perimeter? _____ units

B. Use the same cubes. Make a shape that has a different perimeter. Trace to show your work. Show how long the perimeter is.

- **Mystery Shape Puzzle**
  My perimeter is 16 units long.
  What could I look like?

Use the Clues

Name: _____

Use: linking cubes

- Use the clues to solve each puzzle.

A. Take these cubes: 2 yellow, 2 green, 1 blue, and 1 white.

CLUES
- There is a green cube in both rows.
- There is a blue cube above the white cube and to the right of a green cube.
- One yellow cube is above a green cube.

B. Take these cubes: 2 red, 1 orange, 1 yellow, 1 pink, and 1 black.

CLUES
- The orange cube is above a red cube.
- The orange cube is to the left of the pink cube.
- The yellow cube is between 2 red cubes.

- **Extra Challenge**
  Choose 6 new cubes. Make up your own puzzle with clues. Let a friend solve your puzzle.

More Trains

Use: linking cubes

Linking Cubes

12

A. Make a train 12 cubes long.
Take it apart so each piece is 3 cars long.

How many cars in all? _____

How many cars in each piece? _____

How many pieces? _____

Write a division sentence to show your work.

_____ ÷ _____ = _____
cars in all   cars in   pieces
              each piece

B. Make another train 12 cubes long.
Take it apart a different way.
Each piece must have the same number of cars.

How many cars in all? _____

How many cars in each piece? _____

How many pieces? _____

Write a division sentence to show your work.

_____ ÷ _____ = _____
cars in all   cars in   pieces
              each piece

- **Mystery Train Puzzle**
  You can take me apart and make 6 equal pieces. There will be 4 cars in each piece. What train am I?

Dominoes

Dominoes help students develop these concepts and skills:

Patterns and Algebra Thinking
- Identify and extend number patterns
- Identify function rules

Numbers and Operations
- Count and compare numbers
- Develop concepts of more than, fewer than
- Show and write addition facts
- Show and write "turnaround" facts
- Show and write "doubles" facts
- Show and write "doubles plus 1" facts
- Show and write subtraction facts

Problem solving
- Use logical reasoning to solve Venn circle puzzles
- Solve addition puzzles

What Are Dominoes?

We have used a set of 28 double-six dominoes for these explorations. There is also a set of double-nine dominoes, which has 56 pieces. The double-six set is used more commonly because the number of pieces is more manageable, especially for young children. Following are the dominoes arranged to show the pattern in the numbers of dots.

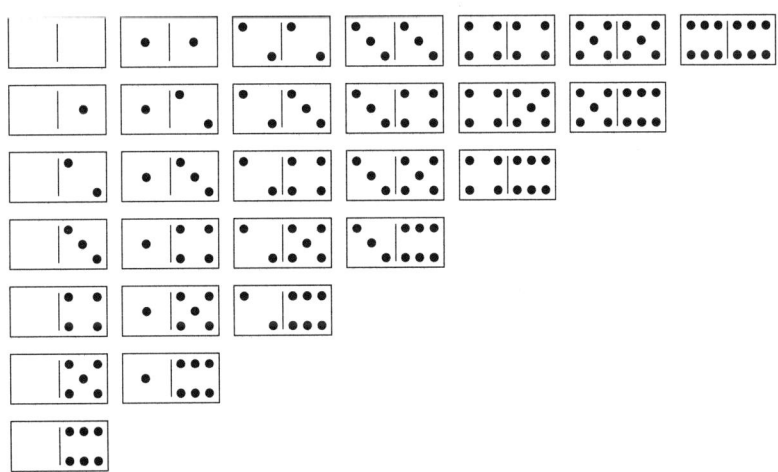

Why Use Dominoes?

Dominoes are an old game, tracing back to about 1800. They are much loved by all ages, and many children will already be familiar with them. Dominoes intrigue children, who love to endlessly arrange the pieces and create structures with them. The pips, or dots, can be used in many ways to build number skills. You can help the children make the connection between the dots and writing the numbers they show. The children will enjoy solving number puzzles with the dominoes, and making up their own puzzles.

Exploring Math With Dominoes

Following are descriptions of 12 explorations that children can do with the dominoes, and the concepts and skills they will be developing. Reproducible masters for the explorations are given on pages 37-48. Most of the explorations end with a challenging puzzle to extend the learning.

1 Count and compare numbers
The children count all the dots on a domino and then look for more dominoes that have the same number of dots.

2 Identify and extend number patterns
The children make a row of dominoes as shown, and look for a pattern in the dots. Then they find the domino that comes next in the pattern.

3 Compare numbers; develop the ideas of more than and fewer than
The children look for dominoes that have 1 more dot on one side than the other. Then they look for dominoes that have 3 fewer dots on one side than the other. They are learning the language of more than and fewer than.

4 Solve addition puzzles
The children solve puzzles by finding three dominoes that together show a given number of dots. Then they find another set of three dominoes that show the same total number of dots.

5 Show and write addition facts
The children choose dominoes and then write the addition fact that each domino shows. They will be linking the dots with the written symbols for addition.

6 Show and write "turnaround" addition facts
The children find dominoes that show a given sum, and then write the two addition facts that each domino shows.

7 Show and write "doubles" addition facts
The children find dominoes that show a given sum and that have the same number of dots on both sides.

8 Show and write "doubles plus 1" addition facts
The children find dominoes that show a given sum, and that have 1 more dot on one side than on the other.

9 Solve subtraction puzzles; show and write subtraction facts
The differences are given for pairs of "turnaround" subtraction facts. The children look for dominoes that fit the numbers given, and finish the two subtraction facts.

10 Solve addition puzzles
The children look for dominoes to solve an addition puzzle. The puzzle is made up of eight dominoes arranged in a rectangle. The sum of the dots on each side of the rectangle must equal a given sum.

11 Use logical reasoning to solve Venn circle puzzles
Two overlapping circles are shown, and a rule is given for each circle. The children find the dominoes that belong in each circle and in the space where the circles overlap.

12 Identify patterns and function rules
The children identify the rules that a fantasy function machine uses to change the number of dots on dominoes coming IN and going OUT of it. Dominoes are shown going IN and coming OUT. The children count the dots on the dominoes and use logical reasoning to identify the rule. Then they use the rule to determine what domino could come OUT when a given domino goes IN.

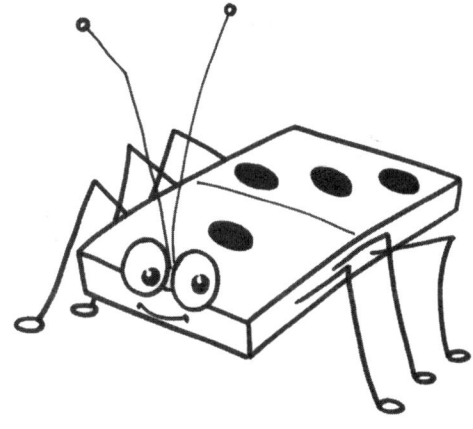

Organizing for Dominoes Explorations

Dominoes explorations can be used effectively with the whole class. Have the children work in pairs sharing materials. Give each pair a set of 28 double-six dominoes. Working in pairs will encourage children to discuss their thinking and develop problem-solving skills.

Dominoes explorations can also be used effectively in centers. Each student or pair of students will need a set of 28 double-six dominoes. Package each set of dominoes separately in a plastic bag or container.

Introducing Dominoes

Let the children begin by just exploring the dominoes. They will want to pile them up, build with them, explore the different sides. When the children are ready, begin by having them describe the dominoes.

Ask these questions:

> Do all the dominoes have dots on them?
> How are the dots arranged on each domino?
> How are the dominoes alike?
> How are the dominoes different?

Then have the children find as many dominoes as they can that have fewer than 5 dots on them. (9) Then have them look for as many dominoes as they can find with more than 7 dots on them. (9)

How Many Dots?

Name: _____

Dominoes

1

Use: dominoes

A. This domino has 5 dots in all: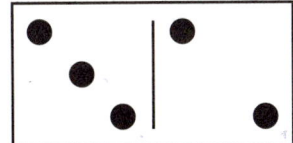

Find two more dominoes that have 5 dots in all.

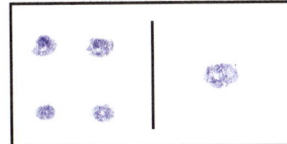 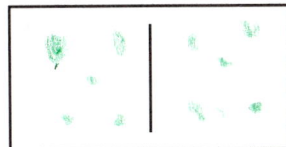

B. This domino has 6 dots in all: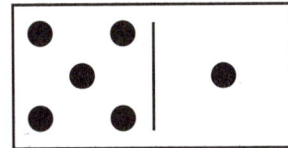

Find two more dominoes that have 6 dots in all.

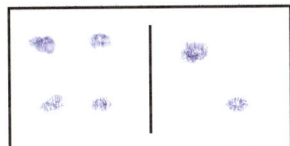 

• **Extra Challenge**
Look for dominoes that have 8 dots in all.
How many can you find?

What Comes Next?

Name: _____

Dominoes

Use: dominoes

A. Make a row of dominoes like this one:

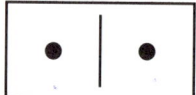 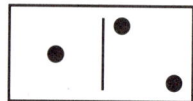  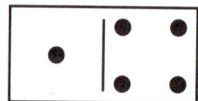 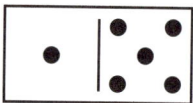

Look for a pattern in the dots on the dominoes.
What domino comes next?

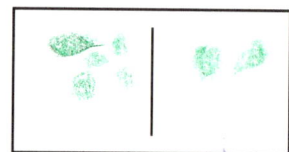

B. Make a row of dominoes like this one:

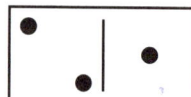 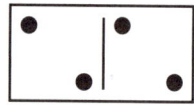 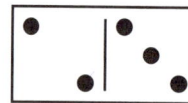 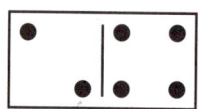 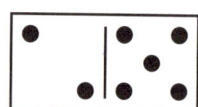

Look for a pattern in the dots on the dominoes.
What domino comes next?

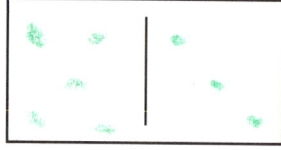

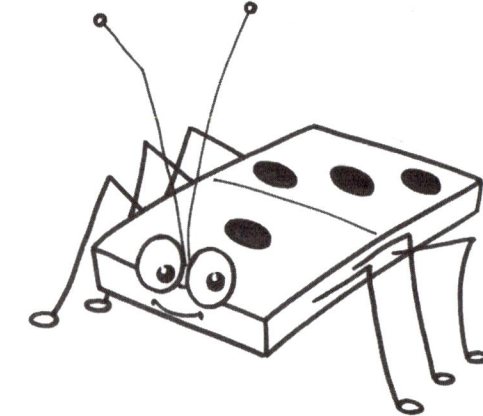

- **Extra Challenge**
  Make up your own pattern. Put your dominoes in a row to show your pattern. Can a friend find your pattern?

More or Fewer

Name: _____

Dominoes

Use: dominoes

A. This domino has 1 more dot on one side than the other.

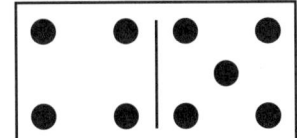

Find 2 more dominoes that have 1 more dot on one side than the other.

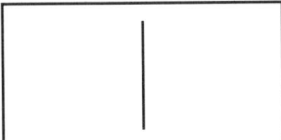 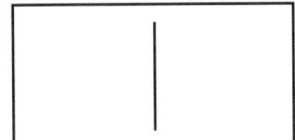

B. This domino has 3 fewer dots on one side than the other.

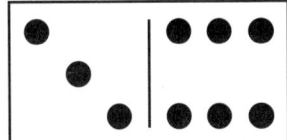

Find 2 more dominoes that have 3 fewer dots on one side than the other.

- **Mystery Domino Puzzle**
  The sum of my dots is more than 5 and less than 9.
  I have 1 more dot on one side than the other side.
  Who am I?

Domino Bugs

Name: _____

Dominoes

4

Use: dominoes

A. Make 2 domino bugs that each have 12 dots in all. Use different dominoes in each bug.

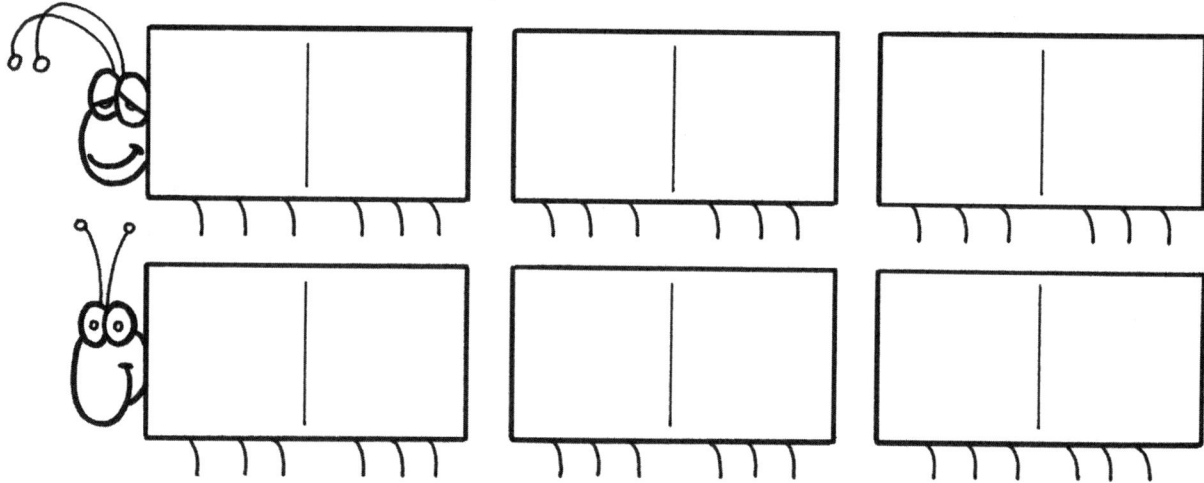

B. Make 2 different domino bugs that each have 15 dots in all.

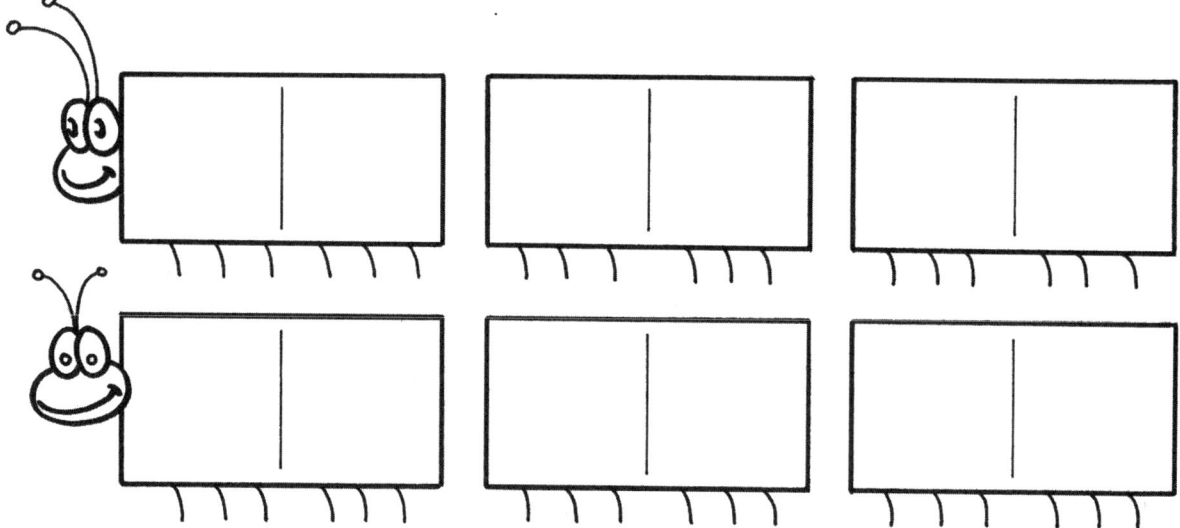

- **Extra Challenge**
  Make up your own domino bugs.
  Choose a new sum for the dots.
  Let someone solve your puzzle.

Name: _____

Domino Addition

Dominoes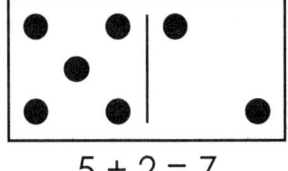

Use: dominoes

- Each domino shows an addition fact.

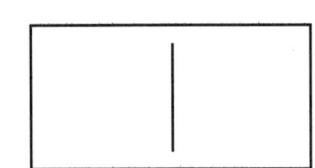

5 + 2 = 7

- Choose 4 dominoes.
  Write the addition fact for each one.

A.

____ + ____ = ____

B.

____ + ____ = ____

C.

____ + ____ = ____

D.

____ + ____ = ____

- **Mystery Domino Puzzle**
  The sum of my dots is 10. I have a different number of dots on each side. Who am I?

41

Turn It Around

Name: _____

Dominoes
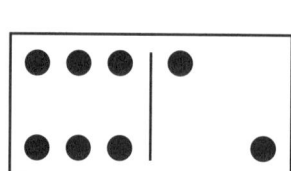

Use: dominoes

- This domino shows 2 addition facts. First it shows 6 + 2 = 8. Then you turn it around to show 2 + 6 = 8.

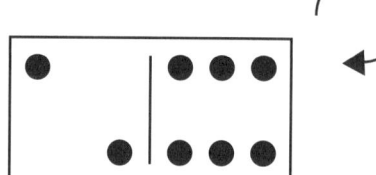

- Find a domino to show each sum. Write the fact. Then write the "turnaround" fact.

A.

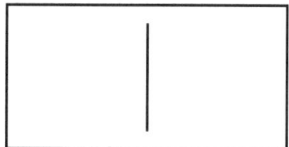  

___ + ___ = 6   ___ + ___ = 6

B.

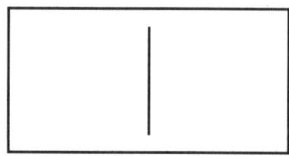 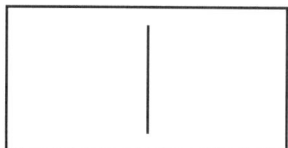

___ + ___ = 10   ___ + ___ = 10

C.

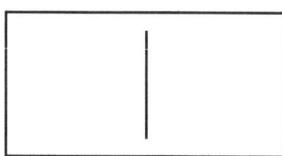 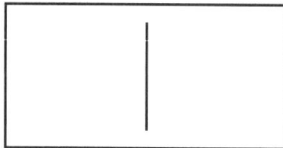

___ + ___ = 9   ___ + ___ = 9

- **Mystery Domino Puzzle**
  The sum of my dots is an odd number greater than 9. Who am I?

Domino Doubles

Name: _____

Dominoes

Use: dominoes

- This domino is a "double." It has the same number of dots on each side.

- Find more "doubles." Write the addition fact that each one shows.

A.
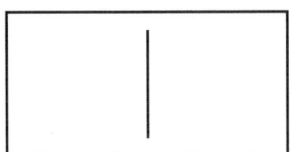

____ + ____ = ____

B.
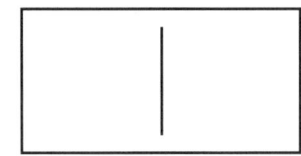

____ + ____ = ____

C.
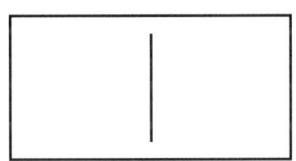

____ + ____ = ____

D.
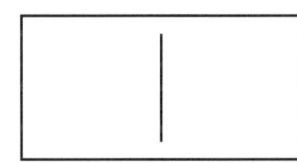

____ + ____ = ____

- **Mystery Domino Puzzle**
  We are both "doubles."
  The sum of all our dots is 12.
  What 2 dominoes could we be?

© Ideal School Supply • A Division of Instructional Fair Group, Inc. • Doing Basic Math with Manipulatives, Grades 1–3 - **Skill:** Addition

One More Than a Double

Name: _____

Dominoes
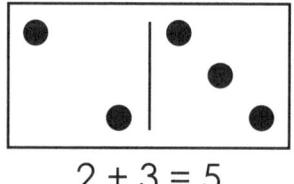

Use: dominoes

- This domino is a "doubles plus 1."
  It has 1 more dot on one side
  than the other.

  2 + 3 = 5

- Find more "doubles plus 1" dominoes.
  Write the addition fact that each one shows.

A.
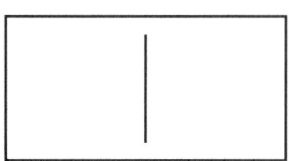
____ + ____ = ____

B.
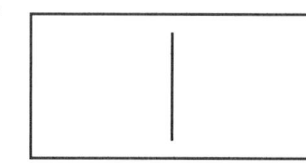
____ + ____ = ____

C.
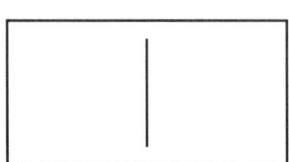
____ + ____ = ____

D.
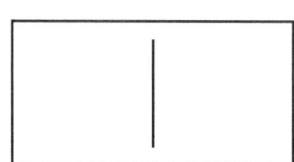
____ + ____ = ____

- **Mystery Domino Puzzle**
  We are both "doubles plus 1" dominoes.
  The sum of all our dots is 12.
  What 2 dominoes could we be?

Name: _____

Subtraction Puzzles

Dominoes

Use: dominoes

- This domino shows the addition fact: 4 + 3 = 7.
  It can also show two subtraction facts:

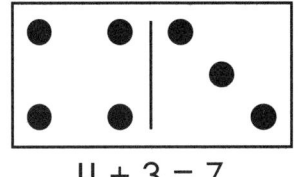
4 + 3 = 7

7 - 4 = 3

7 - 3 = 4

- Look at the two numbers given in each puzzle.
  Find the domino that fits those two numbers.
  Finish writing the subtraction facts.

A.

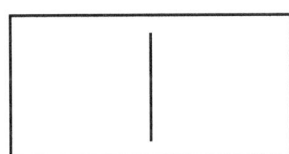

____ - ____ = 6

____ - ____ = 1

B.

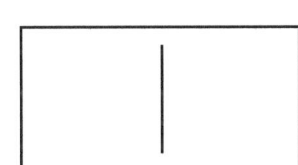

____ - ____ = 5

____ - ____ = 2

C.

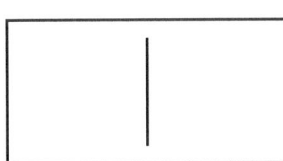

____ - ____ = 6

____ - ____ = 4

D.

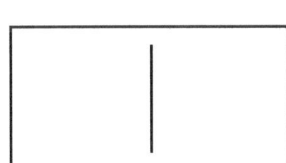

____ - ____ = 4

____ - ____ = 1

© Ideal School Supply • A Division of Instructional Fair Group, Inc. • Doing Basic Math with Manipulatives, Grades 1-3 - **Skill:** Subtraction

45

Name: _____

Domino Rectangle Puzzles

Dominoes

Use: dominoes

- Find dominoes to solve each puzzle.

A. The total number of dots on each side of this rectangle should be 10.

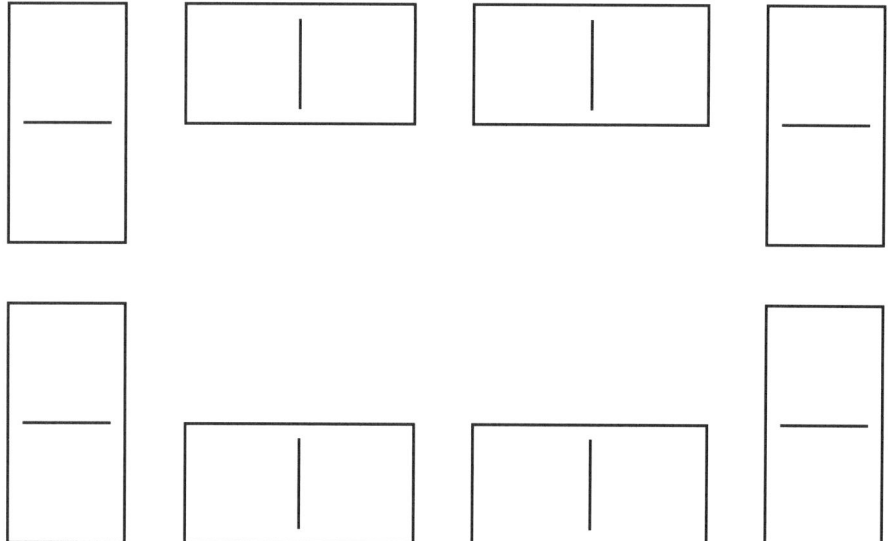

B. The total number of dots on each side of this rectangle should be 16.

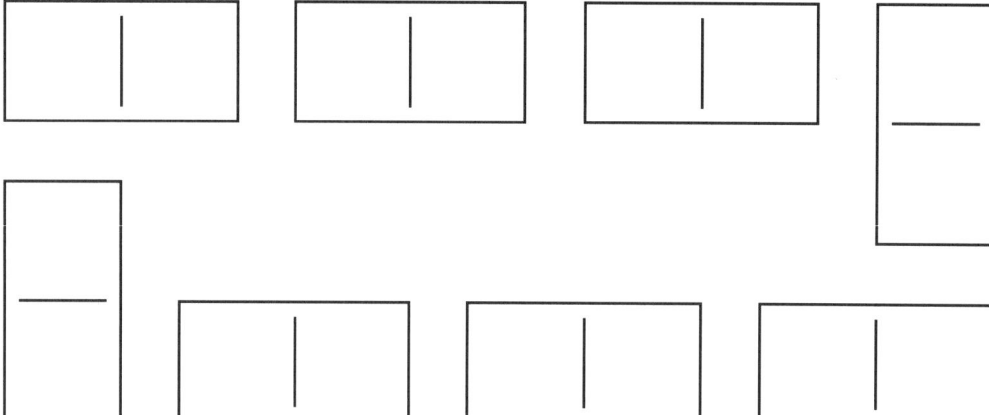

- **Extra Challenge**
  Make up your own domino rectangle puzzle. The total number of dots on each side should be the same. Let someone solve your puzzle.

A Domino Diagram

Name: _____

Dominoes
11

Use: dominoes

- There is a rule for each circle. The rule tells what dominoes belong in the circle. Dominoes that fit both rules belong in part C.

- Find dominoes for parts A, B, and C. Show your dominoes.

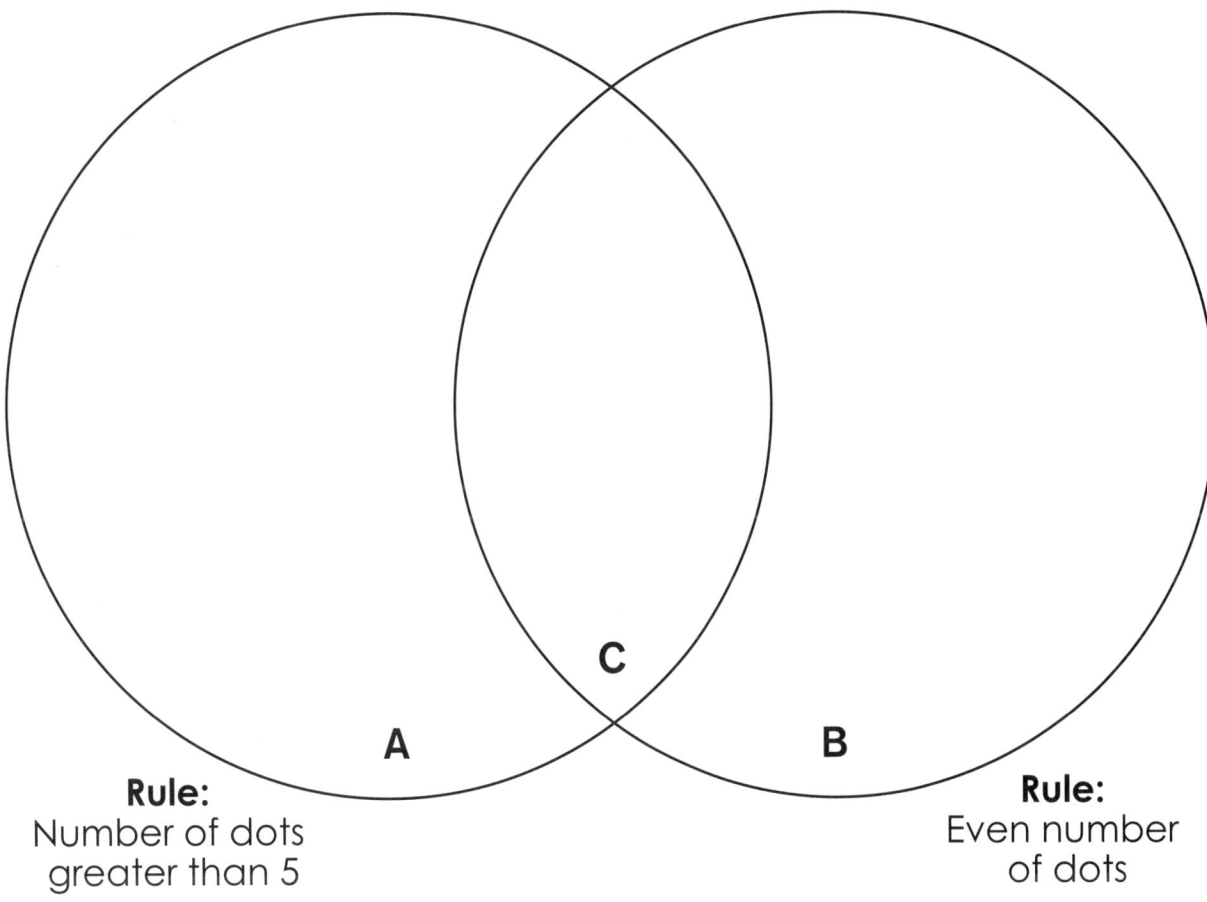

A

C

B

Rule:
Number of dots greater than 5

Rule:
Even number of dots

- **Extra Challenge**
  Make up your own rules for the circles.
  Find dominoes that belong in each part of the circles.

The Troniton

Name: _____

Dominoes
12

Use: dominoes

- When you put a domino IN the Troniton, the machine uses a secret rule to change the number of dots on the domino that comes OUT. Look for a pattern and find the Troniton's rule in each problem. Show the last domino to come OUT.

A.   IN → OUT   Rule

_____
_____
_____
_____

B.   IN → OUT   Rule

_____
_____
_____
_____

- **Extra Challenge**
  Make up your own rules for the Troniton.
  Show some examples. Let someone solve your puzzle.

Learning Clocks

Learning Clocks help children develop these concepts and skills:

Measurement
- Tell time on analog and digital clocks
- Tell time on the hour
- Tell time on the half hour
- Sequence times
- Tell time in 15-minute intervals
- Show elapsed time
- Tell time in 5-minute intervals
- Sequence times from story problems

Data and Graphing
- Use data and clues to solve time puzzles

What Are Learning Clocks?

There are many kinds of Learning Clocks. Some have geared, synchronized hands, while others have hands that move independently. Some Learning Clocks show an analog clock face, while others show a digital clock face; and some show both analog and digital. Most Learning Clocks have the hour and minute hands. Many of the analog clocks have hour and minute hands, and show both hour and minute marks.

Why Use Learning Clocks?

By moving the hands on an analog clock, or numbers on a digital clock, students begin to understand how a clock works. By using hands-on clocks, the students also gain a sense of minutes, and the number of minutes in an hour. Using clocks also helps students gain a sense of the passage of time, and time-related activities that they encounter very early at school; snacks, recess, going home, etc. The children can set the clocks to show the times that are important in their own lives.

Exploring Math With Learning Clocks

Following are descriptions of 12 explorations children can do with Learning Clocks, and the concepts and skills they will be developing. Reproducible masters for the explorations are given on pages 53-64. Many of these explorations end with an extra challenging puzzle to extend the learning.

1 Show time on the hour in two ways
The children show times on the hour on both digital and analog clocks. The times are related to events that occur in their lives.

2 Show times one hour apart
The children read about an animal that starts doing something and then stops an hour later. The times are given. The children show the hour the activity starts, and the hour that the activity stops. They show the times on an analog clock and a digital clock.

3 Show time on the half hour
The children read about animals eating meals, and show times on the half hour. They show the times on an analog clock and a digital clock. The children are learning the vocabulary of time, such as half past and 30 minutes after.

4 Show elapsed time, an hour later
The children read about common situations that take one hour. They show the time the activity starts on their clocks. Then they show the time that it stops one hour later. They show times on analog and digital clocks.

5 Sequence times from a story
The children read a short story. Then they have to find three times in the story and put them in the correct sequence. Two times are given, and the third time is given as elapsed time. They show the times on digital clocks.

6 Show time in 15-minute intervals
The children begin with a starting time. Then they figure out the stopping time, 15 or 45 minutes later. They show the times on digital clocks.

7 Show time in 5-minute intervals; show elapsed time
Students are given a beginning time. Then they find the ending time that is 5, 50, or 40 minutes later. They show the times on digital clocks.

8 Use time clues to solve puzzles
The children are given a clue for a time between two given times. The children can choose any two times that fall between the given times and record them on the clocks. They show the times on digital and analog clocks.

9 Sequence times in a story; show elapsed time
The children read a short story. They sequence times from the story and also find elapsed times. They show the times on digital clocks.

10 Solve time puzzles
The children use various types of clues to identify a time. These clues may relate to number sense as well as to the vocabulary of time.

11 Sequence times in a story; show elapsed time
The children read a short story. Then they sequence times from the story, including times given and elapsed times. They show the times on digital clocks.

12 Use data to solve time puzzles
The children read a schedule of arrival times for the Sun Island ferries. Then they read clues about four different people arriving on the Sun Island ferry. They match a time in the schedule with each clue.

Organizing for Learning Clock Explorations

Learning Clock explorations can be used effectively with the whole class. Have students work in pairs sharing materials. Each pair should have an analog clock face and a digital clock face. Working in pairs will encourage children to discuss their thinking and develop problem-solving skills.

Learning Clock explorations can also be used effectively in centers. Each student or pair of students should have an analog clock face and a digital clock face.

Introducing Learning Clocks

Let the children explore the learning clock, turning the hands. Then talk about the two different kinds of clocks: the round analog clock, and the digital clock. You might use some of these questions:

Where do you see a clock right now? Describe the clock.
What kinds of clocks do you have at home? Describe them.
What kinds of clocks do you see in stores? Describe them.
Do you have a watch? What kind of watch is it?
Does someone in your house have an alarm clock? When do they use it?
Do you get up at the same time each day?
Are there special times that you do things during the day?
Do you do things at the same time on Saturday as you do during the week?

Students may discover that time is something they never thought about, but that it is a major factor in organizing their days. Refer to times that you do things in school. Ask them about all the things they do outside of school that relate to a special time. Children will have lessons, sports practice, etc. Time is a part of math that has a very direct relationship with their everyday lives.

On the Hour

Use: a Learning Clock

- Show each time two ways.

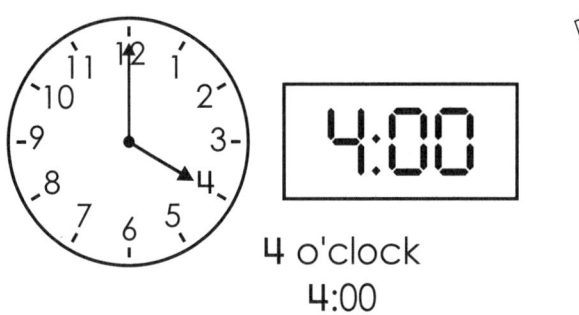

4 o'clock
4:00

A. Milly Mouse eats breakfast at 8 o'clock.

 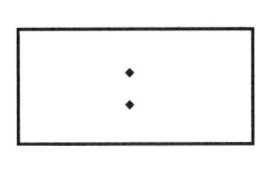 

B. Melinda Mouse goes skating at 10 o'clock.

 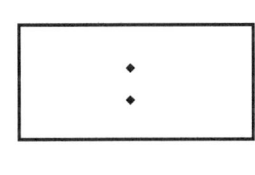

C. Mario Mouse goes to the movies at 3 o'clock.

 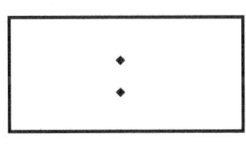

- **Explore Some More**
  What time do you get up on Saturday morning?

An Hour Later

Name: _____

Learning Clocks

2

Use: a Learning Clock

- Show each time two ways.

A. Bella Bear starts playing soccer at 3:00.
She stops playing an hour later, at 4:00.

Start playing   Stop playing

B. Bernie Bear starts washing the dishes at 7:00.
He finishes washing the dishes an hour later, at 8:00.

Start washing   Finish washing

- **Explore Some More**
Think of something you do that takes 1 hour.
Show the time you might start and the time you would stop.

Name: _____

On the Half Hour

Learning Clocks

3

Use: a Learning Clock

- Show each time two ways.

30 minutes after 12
half past 12

A. Rhonda Rabbit eats breakfast at 7:30.

 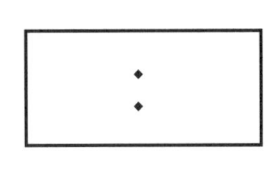

B. Ramos Rabbit eats lunch at 30 minutes after 11:00.

 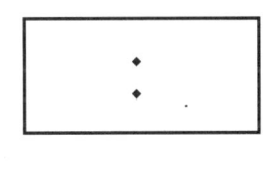

C. Randy Rabbit eats dinner at half past 6:00.

 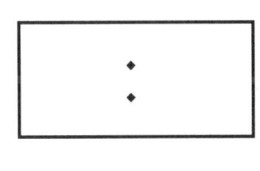

- **Mystery Time Puzzle**
  It is a half hour after one o'clock.
  What time is it?

A Dog and a Basketball

Name: _____

Learning Clocks

Use: a Learning Clock

- Show each time two ways.

A. Jana starts walking the dog at 4:00.
She stops walking the dog one hour later.

Start walking

 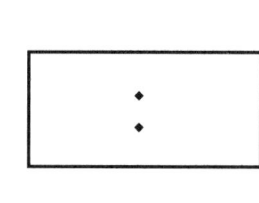

Stop walking

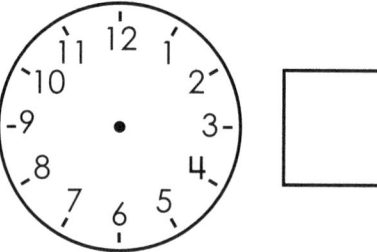 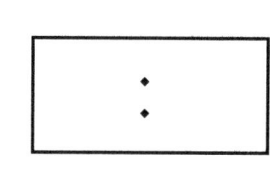

B. Tony starts playing basketball at 5:00.
He stops playing one hour later.

Start playing

 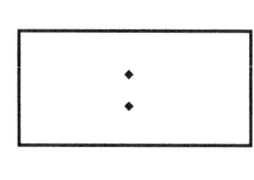

Stop playing

- **Mystery Time Puzzle**
Start on 12 and move ahead 8 hours.
Move to half past the hour.
What time is it?

56 © Ideal School Supply • A Division of Instructional Fair Group, Inc. • Doing Basic Math with Manipulatives, Grades 1-3 - **Skill:** Telling time

Name: _____

Swimming and Biking

Learning Clocks

Use: a Learning Clock

- Read each story.
  Put the story times in order.

A. Megan goes to her friend Lisa's house at 1:00.
Megan and Lisa go swimming at 2:00.
They stop swimming one hour later.

    a. Go to Lisa's house   **b.** _____   **c.** _____

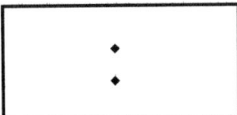   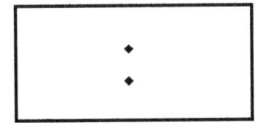   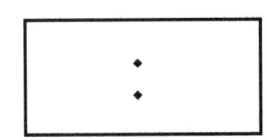

B. Henry meets Pete at the park at 10:30.
They ride their bikes in the park until 11:30.
They get to Pete's house for lunch a half hour later.

    a. Meet at park   **b.** _____   **c.** _____

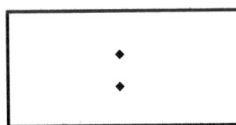   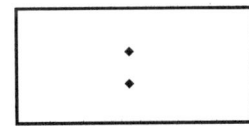   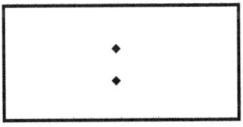

- **Extra Challenge**
  Ted played ball for one hour.
  He stopped playing at 12:00.
  When did Ted begin playing ball?

Starting and Stopping

Name: _____

Learning Clocks

6

Use: a Learning Clock

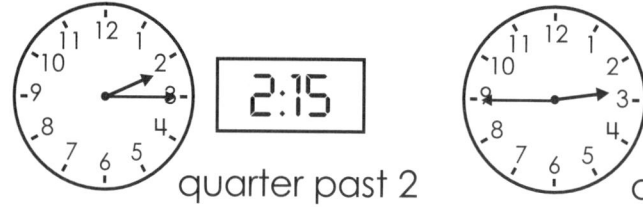

quarter past 2   quarter to 3

- Show when each activity starts and stops.

A. Alberto starts practicing the piano at 7:00.
He stops 45 minutes later.

Start   Stop

B. Marta starts writing e-mail on the computer at 5:30.
She stops 15 minutes later.

Start   Stop

C. Andre starts his tennis lesson at 12:30.
His lesson stops 45 minutes later.

Start   Stop

- **Extra Challenge**
Anita biked for 30 minutes.
She stopped biking at 11:30.
When did Anita begin biking?

Name: _____

What Time Is It Now?

Learning Clocks

Use: a Learning Clock

- Show when each activity begins and ends.

A. Maggie went to get the mail at 4:00. She got back 5 minutes later.

Go get mail
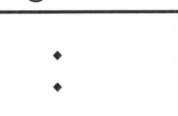

Get back

B. James started making a pie at 6:00. He was finished 50 minutes later.

Start pie
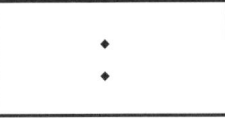

Finish pie

C. Laura started planting vegetables at 9:30. She stopped planting 40 minutes later.

Start planting
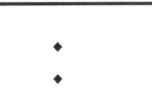

Finish planting

- **Mystery Time Puzzle**
  The number of the hour is an odd number between 8 and 12. The number has two digits. It is quarter past the hour. What time is it?

© Ideal School Supply • A Division of Instructional Fair Group, Inc. • Doing Basic Math with Manipulatives, Grades 1-3 - **Skill: Telling time**

What Time Is Between?

Name: _____

Learning Clocks

Use: a Learning Clock

- Show two different times that fit each clue.

A. Between 9:00 and 10:00

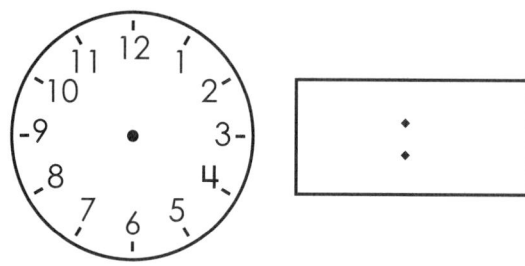

B. Between 30 minutes after 1:00 and 2:00

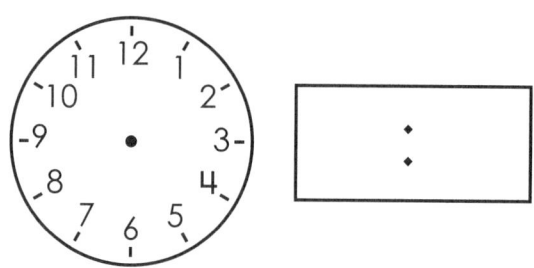

C. Between quarter past 11:00 and 11:45

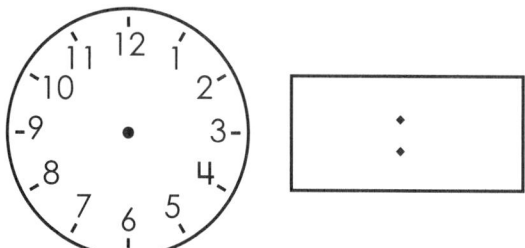

D. Between quarter of 5:00 and quarter after 5:00

- **Extra Challenge**
  Make up your own time clues.
  Let someone find times that fit your clues.

A Camping Trip

Name: _____

Learning Clocks
9

Use: a Learning Clock

- Read the story.
  Put the story times in order.

    David and Louisa get to the lake at 3:00. They help their mother unpack the car and put up the tent. At 4:00 they go fishing. They fish for two hours. Then they cook dinner. The stew is ready in one hour. Time to eat!

A. Get to the lake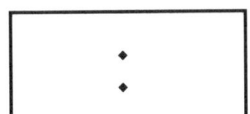

B. _____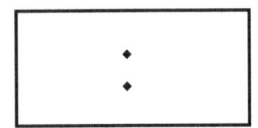

C. _____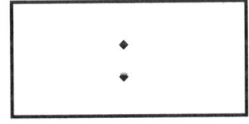

D. _____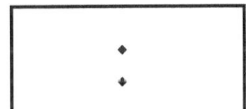

- **Extra Challenge**
  How many hours after they get to the lake do David and Louisa eat dinner?

Name: _____

Mystery Time Puzzles

Learning Clocks

Use: a Learning Clock

• Solve each mystery time puzzle.

A. The hour is 3 hours after 5:00. Count by 5 minutes six times to find the minutes after the hour.

What time is it? _____

B. You say the number of the hour when you count by 2, 3, and 4. Count by 5 minutes ten times to find the minutes after the hour.

What time is it? _____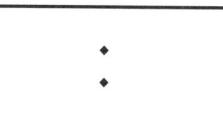

C. The number of the hour is an even number greater than 8. The hour is between 8 o'clock and 11 o'clock. Count by 5 minutes five times to get the minutes after the hour.

What time is it? _____

D. The number of the hour is an odd number. The hour is between 1 o'clock and 4 o'clock. Count by 5 minutes nine times to get the minutes after the hour.

What time is it? _____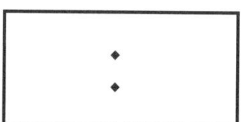

• **Extra Challenge**
Make up 2 mystery time puzzles.
Let someone solve your puzzles.

The Old West Ride

Name: _____

Learning Clocks
11

Use: a Learning Clock

- Read the story.
  Put the story times in order.

Sally and Nancy get on the Wild West tram at 9:30. They get off at Rodeo Roundup after 10 minutes. After 1 hour, they get on the tram again. They get off the tram in 5 minutes at Ghost Town. After one half hour, they stop to eat at the Old Mine Snacks.

A. Get on the tram

B. _____

C. _____

D. _____

E. _____

How long had Sally and Nancy been at the park when they stopped to eat at the Old Mine? _____

- **Extra Challenge**
  Make up your own story about riding the Wild West tram. Where do you stop, and when? How long are you at the park?

Sun Island Ferries

Name: _____

Learning Clocks

12

Use: a Learning Clock

- Look at the schedule of times when the ferry arrives at Sun Island. Read the time clues. Show what time each person arrived at Sun Island.

Ferry Arrives at Sun Island

Saturday	a.m. 8:00, 10:00, 11:00 p.m. 2:30, 5:30
Sunday	p.m. 1:00, 3:00, 4:00, 5:30, 7:00

A. Jerry came Saturday on the ferry that arrived closest to noon.

Jerry arrived at _____

B. Ariel came on Sunday to visit her grandmother. She rode on the ferry that arrived at half past the hour.

Ariel arrived at _____

C. Silloo came to visit her sister and family on Sunday. She rode on the ferry that arrives $4\frac{1}{2}$ hours after the first ferry.

Silloo arrived at _____

D. Andy came on Saturday to work at Ben's Café. He rode on the ferry that arrived 3 hours before the last ferry.

Andy arrived at _____

- **Extra Challenge**
  Make up a new ferry schedule. Write some time clues. Let someone solve your time puzzles.

Play Money

Play coins and bills help children develop these concepts and skills:

Numbers and Operations
- Recognize coins and their values
- Count money
- Use different coins to show equivalent amounts of money
- Find exact amounts of money
- Show the exact amount with different combinations of coins
- Add amounts of money
- Find how much more money is needed
- Pay the exact amount for items
- Make change; trade coins for equivalent coins

Problem solving
- Use clues and logical reasoning to solve mystery coin puzzles
- Solve story problem puzzles

What Is Play Money?

A set of play money has realistic coins made of plastic or cardboard, and paper bills in ones, fives, tens, twenties, fifties, and hundreds. There are many sets of coins and bills available. A beginning set will have about 94 plastic coins and 80 paper bills.

Why Use Play Money?

Using play money is an excellent way for children to learn about the value of coins and bills used in our currency system. It gives the students many opportunities for developing number concepts. As the children group coins and count them to find the values, they discover the relationships between the coins. They will also discover that there are many ways to combine coins to equal a given value. Using play money is an important way for children to develop real-world money skills.

Exploring Math With Play Money

Following are descriptions of 12 explorations that children can do with Play Money, and the concepts and skills they will be developing. Reproducible masters for the explorations are given on pages 69-80. Many of these explorations end with an extra challenging puzzle to extend the learning.

1 Recognize coins and their values; count money
The children match their coins to the ones shown in coin banks. Then they count up the values, beginning with the coin of greatest value. After finding the value of the coins in two banks, the children figure out which bank has more money and how much more.

2 Use different coins to show the same amount of money
An illustration shows a bear and a rabbit. The bear is holding a dime, and the children try to find the rabbit's coins, which have the same value as the dime. The children look for 2 different kinds of coins that together show the same value as the dime. Next, they look for a combination of 3 different kinds of coins that have the same value as a quarter.

3 Pay the exact amount; find how much money is left
The children take a given group of coins and count the money. Then they take away the amount of money shown on the price tag of a toy, and figure out what coins are left and how much money they show.

4 Pay the exact amount in different ways
The children take a given group of coins. They find two or three different combinations of coins they can use to pay the amount shown on the price tag of a toy.

5 Pay the exact amount in different ways
The children choose coins to pay the exact amount shown on the price tag of a toy. Then they choose another group of coins to pay the same amount. They record the combinations of coins.

6 Make combinations of coins to show different amounts of money
The children take a given group of coins. They show as many different amounts of money as they can by making combinations of 2 coins. Then they take a different group of coins and make combinations of 3 coins to show different amounts.

7 Find out how much more money is needed
The children take a given group of coins and bills, then count up their money. They figure out how much more money they will need to pay the amount shown on the price tag of a toy. They write an addition sentence to show the additional money needed.

8 Identify what you can buy with a given amount of money
Six snacks are shown with price tags. The children take a given group of coins and bills, then count up their money. They figure out what snacks they could buy with that amount of money.

9 Find the fewest coins and bills needed to pay an amount
The children find the fewest coins and bills needed to pay for a toy with a given price. They do this for four toys. The children choose the price for one of the toys. They record their work in a chart.

10 Pay the exact amount of money, and make change
The children take a given amount of money, pay for an item, and make the right change. In both problems the students will have to exchange a quarter for dimes, nickels, and pennies in order to make change.

11 Use clues and logical reasoning to solve mystery coins puzzles
The children use clues to identify a group of coins. Then they can write their own mystery coins puzzles.

12 Solve story problem puzzles
The children read a story problem and use the play money to help them find the solution. In one problem they need to add on or subtract. In the next problem they need to divide the given money equally between two people.

Organizing for Play Money Explorations

Play Money explorations can be used effectively with the whole class. Have students work in pairs sharing materials. Each pair should have at least 2 half dollars, 10 quarters, 10 dimes, 20 nickels, 25 pennies, and 5 one-dollar bills. Working in pairs will encourage children to discuss their thinking and develop problem-solving skills.

Play Money explorations can also be used effectively in centers. Each student or pair of students should have the coins and bills listed above. Package each set of coins and bills separately in a plastic bag or container.

Introducing Play Money

First talk about each coin, identifying each one by name. Have the children look at both sides of each coin. Ask the students to describe the coins, telling how they are alike and how they are different.

When the children are comfortable with the names of the coins, hold up a penny and say, **One penny is worth one cent. If we put 5 pennies together, they are worth 5 cents.** Have them count out 5 pennies with you. Then say, **Now we have 5 cents. A nickel is worth 5 pennies or 5 cents.** You can talk about a dime being worth 10 cents and a quarter having a value of 25 cents. The children can count out the number of pennies equal to the dime and then to the quarter.

Show the students a nickel, a dime, and a quarter. Ask them which is worth the fewest pennies and which is worth the most pennies. Then go on to talk about half dollars and dollars. Talk about coins equal to a half dollar and coins equal to one dollar.

Coin Banks

Name: _____

Play Money 1

Use: play coins

penny 1¢   nickel 5¢   dime 10¢   quarter 25¢

• Match the coins. Count the money.

A. Begin with the dime, then nickels, then pennies.

__10__, __15__, _____, _____, _____   Amount: _____¢

B. Begin with the quarter, then dimes, then nickels, then pennies.

_____, _____, _____, _____, _____, _____, _____   Amount: _____¢

Name: _____

Rabbit and Bear

Play Money

Use: play coins

penny 1¢   nickel 5¢   dime 10¢   quarter 25¢

• Rabbit and Bear have the same amount of money, but they have different coins.

A. Rabbit has 2 different kinds of coins. What coins does Rabbit have?

   Bear   Rabbit   

B. Rabbit has 3 different kinds of coins. What coins could Rabbit have?

   Bear      Rabbit   

• **Mystery Coins Puzzle**
Owl has 4 coins. Together they are worth 25¢.
What coins does Owl have?

Cars and Bugs

Name: _____

Play Money
3

Use: play coins

- Take the coins shown.
  Pay the exact amount for each toy.

A.

1 quarter   1 dime   4 nickel   11 penny

28 ¢

Amount you have: _____ ¢

Amount you pay: _____ ¢

Coins left: _____

Money left: _____ ¢

B.

1 quarter   2 dime   4 nickel   8 penny

45 ¢

Amount you have: _____ ¢

Amount you pay: _____ ¢

Coins left: _____

Money left: _____ ¢

- **Mystery Coins Puzzle**
  Josie paid 30¢ for colored pens.
  She used 4 coins.
  What coins did she use?

Wind it Up!

Name: _____

Play Money

Use: play coins

A. Take

    1 quarter   3 dime   2 nickel   2 penny

Show 2 ways to pay exactly 40¢.

Way 1:

Way 2:

B. Take

  1 half dollar   2 quarter   2 dime   1 nickel   2 penny

Show 3 ways to pay exactly 50¢.

Way 1:

Way 2:

Way 3:

- **Mystery Coins Puzzle**
  Jamie paid 45¢ for stickers.
  He used 4 coins.
  What coins did he use?

Two Ways

Name: _____

Play Money 5

Use: play coins

- Find two ways to pay for each toy. Show what coins you use.

A.

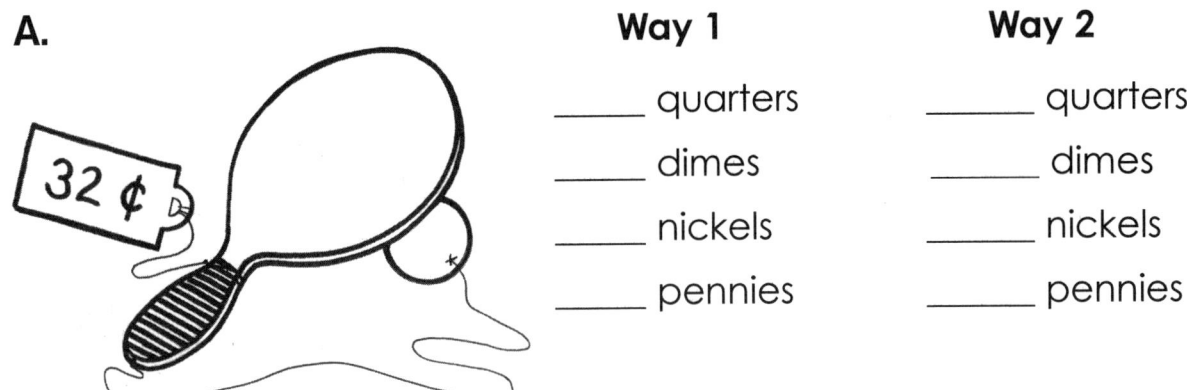

32 ¢

Way 1	Way 2
____ quarters	____ quarters
____ dimes	____ dimes
____ nickels	____ nickels
____ pennies	____ pennies

B.

65 ¢

Way 1	Way 2
____ quarters	____ quarters
____ dimes	____ dimes
____ nickels	____ nickels
____ pennies	____ pennies

- **Mystery Coins Puzzle**
  We are 3 coins. Together we are worth more than 15¢ and less than 20¢. What coins are we?

Skill: Counting money 73

Name: _____

Different Amounts of Money

Play Money

6

Use: play coins

A. Take

Use 2 coins to show an amount of money.
What different amounts can you show?

B. Take

Use 3 coins to show an amount of money.
What different amounts can you show?

- **Mystery Coins Puzzle**
  We are 5 coins. Together we are worth
  an odd number of cents. We are
  worth more than 50¢, but less than 60¢.
  What coins could we be?

Name: _____

How Much More?

Play Money
7

Use: play coins and bills

- Take the coins and bills shown. How much more money do you need to pay the exact amount?

A.

    1 half dollar   1 quarter   1 dime

How much money do you have? _____ ¢
How much more money do you need? _____ ¢

_____ + _____ = 99¢

What coins do you need?

B.

    1 dollar   1 quarter   2 penny

How much money do you have? _____ ¢
How much more money do you need? _____ ¢

_____ + _____ = $1.50

What coins do you need?

- **Mystery Money Puzzle**
  I have 4 dimes and 1 quarter.
  I need 1 more coin to pay for a ball.
  How much could the ball cost?

© Ideal School Supply • A Division of Instructional Fair Group, Inc. • Doing Basic Math with Manipulatives, Grades 1-3 - **Skill:** Counting money

The Snack Stop

Name: _____

Play Money
8

Use: play coins and bills

- Take the coins and bills.
  If you spend all your money, what snacks can you buy?

A. Take 1 one-dollar bill and 2 quarters.
Amount to spend: $_____

Snacks you can buy:

_____

_____

B. Take 1 one-dollar bill, 1 half dollar, and 3 dimes.
Amount to spend: $_____

Snacks you can buy:

_____

_____

- **Extra Challenge**
  Celia had 2 half dollars and 1 quarter.
  She bought 2 snacks. She has less than
  20 cents left, but more than 10 cents.
  What snacks did she buy?

Name: _____

Bears, Bears, Bears

Play Money

9

Use: play coins and bills

- Pay for each bear.
  Use as few coins and bills as you can.
  Show what you use.

	 $1 bill	 quarter	 dime	 nickel	How many pieces of money?
A.  $1.75					
B.  $1.95					
C.  $2.50					
D. Choose a price. Write it on the tag. 					

© Ideal School Supply • A Division of Instructional Fair Group, Inc. • Doing Basic Math with Manipulatives, Grades 1-3 - **Skill:** Counting money

Kites

Name: _____

Play Money
10

Use: play coins and bills

- Take the money. Pay the exact amount.
  Trade coins for other coins of equal value when you need to.
  What change do you get back?

A. Take 4 quarters.

Coins you get back:

Amount you get back: ____

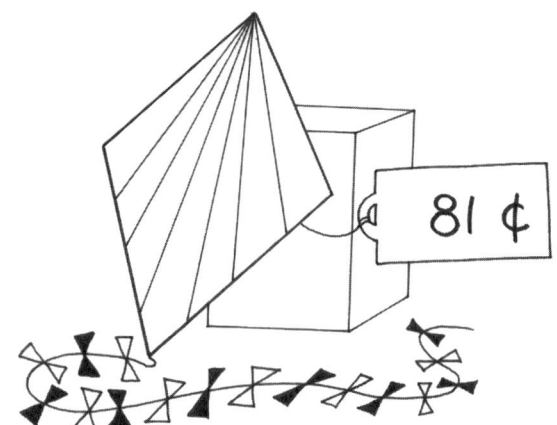

B. Take 1 one-dollar bill and 1 quarter.

Coins you get back:

Amount you get back: ____

- **Extra Challenge**
  I paid one dollar and 1 quarter for my kite.
  I got back 1 dime and 2 pennies.
  What did I pay for my kite?

Mystery Coins

Name: _____

Play Money

11

Use: play coins

- Read the clues for each puzzle.
  Find the mystery coins.

A. CLUES
- There is an odd number of coins.
- Together they are worth 45¢.
- There are 2 kinds of coins.
- There are no pennies.

What coins are they?

B. CLUES
- There is an even number of coins.
- Together they are worth 71¢.
- There are 4 kinds of coins.
- There are fewer than 10 coins.

What coins are they?

C. CLUES
- There is an even number of coins.
- Together they are worth 75¢.
- There are no pennies.
- There are fewer than 8 coins.

What coins are they?

- **Extra Challenge**
  Write your own mystery coins puzzle.
  Let someone solve your puzzle.

Money Puzzles

Name: _____

Play Money

12

Use: play coins and bills

- Solve each puzzle.

A. Jose was saving money. He had saved $7.85. Jose had saved $2.40 more than his friend Nathan. How much money had Nathan saved?

B. Olga and Darla were feeding their neighbor's cats and watering her plants. When the neighbor got home, she gave them 3 one-dollar bills, 3 quarters, 3 dimes, and 3 nickels. They divided the money equally. How did they do this so that they each got the same amount?

- **Extra Challenge**
  Write your own money puzzle.
  Let someone solve your puzzle.

Colored Cubes

Colored Cubes help children develop these concepts and skills:

Patterns and Algebra Thinking
- Create color patterns
- Recognize and extend number patterns

Numbers and Operations
- Count and show numbers
- Show addition
- Show subtraction
- Use repeated addition to explore multiplication
- Show a fraction of a group

Measurement
- Measure perimeter using one-inch cubes
- Measure area using one-inch cubes
- Measure volume using one-inch cubes

Data, Probability, and Graphing
- Experiment to explore probability; graph the results

Problem Solving
- Make different combinations using an organized list

What Are Colored Cubes?

Colored Cubes are one-inch plastic or wooden cubes that come in 9 bright colors: red, orange, black, white, purple, yellow, green, blue, and brown. These cubes are packaged in groups of 100.

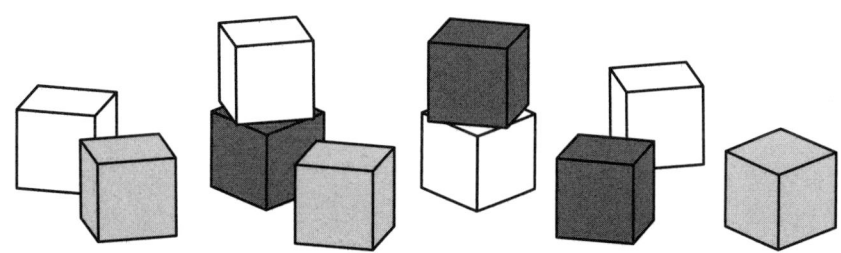

Why Use Colored Cubes?

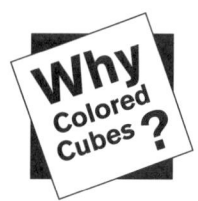

Some manipulatives are particularly useful for math class because they can help children see and understand a variety of concepts. Colored Cubes are one of these manipulatives, as they can be used to represent numbers of objects, to show patterns, to show fractional parts of groups, and to measure length, perimeter, area, and volume. They can also be used for solving logical reasoning problems and exploring probability. The one-inch cubes are perfect for small hands to move around, but are equally appropriate for older children to use.

Exploring Math With Colored Cubes

Following are descriptions of 12 explorations that children can do with Colored Cubes, and the concepts and skills they will be developing. Reproducible masters for the explorations are given on pages 85-96. Many of the explorations end with an extra challenging puzzle to extend the learning.

1 **Compare numbers: same number as, more than, fewer than; count how many altogether**
The children take 6 yellow cubes, then add the same number of green cubes to them, and count how many cubes there are altogether. They do the same kind of problem again, adding more cubes or fewer cubes than the first color.

2 **Create color patterns**
The children use 6 red cubes and 3 white cubes to create color patterns in a 3 x 3 grid. They color the grids to show their patterns.

3 **Combine groups to show addition; write addition sentences**
The children make 3 groups of cubes using different colors. They combine two groups at a time to show addition, and write addition sentences to show their work. They end by combining all three groups and writing the addition sentence.

4 **Show subtraction; write subtraction sentences**
The children take a group of cubes, then take away cubes and find out how many cubes are left. They write subtraction sentences to show their work.

5 Use repeated addition to explore multiplication
The children make 2 two-layer cakes, using 4 cubes for each cake. They record an addition sentence to show this. They also write a multiplication sentence to show this. A visual representation with the cubes will help children see the relationship between repeated addition and multiplication. They go on to make 3 two-layer cakes, and write the addition and multiplication sentences to show their work.

6 Show fractional parts of a group
The children make groups of cubes with two different colors. Then they find out what fraction of the group each color shows. They show fourths and thirds in the exploration, then sixths in the extra challenge at the end of the exploration.

7 Measure perimeter, using one-inch cubes
The children estimate the length of the perimeter of a rectangular pool in a picture, then use the one-inch cubes to measure. Then they estimate and measure the perimeter of one of their shoes.

8 Measure area, using one-inch cubes
The children estimate the area of a shape, then use cubes to measure it. Then they estimate and measure the area of the sheet of paper they are working on.

9 Identify and extend number patterns
The children build a series of robots, using 5 cubes for each robot. They keep track of the number of robots and cubes used in a table, then look for a pattern in the numbers. They extend the pattern to find out how many cubes it would take to make 8 and 10 robots.

10 Measure volume, using one-inch cubes
The children use cubes to cover a rectangular "floor" of a building. They begin by counting the cubic units of space on one floor. As they add a second and third floor, they record the cubic units of space in the building. Finally, they figure out the cubic units of space in a five-floor building, and use that as the measure of the volume of the building.

11 Act out story problems; show different combinations in an organized list
The children take cubes of different colors to act out the problems. First they combine cubes to make three different pairs of fish. They record their pairs in an organized list. Then they combine cubes to make five different groups of 4 fish.

12 Experiment to explore probability; graph the results

The children put one each of four different-colored cubes in a bag. They shake the bag, then draw out 1 cube, record the color, and put the cube back into the bag. They repeat this for a total of 20 draws. Then they look at the results of the experiment as shown in their graph. For the next experiment, they put two cubes of one color and one each of two other colors in the bag. They do the same experiment as before. They should get different results for the colors; however, sometimes it may require repeating the experiment many more times than 20 to come close to the expected results. The exploration should give children a sense of how the chances of drawing a particular color relate to the number of cubes of each color in the bag.

Organizing for Colored Cubes Explorations

Colored Cubes explorations can be used effectively with the whole class. Have students work in groups of two to three sharing materials. Give every group 10 cubes each of 9 different colors, or 90 cubes. Working in pairs or small groups will encourage children to discuss their thinking and develop problem-solving skills together.

Colored Cubes explorations can also be used effectively in centers. Each student or pair of students will need 10 cubes each of the 9 different colors, or 90 cubes. Package each set of cubes separately in a plastic bag or container.

Introducing Colored Cubes

Let the children begin by just exploring the cubes–sorting them by color or making towers with them. When the children are ready for more activities, have them use the cubes to act out this story:

> There were 6 red rabbits skating at the park. Then 3 blue cats came to skate with them. Soon 2 of the red rabbits went home. Then 4 yellow ducks started skating with the rabbits and cats. Two blue cats got tired and went home. How many animals altogether are skating now? (6 + 3 - 2 + 4 - 2 = 9)

Encourage the children to make up their own stories and share them with the class. The class can act out each story.

In the Box

Use: colored cubes

A. Put 6 yellow cubes in the box. Put the same number of green cubes as yellow cubes in the box. Count the cubes.

How many cubes are there altogether in the box? _____

B. Put 4 blue cubes in the box. Put 2 more orange cubes than blue cubes in the box. Count the cubes.

How many cubes are there altogether in the box? _____

C. Put 5 white cubes in the box. Put 3 fewer brown cubes than white cubes in the box. Count the cubes.

How many cubes are there altogether in the box? _____

- **Explore Some More**
  Put red cubes, blue cubes, and green cubes in the box. Use more green cubes than blue cubes. Use more red cubes than green cubes. How many cubes do you have in all?

Square Patterns

Name: _____

Colored Cubes

Use: colored cubes and crayons or markers

- Take 6 red cubes and 3 white cubes. What kinds of patterns can you make in the squares?

- Color to show two patterns.

- **Explore Some More**
  Make a pattern in a long train of cubes. Use 6 blue cubes, 3 yellow cubes, and 3 green cubes.

Putting Cubes Together

Name: _____

Colored Cubes

3

Use: colored cubes

• Take 8 purple, 5 white, and 6 orange cubes.

A. Put the purple cubes and the white cubes together.
What sum do they show? _____
Write an addition sentence to show your work.

_____ + _____ = _____

B. Use the cubes to show different sums.
Write an addition sentence for each sum.

_____ + _____ = _____

_____ + _____ = _____

_____ + _____ + _____ = _____

• **Mystery Cubes Puzzle**
There are 16 cubes in all. There is the same
number of yellow cubes as blue cubes.
There are 4 more red cubes than blue cubes.
What are the mystery cubes?

Taking Cubes Away

Name: _____

Colored Cubes

Use: colored cubes

A. Take 9 red cubes.
Take away 4 of the cubes.
How many cubes are left? ____
Write a subtraction sentence to show your work.

____ – ____ = ____

B. Take 10 brown cubes.
Take away 7 of the cubes.
How many cubes are left? ____
Write a subtraction sentence to show your work.

____ – ____ = ____

- **Mystery Cubes Puzzle**
  There are 7 cubes left.
  There were 12 cubes to begin with.
  How many cubes were taken away?

Two-Layer Cakes

Name: _____

Colored Cubes

5

Use: colored cubes

A. It takes 4 cubes to make a two-layer cake.
How many cubes do you need for 2 cakes? _____

Write an addition sentence about the cakes.

____ + ____ = ____

Write a multiplication sentence about the cakes.

____ x ____ = ____
number   number   total
of cakes of cubes in number
         each cake   of cubes

B. How many cubes do you need for 3 cakes? _____
Write an addition sentence.

____ + ____ + ____ = ____

Write a multiplication sentence.

____ x ____ = ____
number   number   total
of cakes of cubes in number
         each cake   of cubes

• **Extra Challenge**
How many cubes do you need for 5 cakes?

© Ideal School Supply • A Division of Instructional Fair Group, Inc. • Doing Basic Math with Manipulatives, Grades 1-3 - **Skill: Multiplication**

What Part of the Group?

Name: _____

Colored Cubes

6

Use: colored cubes

A. Put 2 green cubes and 2 yellow cubes in a group.
Each cube is 1 of 4 equal parts of the group.
Each cube is $\frac{1}{4}$ of 4 cubes.
Find what fraction each color shows.

$\frac{}{4}$ of the cubes are yellow   — of the cubes are green

B. Put 2 blue cubes and 1 red cube in a group.
Each cube is 1 of 3 equal parts of the group.
Each cube is $\frac{1}{3}$ of 3 cubes.
Find what fraction each color shows.

— of the cubes is red   — of the cubes are blue

C. Put 3 black cubes and 1 orange cube in a group.
Each cube is 1 of 4 equal parts of the group.
Each cube is $\frac{1}{4}$ of 4 cubes.
Find what fraction each color shows.

— of the cubes are black   — of the cubes is orange

- **Extra Challenge**
  Each animal is $\frac{1}{6}$ of the group.
  What fraction do the dogs show?
  What fraction do the cats show?

How Many Around?

Name: _____

Colored Cubes

Use: colored cubes

- Each edge of a colored cube is 1 inch long.

- **Perimeter** is the distance around the outside of an object or a shape.

1 inch long

A. How many inches long is the distance around the pool?

Guess _____ inches

Use the cubes to measure the perimeter around the pool.

Measure _____ inches

B. How many inches long is the distance around your shoe?

Guess _____ inches

Use the cubes to measure the perimeter of your shoe.

Measure _____ inches

- **Explore Some More**
  Measure around 3 more things in your room.
  Use cubes to measure the perimeter of each one.

© Ideal School Supply • A Division of Instructional Fair Group, Inc. • Doing Basic Math with Manipulatives, Grades 1-3 - Skill: Measurement

Cover Up

Name: _____

Use: colored cubes

- Each face of a colored cube covers 1 square inch of **area**.

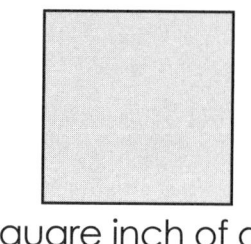

1 square inch of area

A. How many cubes will cover this shape?

Guess _____   Measure _____

How many square inches of area does the shape have?

_____ square inches

B. Take a piece of paper. How many cubes will cover it?

Guess _____   Measure _____

The paper has _____ square inches of area.

- **Explore Some More**

  Trace around your hand on paper. How many cubes will cover the picture of your hand? Guess, then measure. About how many square inches of area does your hand have?

Building Robots

Name: _____

Colored Cubes
9

Use: colored cubes

A. Use cubes to build the robots.

It takes 5 cubes to make 1 robot.

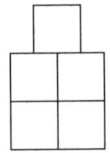

It takes 10 cubes to make 2 robots.

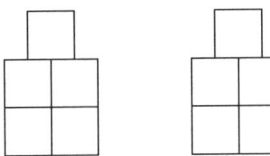

It takes ____ cubes to make 3 robots.

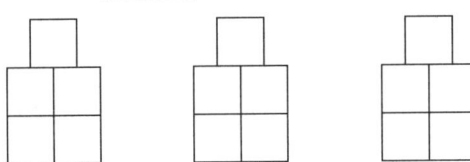

Number of robots	Number of cubes
1	5

B. Fill in the table. Look for a pattern in the numbers.

How many cubes would you need to make 8 robots? ____

How many cubes would you need to make 10 robots? ____

- **Extra Challenge**
  How many cubes would you need to make 20 robots?

The Cube Center

Name: _____

Colored Cubes

Use: colored cubes

A. Cover the shape with cubes. Let's say that each cube is a room.

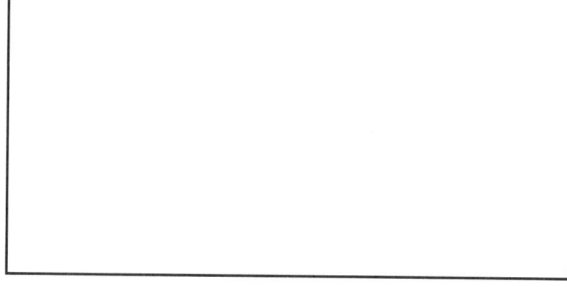

You made the first floor. How many rooms are in a 1-floor Cube Center? _____

Make a second floor. How many rooms are in a 2-floor Cube Center? _____

Make a third floor. How many rooms are in a 3-floor Cube Center? _____

B. How many rooms do you think there are in a 5-floor Cube Center? _____ Make the fourth and fifth floors. How many rooms are in a 5-floor Cube Center? _____

C. Each cube fills 1 **cubic unit** of space.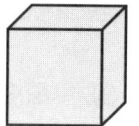

Volume is the number of cubic units of space inside something.

What is the volume of a 3-floor Cube Center? _____ cubic units

What is the volume of a 5-floor Cube Center? _____ cubic units

• **Extra Challenge**
Make a building that has 4 floors and a volume of 16 cubic units. How many rooms does each floor have?

Funtastic Fish

Name: _____

Colored Cubes

11

Use: colored cubes

A. On Monday, the Funtastic Fish Shop got 2 green spotted fish, 2 yellow fish, and 2 white striped fish. Freida put 2 of the fish into each tank. Each pair of 2 fish was different. What were the pairs? Make an organized list to show your pairs.

   1 green and 1 yellow
   _____
   _____

B. On Tuesday, Funtastic Fish got 10 blue-eyed fish and 10 green-eyed fish. Franklin put 4 of the fish into each tank. Each group of 4 fish was different. What were the groups? Make an organized list to show your groups.

   _____
   _____
   _____
   _____
   _____

- **Extra Challenge**
  Today Funtastic Fish gets 3 yellow fish, 3 green fish, 3 red, and 3 blue fish. Flora puts them into different pairs. What are the pairs?

Name: _____

What Are Your Chances?

Colored Cubes

12

Use: colored cubes and a paper bag

A. Put 1 red cube, 1 green cube, 1 yellow cube, and 1 blue cube in a paper bag. Shake the bag. Draw one cube out of the bag without looking. Record the color of your cube in the graph below, then put your cube back in the bag. Do this 20 times in all.

red																				
green																				
yellow																				
blue																				

Look at your graph. Did you get one color more than another? _____ Did you get each color about the same number of times? _____ Do you think you had the same chance of getting each color? _____

B. Put 1 red, 1 yellow, and 2 blue cubes in the bag. Shake the bag. Without looking, draw one cube out of the bag. Record the color in the graph. Put the cube back into the bag. Do this 20 times.

red																				
yellow																				
blue																				

Look at your graph. Did you get one color more than the other colors? _____ Did you have a greater chance of drawing one color than the others? _____ What color? _____

- **Explore Some More**
  What do you think your graph would look like if you drew cubes 100 times in Experiment B? Try it.

Base Ten Blocks

Base Ten Blocks help children develop these concepts and skills:

Numbers and Operations
- Estimate, count, and write numbers
- Show a number in different ways, using tens and ones
- Explore place value of ones, tens, and hundreds
- Trade ones for tens and tens for ones
- Use number sense to identify mystery numbers
- Show addition; write addition sentences
- Show subtraction; write subtraction sentences
- Show multiplication using repeated addition; write multiplication sentences
- Show division using equal groups; write division sentences

Patterns and Algebra Thinking
- Recognize and extend number patterns
- Use algebra thinking to solve problems

Problem Solving
- Use clues and logical reasoning to solve problems

What Are Base Ten Blocks?

Base Ten Blocks are concrete models of our base ten number system. Ten ones-blocks together form a tens-block. Ten tens-blocks together form a hundreds-block. Ten hundreds-blocks together form a thousands-block. A beginning set has 100 cubes (ones-blocks), 20 rods (tens-blocks), and 10 flats (hundreds-blocks), and 1 block (thousands-block).

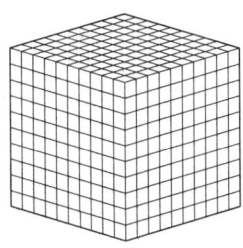
thousands-block

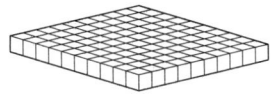
hundreds-block

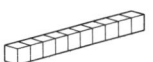
tens-block

ones-block

Why Use Base Ten Blocks?

The concept of the ones place, tens place, and hundreds place in numbers is abstract. If children can see that when you put 10 ones together they equal a tens-block, this helps them to understand how numbers are constructed. As children count and group the blocks by ones, tens, and hundreds, they build strong mental images of numbers. As they learn to trade 10 ones-blocks for a tens-block, or a tens-block for 10 ones-blocks, they begin to understand regrouping in addition and subtraction. It is vital that at each stage the children attach meaning to what they are doing with the blocks, and that they write numbers to represent groups of blocks. It is also important that children write addition, subtraction, multiplication, and division sentences to represent what they are doing as they combine blocks, take blocks away, and make equal groups of blocks. The children should always be using the blocks to help them with writing the symbols.

Exploring Math With Base Ten Blocks

Following are descriptions of 12 explorations that children can do with Base Ten Blocks, and the concepts and skills they will be developing. Reproducible masters for the explorations are given on pages 101-112. Many of the explorations end with an extra challenging puzzle to extend the learning.

1 Estimate, count, and write numbers
The children first look at a shape and guess how many ones-blocks or tens-blocks will cover it. Then they cover the shape, count the blocks, and write the number that the blocks show.

2 Show a number in different ways
The children cover a shape in three different ways, using different groups of blocks for each way. They record the tens and ones for each way, and they write the number shown by the blocks.

3 Use blocks to show different numbers
The children begin with a group of blocks. They look for all the different numbers they can show with one or more of the blocks.

4 Trade ones for tens and tens for ones
The children first trade a group of ones-blocks for as many ten-blocks as they can. Then they trade tens-blocks for ones-blocks. They record their blocks before and after their trades, and write the numbers shown by the blocks.

5 Use clues and logical reasoning to identify mystery numbers
The children begin with a group of blocks. Then they read clues to decide which blocks to use to show a mystery number. They find the blocks and write the mystery number.

6 Combine groups of blocks to show addition; write addition sentences
The children first make three groups of blocks, and write the numbers they show. Then they estimate which two groups together will show a number greater than 130, or less than 100. Next they find the sums of the four different ways that they can combine the groups. They write an addition sentence for each combination.

7 Add on blocks to show addition; write addition sentences
The children begin with a group of blocks. Then they add more blocks to show a number within a given range, such as between 50 and 60. They write an addition sentence to show their work.

8 Recognize and extend number patterns
The children make a series of three groups of blocks, and write the number that each group shows. They look for a pattern in the numbers and the blocks. Then they show what the next group of blocks in the pattern would be and write the number that the blocks show.

9 Take away blocks to show subtraction; write subtraction sentences
The children begin with a group of blocks and then take away blocks to show a number in a given range. They write a subtraction sentence to show their work.

10 Use repeated addition to show multiplication; write addition and multiplication sentences
The children make a bug with a given group of blocks, and then make three more bugs that are the same. They write an addition sentence to show what number the bugs show altogether. Then they write a multiplication sentence to show this.

11 Put blocks in equal groups to show division; write division sentences
The children begin with a group of blocks (12 ones-blocks) which they separate into equal groups. Then they write a division sentence that shows this. They look for another way to divide the same blocks into equal groups.

12 Use algebra thinking to solve problems
The children look at the blocks that are left after the Mystery Muncher steals some blocks. They have to figure out which blocks each person started with. They can use subtraction or count on to find the unknown number.

Organizing for Base Ten Blocks Explorations

Base Ten Blocks explorations can be used effectively with the whole class. Have students work in groups of 2 or 3 sharing materials. Each group should have 100 cubes, 20 rods, and 4 flats. They will mostly be using the cubes and rods in these activities. Working in pairs or small groups will encourage children to discuss their thinking and develop problem-solving skills.

Base Ten Blocks explorations can also be used effectively in centers. Each student or pair of students should have 100 cubes, 20 rods, and 4 flats. Package each set of blocks separately in a plastic bag or container.

Introducing Base Ten Blocks

Let the children begin by just exploring the Base Ten Blocks. They can put them together into groups or build with them. When the children are ready, begin by talking about the relationships between the blocks.

Take a ones-block and say, **The smallest block is called a ones-block. Take ten of these and line them up together.** Give the children a chance to do this and then hold up a tens-block and say, **This block is called a tens-block. Take one of these and put it next to the blocks you just lined up. Why is this called a tens-block?** They should be able to see that when the 10 ones-blocks are lined up, they equal one tens-block.

Next, have the children lay 10 of the tens-blocks side by side. Then hold up the hundreds-block and say, **This is the next larger block. See if it covers your 10 tens-blocks. What do you think we call this block?** Then have the children count by 10s to 100.

Show the children this easy way to record the blocks instead of drawing pictures of them:

•	|	☐
ones-block	tens-block	hundreds-block

Name: _____

How Many Blocks?

Base Ten Blocks

Use: Base Ten Blocks

- Guess how many blocks will cover each shape. Then cover the shape. Count the blocks. Write the number they show.

ones-block   tens-block

A.

Guess _____

Count _____

What number do the blocks show? _____

B.

Guess _____

Count _____

What number do the blocks show? _____

C.

Guess _____

Count _____

What number do the blocks show? _____

© Ideal School Supply • A Division of Instructional Fair Group, Inc. • Doing Basic Math with Manipulatives, Grades 1-3 - **Skill:** Estimation

Different Ways

Name: ____________________

Base Ten Blocks

2

Use: Base Ten Blocks

- Cover each shape with blocks.
  Find three different ways.

ones-block tens-block

A.

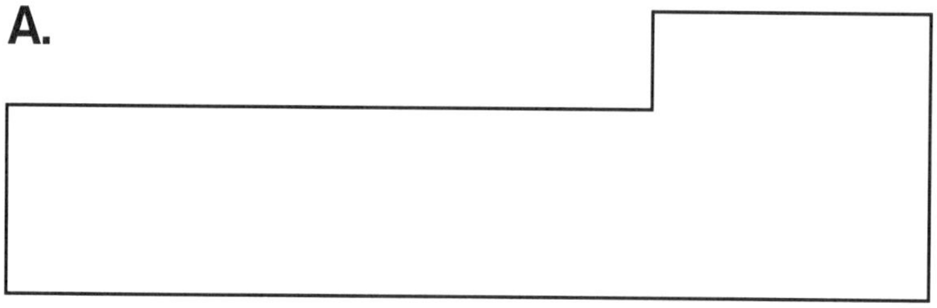

	tens	ones
Way 1		
Way 2		
Way 3		

What number do the blocks show? _____

B.

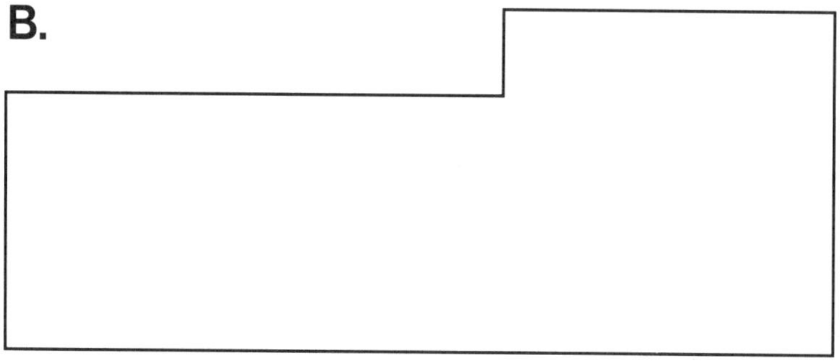

	tens	ones
Way 1		
Way 2		
Way 3		

What number do the blocks show? _____

- **Explore Some More**
  Use tens-blocks and ones blocks.
  Make a shape. Trace around the shape.
  How many different ways can you cover it?

 - **Skill: Showing numbers**

How Many Numbers?

Name: _____

Base Ten Blocks

Use: Base Ten Blocks

- Take the blocks shown.
  Show different numbers.
  Use 1 or more blocks to show each number.

Record like this:
• = ones-block
| = tens-block

A.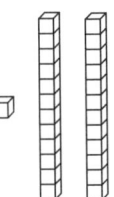

Blocks	Number shown

B.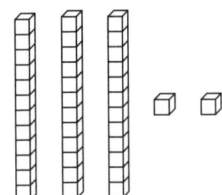

Blocks	Number shown

- **Mystery Blocks Puzzle**
  We show a number between 20 and 30.
  We have 1 more ones-block than tens-blocks.
  What blocks are we?

Skill: Showing numbers   103

A Bear Trader

Name: _____

Base Ten Blocks

Use: Base Ten Blocks

- • = ones-block
- | = tens-block
- ☐ = hundreds-block

A. Bear likes to trade blocks. Today he's trading ones for tens. Take the blocks shown. Count the ones-blocks. Trade 10 ones-blocks for 1 tens-block. Trade as many times as you can.

[25 ones-blocks shown]

Before trade

tens	ones

After trade

tens	ones

What number do the blocks show? ____

B. Today Bear is trading tens-blocks for ones-blocks. Trade each tens-block for 10 ones-blocks. Trade as many times as you can.

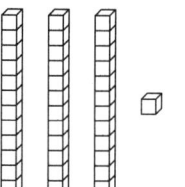

Before trade

tens	ones

After trade

tens	ones

What number do the blocks show? ____

• **Mystery Blocks Puzzle**
We show a number between 40 and 50. We have the same number of ones-blocks as tens-blocks. What blocks are we?

104 © Ideal School Supply • A Division of Instructional Fair Group, Inc. • Doing Basic Math with Manipulatives, Grades 1-3 - **Skill: Place value**

Mystery Numbers

Name: _____

Base Ten Blocks

Use: Base Ten Blocks

- Read the clues.
  Find the mystery numbers.

| • = ones-block |
| l = tens-block |
| ☐ = hundreds-block |

A. Take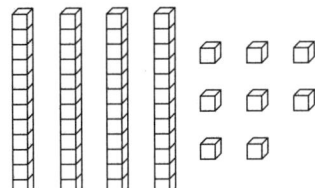

CLUES
- The number is greater than 20 and less than 30.
- Use 5 of the blocks.
  What is the mystery number? _____

B. Take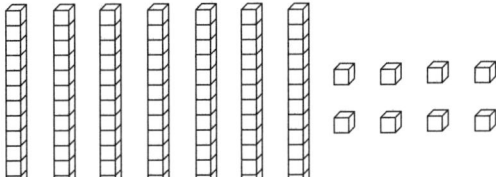

CLUES
- The number is >60 and <70.
- Use 11 of the blocks.
  What is the mystery number? _____

C. Take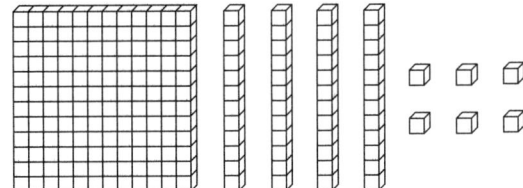

CLUES
- The number is >120 and <130.
- Use 9 of the blocks.
  What is the mystery number? _____

- **Extra Challenge**
  Make up your own mystery numbers clues.
  Let someone solve your mystery numbers puzzle.

Putting Groups Together

Name: _____

Base Ten Blocks

Use: Base Ten Blocks

- Make these groups of blocks and write the numbers they show.

> • = ones-block
> | = tens-block
> □ = hundreds-block

a. 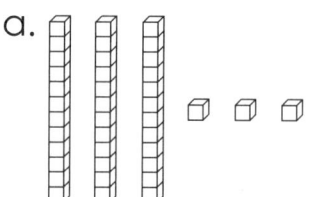   b. 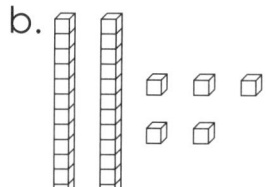   c.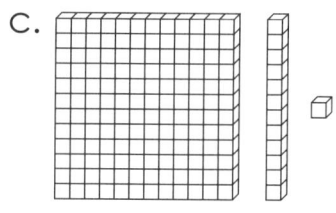

shows number ____   shows number ____   shows number ____

A. Which two groups together show a number >140?
Guess ____ and ____

Which two groups together show a number <100?
Guess ____ and ____

B. Put the groups of blocks together to show different sums.
Write addition sentences to show your work.

____ + ____ = ____

____ + ____ = ____

____ + ____ = ____

____ + ____ + ____ = ____

- **Mystery Blocks Puzzle**
We show a number between 110 and 120.
We have the same number of tens-blocks as hundreds-blocks.
We have 6 more ones-blocks than tens-blocks.
What blocks are we?

Adding On

Name: _____

Use: Base Ten Blocks

• = ones-block
| = tens-block
□ = hundreds-block

A. Take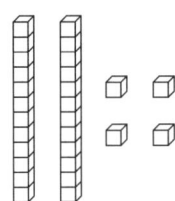

What number do the blocks show? _____

Add more blocks to show a number between 50 and 60. What blocks did you add?

Write an addition sentence to show your work.

_____ + _____ = _____

B. Take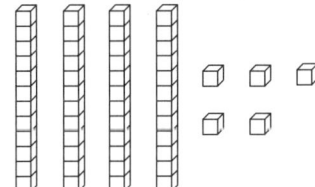

What number do the blocks show? _____

Add more blocks to show a number between 140 and 150. What blocks did you add?

Write an addition sentence to show your work.

_____ + _____ = _____

• **Mystery Blocks Puzzle**
We are 4 blocks. If you add on 2 tens-blocks, we will show a number between 130 and 140. What blocks are we?

© Ideal School Supply • A Division of Instructional Fair Group, Inc. • Doing Basic Math with Manipulatives, Grades 1-3 - **Skill: Addition**

Name: _____

Number Patterns

Base Ten Blocks

Use: Base Ten Blocks

- Make each group of blocks and write the number they show. Look for a pattern in the groups. Find the group of blocks that comes next. Write the number it shows.

A.

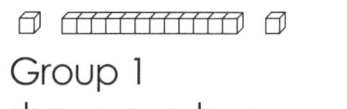

Group 1
shows number _____

Group 2
shows number _____

Group 3
shows number _____

Group 4
shows number _____

B.

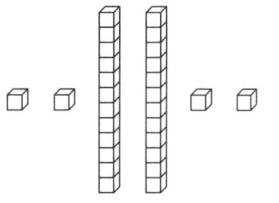   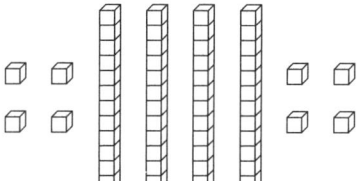

Group 1
shows number _____

Group 2
shows number _____

Group 3
shows number _____

Group 4
shows number _____

- **Extra Challenge**
Make up your own block pattern puzzle.

Take Some Away

Name: _____

Base Ten Blocks

Use: Base Ten Blocks

A. Take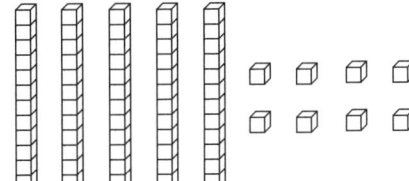

What number do the blocks show? _____

Take away blocks to show a number between 35 and 45. What blocks did you take away?

Write a subtraction sentence to show your work.

_____ − _____ = _____

B. Take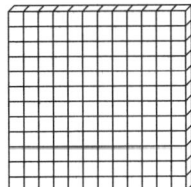

What number does the block show? _____

Trade for tens-blocks and ones-blocks.

Take away blocks to show a number between 70 and 80. What blocks did you take away?

Write a subtraction sentence to show your work.

_____ − _____ = _____

• **Mystery Blocks Puzzle**
We are 5 blocks. If you take away a tens-block, we show a number between 30 and 40. What blocks are we?

Block Bugs

Use: Base Ten Blocks

Base Ten Blocks

A. Make this block bug.

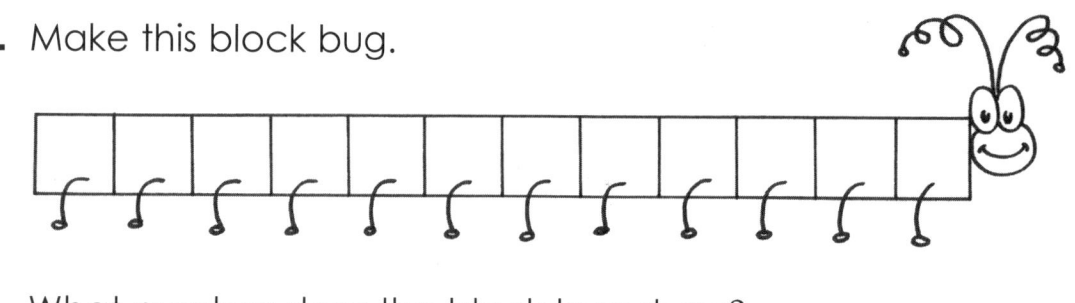

What number does the block bug show? _____

Make 3 more block bugs.
What number do the blocks show altogether? _____
Write an addition sentence to show your work.

_____ + _____ + _____ + _____ = _____

How many block bugs did you make? _____
What number does each bug show? _____
What number do the bugs show altogether? _____

Write a multiplication sentence to show your work.

_____ x _____ = _____

B. Make your own block bug. Then make 3 more of them.
Write an addition sentence to show your work.
Write a multiplication sentence to show your work.

_____ + _____ + _____ + _____ = _____

_____ x _____ = _____

- **Mystery Bug Puzzle**
  I am a mystery bug. I have the same number
  of ones-blocks as tens-blocks. When there are 4
  of us, we show a number between 80 and 90.
  What blocks am I made of?

Block Teams

Use: Base Ten Blocks

- Take 🧊🧊🧊🧊🧊🧊🧊🧊🧊🧊🧊🧊

Base Ten Blocks

11

A. Make equal groups with the blocks.
Each group must show the same number.

What number do the blocks show altogether? _____
What number does each group show? _____
How many groups? _____

Write a division sentence to show your work.

_____ ÷ _____ = _____

B. Find another way to make equal groups.
Each group must show the same number.

Write a division sentence to show your work.

_____ ÷ _____ = _____

- **Mystery Blocks Puzzle**
We are 16 blocks. When you put us into 2 equal groups, each group shows a number between 15 and 20. What blocks are we?

The Mystery Muncher

Name: _____

Use: Base Ten Blocks

- The Mystery Muncher steals blocks.

A. Jeff had 18 blocks that showed the number 54.
After the Muncher came, Jeff had these blocks left:

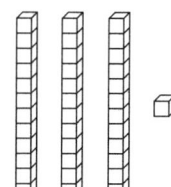

What blocks did the Muncher take?

B. Janell had 32 blocks that showed the number 86.
After the Muncher came, Janell had these blocks left:

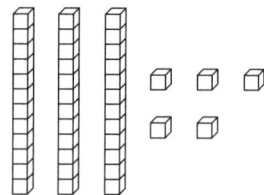

What blocks did the Muncher take?

C. Jody had 17 blocks that showed the number 125.
After the Muncher came, Jody had these blocks left:

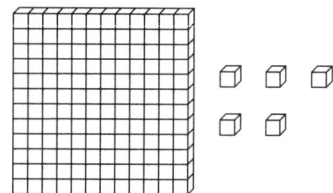

What blocks did the Muncher take?

- **Extra Challenge**
Make up a Mystery Muncher puzzle.
Ask someone to solve your puzzle.

Hundred Number Chart

The Hundred Number Chart helps children develop these concepts and skills:

Numbers and Operations
- Count by ones; skip-count by twos, fives, and tens
- Develop number sense
- Develop an understanding of the base ten number system
- Explore number relationships
- Compare and order numbers
- Explore beginning place value
- Add and subtract 1- and 2-digit numbers
- Multiply, using repeated addition
- Identify odd and even numbers
- Explore multiples

Patterns and Algebra Thinking
- Identify and extend number patterns
- Use algebraic thinking to solve problems

Problem Solving
- Use logical reasoning to solve problems

What Is the Hundred Number Chart?

The Hundred Number Chart used in this book is a chart showing the numbers 1 through 100.

1	2	3	4	5	6	7	8	9	10
11	12	13	14	15	16	17	18	19	20
21	22	23	24	25	26	27	28	29	30
31	32	33	34	35	36	37	38	39	40
41	42	43	44	45	46	47	48	49	50
51	52	53	54	55	56	57	58	59	60
61	62	63	64	65	66	67	68	69	70
71	72	73	74	75	76	77	78	79	80
81	82	83	84	85	86	87	88	89	90
91	92	93	94	95	96	97	98	99	100

The Hundred Number Chart is available in many forms, including charts numbered 0 through 99 and 1 through 100, a pocket chart with number inserts, and a plastic board accompanied by tiles numbered 1 through 100.

Why Use a Hundred Number Chart?

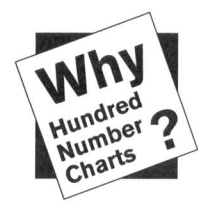

Hundred number charts are excellent models for children to use to explore our base ten system. They present numbers 1 through 100 in ten rows of ten, which helps children build a mental picture of place value.

Hundred number charts help children see relationships between numbers and discover patterns in them. The charts also help children build an understanding of addition, subtraction, and multiplication, and allow them to develop useful strategies for mental computation. Children will also find that the hundred number chart is a handy reference when they are solving a variety of number puzzles.

Exploring Math With Hundred Number Charts

Following are descriptions of 12 explorations that children can do with the hundred number chart, and the concepts and skills they will be developing. Reproducible masters for the explorations are given on pages 117-128. Many of the explorations end with an extra challenging puzzle to extend the learning.

1 **Find numbers that are one more than or one less than numbers shown**
The children find numbers that are one more or one less than given numbers. This exploration introduces the children to numbers 1 through 50 on the hundred number chart, and helps them discover relationships between the numbers.

2 **Find numbers that are ten more than or ten less than numbers shown**
The children find numbers that are ten more or ten less than given numbers.

3 **Use clues about number relationships to identify missing numbers**
The children use what they know about number relationships to fill in missing numbers.

4 **Identify and extend patterns in odd numbers**
The children look at odd numbers 1 through 25, then fill in the missing odd numbers from 27 through 49. They look for the pattern in the ones digits of the odd numbers, and use that pattern to identify more odd numbers.

5 Identify and extend patterns in even numbers
The children look at even numbers 2 through 20, then fill in the missing even numbers from 22 through 50. They look for the pattern in the ones digits of the even numbers, and use that pattern and clues to identify mystery numbers.

6 Skip-count by fives; identify and extend the number pattern
The children skip-count by fives on the hundred number chart, and write the numbers they stop on. They look for a pattern in the numbers, then use the pattern to identify three-digit numbers that fit the pattern.

7 Count on and count back to add and subtract
The children count on or count back to find the sum of two numbers or the difference between two numbers. This exploration gives children practice with basic addition and subtraction facts, but also introduces a useful mental computation strategy.

8 Count on and count back to add and subtract two-digit numbers; use computation strategies
The children count on to find the sum of two 2-digit numbers. An illustration is given of a computation strategy: first counting on by tens, then by the extra ones. The children then count back to find the differences between two 2-digit numbers, and show any shortcut strategies they find.

9 Explore number patterns
The children begin by choosing groups of four number neighbors. They find the sum of each pair of diagonal neighbors, then look for a pattern in the sums.

| 1 | 2 | 1 + 12 = 13
|---|---|
| 11 | 12 | 2 + 11 = 13

Next, they choose groups of five number neighbors. They find the sum of each trio of diagonal neighbors, then look for a pattern in the sums.

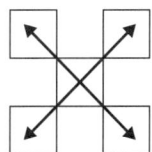

10 Identify and extend number patterns
The children look for patterns in number sequences, then extend the patterns. There are number sequences with repeated increases or decreases, and also a sequence with a growing increase.

11 Use clues about place value to identify mystery numbers
The children use clues about tens and ones to identify mystery numbers.

12 Use logical reasoning to solve Venn circle problems
They look at numbers shown in a Venn circle puzzle, and identify what skip-counting pattern these numbers fit. Then they find more numbers that belong in the two circles and in their intersection.

Organizing for Hundred Number Chart Explorations

Hundred number chart explorations can be used effectively with the whole class, with small groups, and in learning centers. Have the children work in pairs, sharing materials. Working as partners will encourage the children to discuss their thinking and share problem-solving strategies. Each pair should have a hundred number chart. A reproducible master for a hundred number chart is given on page xv.

Introducing the Hundred Number Chart

Let the children begin by just looking at the hundred number chart or putting number tiles on a hundred number board. When the children are ready, ask them questions such as these:

> What can you tell me about the hundred number chart?
> How many numbers are on the chart?
> How many rows of numbers are there? How many numbers are there in each row?
> How are all the numbers in the second row alike? In the third row?
> How are all the numbers in the first column alike?

You might also have the children do the following activities. Give each pair of partners a pencil and a copy of the hundred number chart on page xv. Have the children take turns counting by ones, with one child counting from 1 to 10, the other child from 11 to 20, and so on to 100. Then challenge the children to count backwards from 100 to 1 in the same way.

Next, have the children skip-count by twos and mark each number they say. Tell them to start at 2, mark it, then count on 2 and mark that number, and so on to 100. Ask the partners to look for a pattern in the numbers they marked and to talk about the pattern they find.

Name: _____

Before and After

Hundred Number Charts

Use: a hundred number chart

A. Find each number on the hundred number chart. Then find the number that is 1 more.

| 6 | 7 | | 18 | 19 | | 29 | 30 |

| 10 | 11 | | 43 | 44 | | 31 | 32 |

B. Find each number on the hundred number chart. Then find the number that is 1 less.

| 2 | 3 | | ~~18/16~~ 16 | 17 | | ~~40~~ | 41 |

| ~~49~~ | 50 | | 25 | 26 | | ~~34~~ | 35 |

- **Mystery Number Puzzle**
  I am 1 more than 9. 10
  I am 1 less than 11. 10
  What number am I?

117

Name: _____

Above and Below

Hundred Number Charts

Use: a hundred number chart

A. Find each number on the hundred number chart.
Then find the number that is 10 more.

1	10	26	45	89

B. Find each number on the hundred number chart.
Then find the number that is 10 less.

75	52	38	19	100

- **Mystery Number Puzzle**
  I am 10 more than 9.
  I am 10 less than 29.
  What number am I?

118 © Ideal School Supply • A Division of Instructional Fair Group, Inc. • Doing Basic Math with Manipulatives, Grades 1-3 - **Skill:** Comparing numbers

What's Missing?

Name: _____

Hundred Number Charts

Use: a hundred number chart

- Fill in the missing numbers.
  Don't look at the hundred number chart.

A.
11	12	13	14
21	22	23	24
31	32	33	34
41	42	43	44

B.
57	58	59	60
67	68	69	70
77	78	79	80
87	88	89	90

Now use the hundred number chart to check your numbers.

- **Extra Challenge**
  Can you fill in the missing numbers?

1	2	3	4

14	15	16

26	27	28

38	39	40

Odd Numbers

Name: _____

Hundred Number Charts

4

Use: a hundred number chart

A. The numbers below are called **odd numbers**.
Fill in the rest of the odd numbers.

1		3		5		7		9	
11		13		15		17		19	
21		23		25					
								49	

B. Look for a pattern in the odd numbers.
Hint: Look at the last digit in each number.

1   3   5   7   9   11   13

What pattern do you see?

C. Think about the pattern you found.
Circle the numbers that are odd.

65   68   80   87   91   92   93   95   99

120   © Ideal School Supply • A Division of Instructional Fair Group, Inc. • Doing Basic Math with Manipulatives, Grades 1-3 - Skill: Patterns

Even Numbers

Name: _____

Hundred Number Charts

5

Use: a hundred number chart

A. The numbers below are called even numbers.
Fill in the rest of the even numbers.

	2		4		6		8		10
	12		14		16		18		20
									50

B. Look for a pattern in the even numbers.
Hint: Look at the last digit in each number.

2   4   6   8   10   12   14

What pattern do you see?

- **Mystery Number Puzzle**
  I am an even number.
  I am between 50 and 56.
  I am not 52.
  What number am I?

121

Fives

Name: _____

Hundred Number Charts

6

Use: a hundred number chart

A. Begin at 1 on the hundred number chart. Skip-count by fives. Write the numbers you stop on.

__5__, ____, ____, ____, ____,

____, ____, ____, ____, ____,

____, ____, ____, ____, ____,

____, ____, ____, ____, ____

B. Look for a pattern in the numbers you wrote. What is the pattern?

C. Think about the pattern you found. Which of these numbers belong in the "fives" pattern?

101   102   105   110   115   117   120

- **Mystery Number Puzzle**
  I am an odd number.
  I am between 36 and 46.
  You say my name when you skip-count by fives.
  What number am I?

Name: _____

Count On, Count Back

Hundred Number Charts

7

Use: a hundred number chart

A. Use the hundred number chart to help you add.
Count on to find each sum.

Start on 3, count on 5.
The sum is 8.

```
  3     5     2     4     1     9
+ 5   + 3   + 4   + 2   + 9   + 1
───   ───   ───   ───   ───   ───
  8
```

B. Count back to find each difference.

Start on 10, count back 9.
The difference is 1.

```
 10     8     6     9     7     6
- 9   - 3   - 2   - 1   - 5   - 3
───   ───   ───   ───   ───   ───
```

- **Mystery Number Puzzle**
  If you start on me and subtract 4, you end on 4.
  What number am I?

- **Extra Challenge**
  Write clues about a mystery number.
  Let someone solve your mystery number puzzle.

Add and Subtract

Name: _____

Hundred Number Charts

Use: a hundred number chart

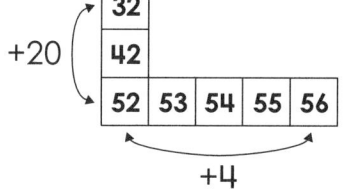

A. Use the chart to help you add.
Count on to find each sum.

I use a shortcut.

```
  32      28      21      49      19      85
+ 24    + 36    + 45    + 11    + 43    + 15
-----   -----   -----   -----   -----   -----
  56
```

Did you use a different shortcut?
Show it here and talk about it with a friend.

B. Count back to find each difference.

```
  40      85      64      93      50      61
- 29    - 32    - 27    - 18    - 25    - 35
-----   -----   -----   -----   -----   -----
```

Did you find a shortcut? Show it here.

- **Mystery Number Puzzle**
  If you start on me and add 50, you end on 75.
  What number am I?

- **Extra Challenge**
  Write clues about a mystery number.
  Let someone solve your mystery number puzzle.

Number Patterns

Name: _____

Hundred Number Charts

9

Use: a hundred number chart

A. Choose 2 groups of 4 number
neighbors on the chart, like this:

Show your numbers. Then find the sum
of each pair of diagonal neighbors.

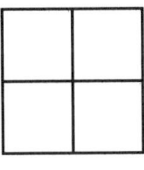   ___ + ___ = ___   ___ + ___ = ___

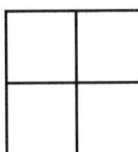   ___ + ___ = ___   ___ + ___ = ___

What pattern did you find?

Is the same pattern in other diagonal neighbors?

B. Choose 2 groups of 5 number neighbors, like this: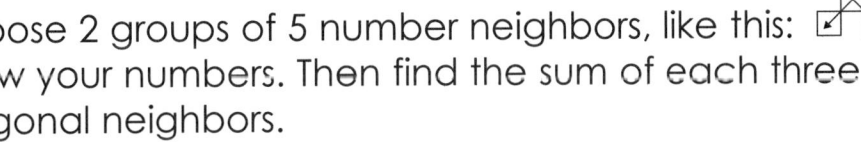
Show your numbers. Then find the sum of each three
diagonal neighbors.

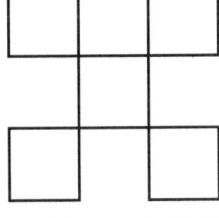   ___ + ___ + ___ = ___   ___ + ___ + ___ = ___

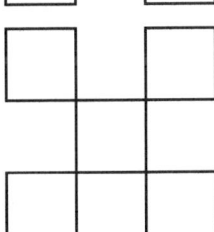   ___ + ___ + ___ = ___   ___ + ___ + ___ = ___

What pattern did you find?

• **Explore Some More**
What other patterns can you find on the chart?

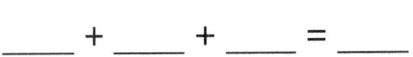

125

What's My Pattern?

Name: _____

Hundred Number Charts

Use: a hundred number chart

A. Find the pattern in each number sequence. Add numbers to continue the pattern.

3, 6, 9, 12, 15, ____, ____, ____, ____, ____, ____

8, 16, 24, 32, 40, ____, ____, ____, ____, ____, ____

100, 90, 80, 70, ____, ____, ____, ____, ____, ____

99, 88, 77, ____, ____, ____, ____, ____, ____

80, 75, 70, 65, ____, ____, ____, ____, ____, ____

B. Find the pattern in this number sequence. Add numbers to continue the pattern.

Hint: The skip-count number grows!

1, 2, 4, 7, 11, 16, 22, 29, ____, ____, ____, ____, ____, ____

- **Extra Challenge**
  Choose a pattern. Write a number sequence that follows your pattern. Let someone find your pattern and add more numbers.

Name: _____

Tens and Ones

Hundred Number Charts

Use: a hundred number chart

A. Find each number.

1 ten and 2 ones
That means 1 row of ten and 2 ones.
That's number 12.

2 tens and 5 ones = ___   1 ten and 4 ones = ___

4 tens and 9 ones = ___   3 tens and 1 one = ___

B. Find each number.

7 tens and 0 ones = ___   9 tens and 9 ones = ___

0 tens and 7 ones = ___   6 tens and 0 ones = ___

- **Mystery Number Puzzle**
  I have more tens than ones.
  I am between 52 and 60.
  I am an even number.
  What number am I?

- **Extra Challenge**
  Write clues about a mystery number.
  Let someone find your mystery number.

Name: _____

Missing Number Puzzles

Hundred Number Charts

Use: a hundred number chart

- Look at the numbers in each circle. What is the skip-count pattern for each circle? What numbers belong in **both** circles? Write them in the space where the circles overlap. Then find more numbers from 51 through 100 that belong in the circles.

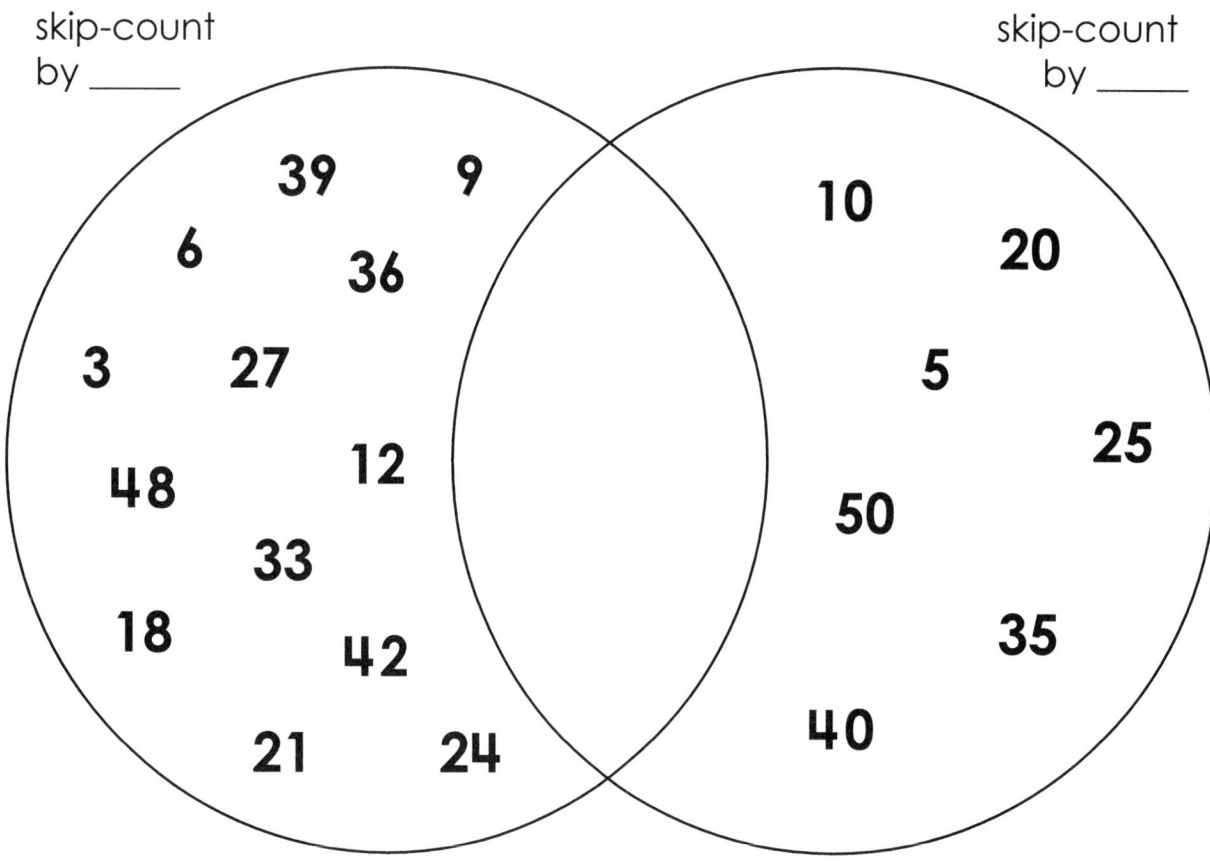

skip-count by _____   skip-count by _____

- **Extra Challenge**
  Draw 2 overlapping circles. Use different rules for the circles. Write some numbers in the circles. Let someone find your rules and add numbers.

128   © Ideal School Supply • A Division of Instructional Fair Group, Inc. • Doing Basic Math with Manipulatives, Grades 1-3 - **Skill:** Problem solving

Fraction Pieces

Fraction pieces help children develop these concepts and skills:

Fractions
- Find equal parts of a whole
- Recognize and name fractions
- Compare fractions
- Find equivalent fractions
- Add fractions with like denominators
- Subtract fractions with like denominators

What Are Fraction Pieces?

In the explorations, we use two plastic fraction models: Deluxe Fraction Circles (circle) and Fraction Builder® (rectangle). The fraction pieces show equal parts of a whole shape. Both of these fraction models include these pieces: 1 whole, 2 halves, 3 thirds, 4 fourths, 5 fifths, 6 sixths, 8 eighths, 10 tenths, and 12 twelfths. The Fraction Builder® pieces have the fraction notation marked on each piece. In both sets, pieces that show the same fractional part are the same color. For example, the fourths in both models are purple.

Color Code for Fraction Pieces

whole - black	fourths - purple	eighths - brown
halves - orange	fifths - blue	tenths - yellow
thirds - green	sixths - red	twelfths - tan

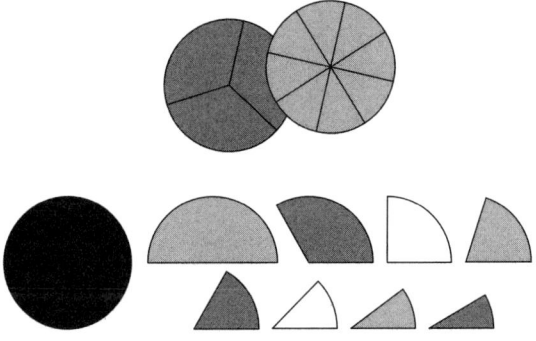
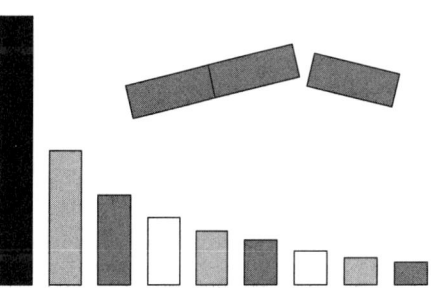

© Ideal School Supply • A Division of Instructional Fair Group, Inc. • Doing Basic Math with Manipulatives, Grades 1-3

Why Use Fraction Pieces?

The concept of fractions is difficult for many children to grasp. Using colorful, concrete models can help children form mental images of fractions as equal parts of a whole area. As children explore with the pieces, they will begin to understand the meaning of fractions as equal parts of a whole. They will begin to recognize and develop mental images of common fractions, and will begin to connect the fraction pieces with the symbolic way of writing fractions. The children can lay fraction pieces on top of other pieces to compare sizes of fractions and to find equivalent fractions. They can put fraction pieces together to add fractions, and take away pieces to subtract.

Exploring Math With Fraction Pieces

Following are descriptions of 12 explorations that children can do with the fraction pieces, and the concepts and skills they will be developing. Reproducible masters for the explorations are given on pages 133-144. Children can trace around the pieces and color to show their work. The Deluxe Fraction Circles pieces are used in the first six explorations, and Fraction Builder® pieces are used in the last six explorations. Many of the explorations end with an extra challenging puzzle to extend the learning.

Deluxe Fraction Circles (circle model)

1 Match fraction pieces to parts of a whole
The children match fraction pieces to shaded parts shown on the circle. They cover the circle with halves, and then thirds. The language of fractions is stressed here: two halves, 2 equal parts of 1 whole. They color to record the pieces and write the missing numbers.

2 Match fraction pieces to parts of a whole
The children match fraction pieces to shaded parts shown on the circle. First they cover the whole with fourths, and then sixths. They color to record the pieces and write the missing numbers.

3 Show fractional parts of a whole
The children find one fourth, and then one third, and trace them on the circles. They color to record the pieces and write the missing numbers.

4 Show fractional parts of a whole
The children find two fifths, and then three sixths, and trace them on the circles. They color to record the pieces and write the missing numbers.

5 Show equivalent fractions
The children first cover the shaded half with the $\frac{1}{2}$ piece on the first circle. Then they use fourths to cover the shaded half on the second circle. They color to record the pieces and write the missing numbers.

6 Show equivalent fractions
The children first find one third, and trace and color to record on the first circle. Then they find the sixths that equal $\frac{1}{3}$ and show these on the second circle. They fill in the missing numbers.

Fraction Builder® (rectangle model)

7 Match fraction pieces to parts of a whole
The children find fraction pieces to cover the shaded parts of each rectangle. First they use $\frac{8}{8}$, then $\frac{3}{5}$, and next $\frac{4}{10}$. They color to match the pieces and fill in the missing numbers.

8 Show equivalent fractions
The children look for different fractions that are equivalent to one fourth: two eighths and three twelfths. They trace their pieces, color, and write the missing numbers.

9 Compare fractions
The children trace and shade one half of the rectangle. Then they use fraction pieces to show a fraction that is less than $\frac{1}{2}$, and a fraction that is greater than $\frac{1}{2}$. They trace and color to record the pieces, then write the fractions.

10 Compare fractions
The children first show one sixth and one fourth, trace and color them, and write the missing numbers. Then they compare the two fractions to see which one is greater.

11 Add fractions with like denominators; write addition sentences
The children cover each shaded part with fraction pieces. Then they add pieces and find out how many pieces there are in all. They color to show the fraction pieces. They write the missing numbers and addition sentences.

12 Subtract fractions with like denominators; write subtraction sentences
The children put pieces on the whole to show a fraction. Then they take pieces away and color to show what is left. They write the missing numbers and subtraction sentences.

Organizing for Fraction Pieces Explorations

The students can work as a whole class to explore fractions with the fraction pieces. Have students work in groups of four sharing materials. Have the students work in pairs within each group. Each pair of students should have one set of Deluxe Fraction Circles pieces for the first six explorations, and one set of Fraction Builder® pieces for the last six explorations. Working in pairs and small groups encourages the children to share their ideas and problem-solving strategies.

The students can also work with fraction pieces in learning centers. Each student or pair of students should have one set of Deluxe Fraction Circles pieces and one set of Fraction Builder® pieces. Package each set of fraction pieces separately in a plastic bag or container. This helps students check to be sure they have a complete set.

Introducing Deluxe Fraction Circles Pieces and Fraction Builder® Pieces

Give the children time to just explore the pieces of one of the models. After they spend some time playing with the pieces, ask them to sort the pieces by color. Then ask them to find the black piece and say, **This piece stands for the whole.** Next say, **Find two pieces that are the same color that will cover the whole.** You can explain, **These pieces are two equal parts of the whole. Each piece is one half.** You can continue with 3 pieces, 4 pieces, and so on.

It is important that the children make the connection between the fraction pieces and the ways we can write each fraction – with words and with the symbol. Use the example of one half again, showing the words and $\frac{1}{2}$.

Cover-up

Name: _____

Fraction Pieces

Use: 1 set of Deluxe Fraction Circles pieces and crayons

- Match fraction pieces to the parts of each circle. Color to show the pieces. Write the missing numbers.

A.

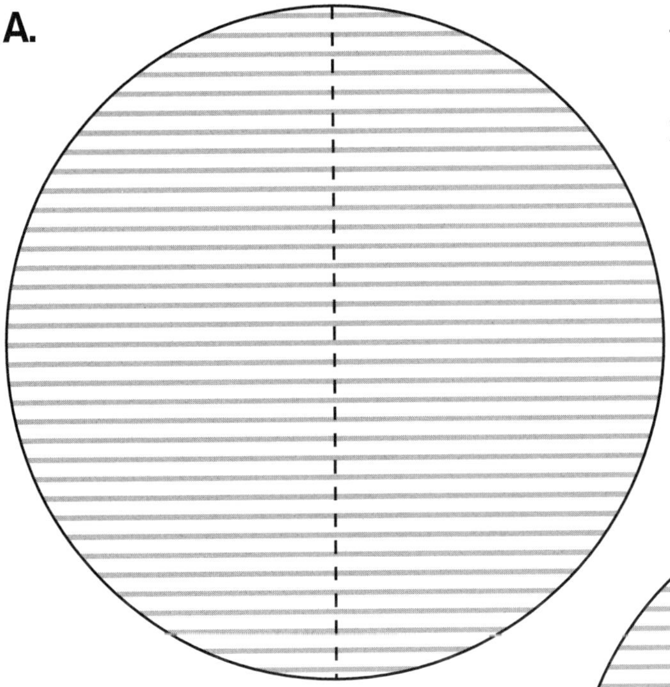

two halves $\dfrac{2}{2}$

2 equal parts of 1 whole

B.

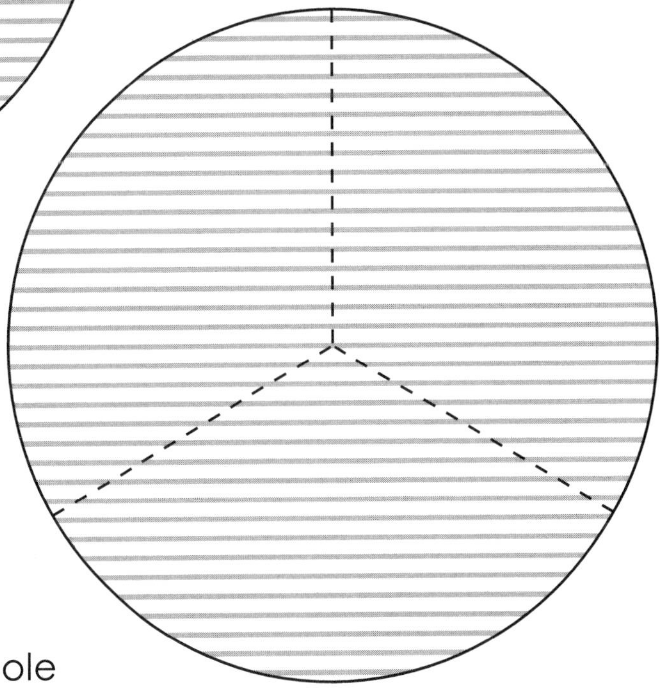

three thirds $\dfrac{3}{3}$

___ equal parts of ___ whole

- **Mystery Fraction Puzzle**
  I show 5 equal parts of a circle.
  What fraction am I?

133

More Cover-Ups

Name: ____________________

Fraction Pieces 2

Use: 1 set of Deluxe Fraction Circles pieces and crayons

- Match fraction pieces to the parts of each circle. Color to show the pieces. Write the missing numbers.

A.

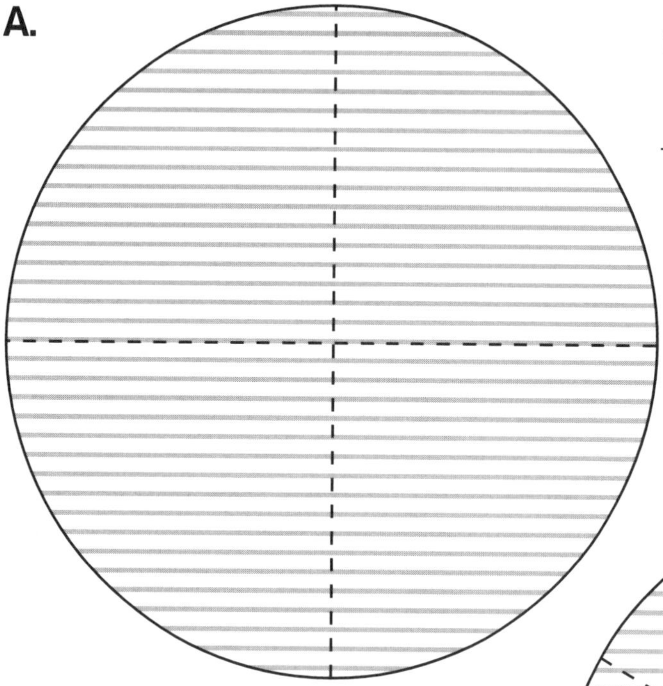

four fourths $\frac{4}{4}$

____ equal parts of ____ whole

B.

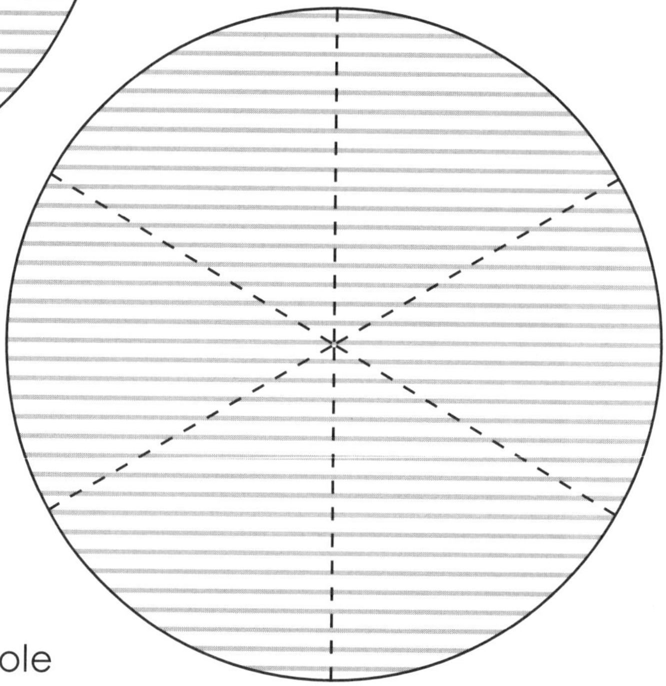

six sixths $\frac{6}{6}$

____ equal parts of ____ whole

- **Mystery Fraction Puzzle**
  I show 8 equal parts of a circle.
  What fraction am I?

 - **Skill: Matching fractions**

Which Part?

Name: _____

Fraction Pieces
3

Use: 1 set of Deluxe Fraction Circles pieces and crayons

- Find the fraction pieces.
  Trace and color to show them.
  Write the missing numbers.

A.

one fourth $\frac{1}{4}$

1 of ___ equal parts

B.

one third $\frac{1}{3}$

___ of ___ equal parts

- **Explore Some More**
  Color $\frac{2}{3}$ of the bugs.

© Ideal School Supply • A Division of Instructional Fair Group, Inc. • Doing Basic Math with Manipulatives, Grades 1-3 - Skill: Showing fractions

Which Parts?

Name: _____

Fraction Pieces

Use: 1 set of Deluxe Fraction Circles pieces and crayons

- Find the fraction pieces.
  Trace and color to show them.
  Write the missing numbers.

A.

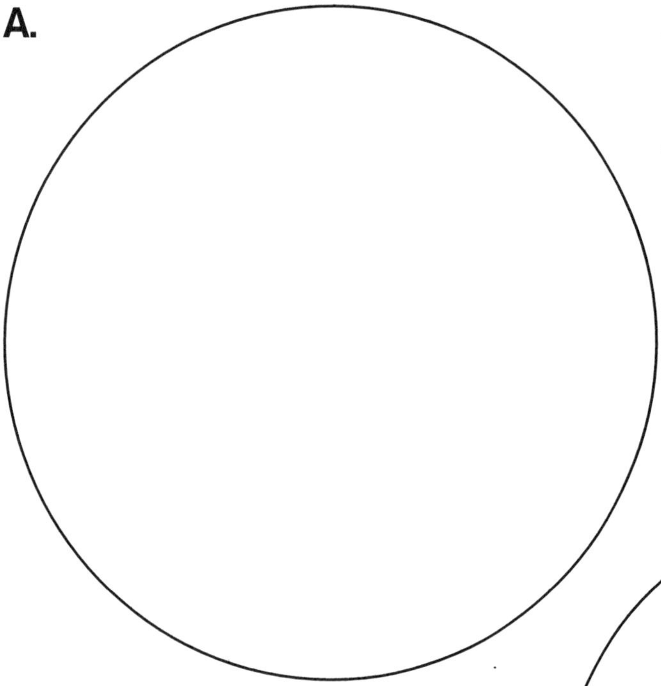

two fifths $\dfrac{}{5}$

___ of ___ equal parts

B.

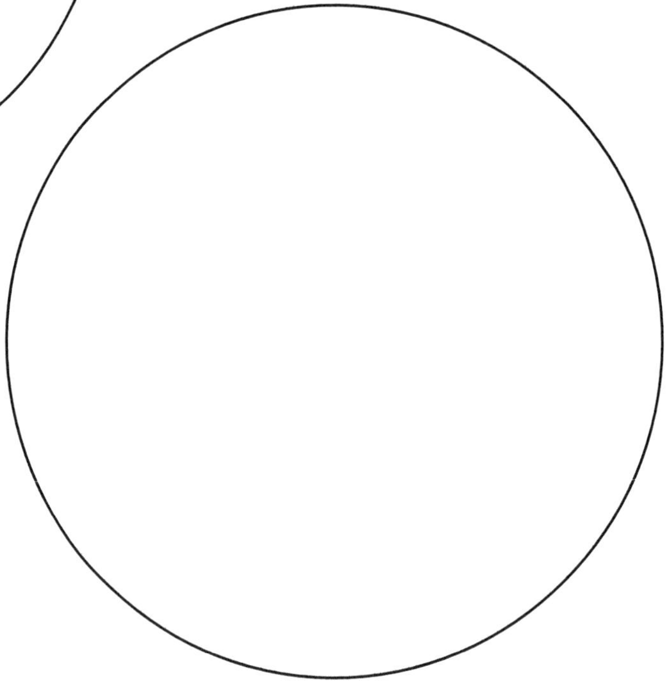

three sixths $\dfrac{}{6}$

___ of ___ equal parts

- **Explore Some More**

  Color $\dfrac{2}{6}$ of the spiders.

136 © Ideal School Supply • A Division of Instructional Fair Group, Inc. • Doing Basic Math with Manipulatives, Grades 1-3 - **Skill:** Showing fractions

Name: _____

Equal Parts

Fraction Pieces

Use: 1 set of Deluxe Fraction Circles pieces and crayons

- Find the fraction pieces. Cover the shaded part of each circle. Trace and color to match. Fill in the missing numbers.

A.

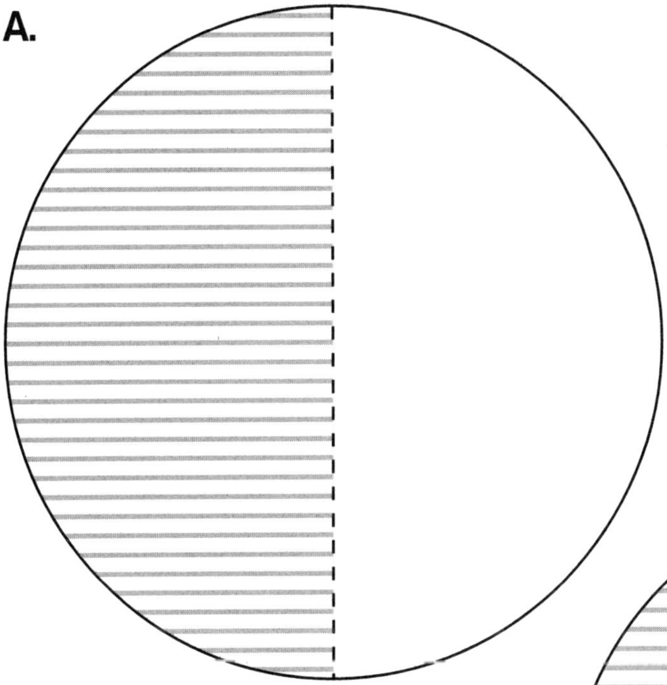

one half $\dfrac{}{2}$

___ of ___ equal parts

B.

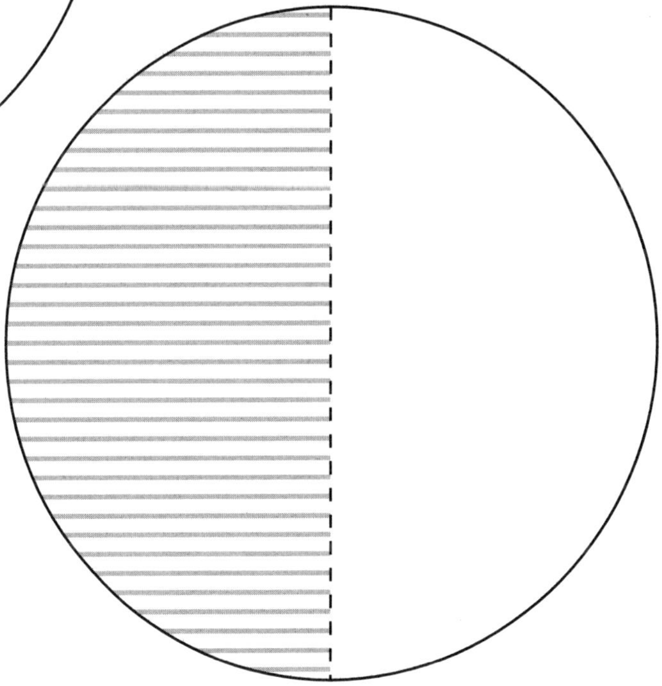

___ fourths $\dfrac{}{4}$

___ of ___ equal parts

$\dfrac{}{2}$ is the same size as $\dfrac{}{}$

- **Explore Some More**
Color one half of the fish.

© Ideal School Supply • A Division of Instructional Fair Group, Inc. • Doing Basic Math with Manipulatives, Grades 1-3 - Skill: Showing fractions

Name: ______________________

More Equal Parts

Fraction Pieces

6

Use: 1 set of Deluxe Fraction Circles pieces and crayons

- Find and show one third. Trace and color to match.
  Then find sixths that equal one third. Trace and color.
  Write the missing numbers.

A.

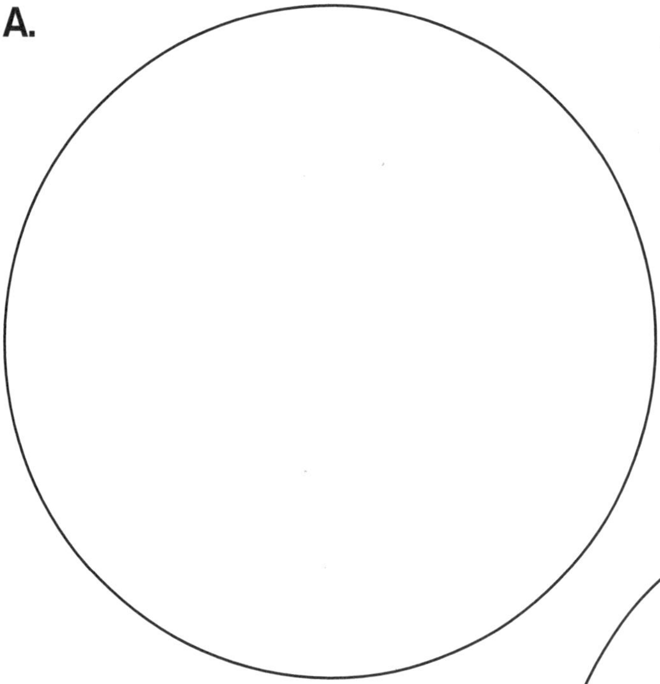

one third $\frac{__}{3}$

____ of ____ equal parts

B.

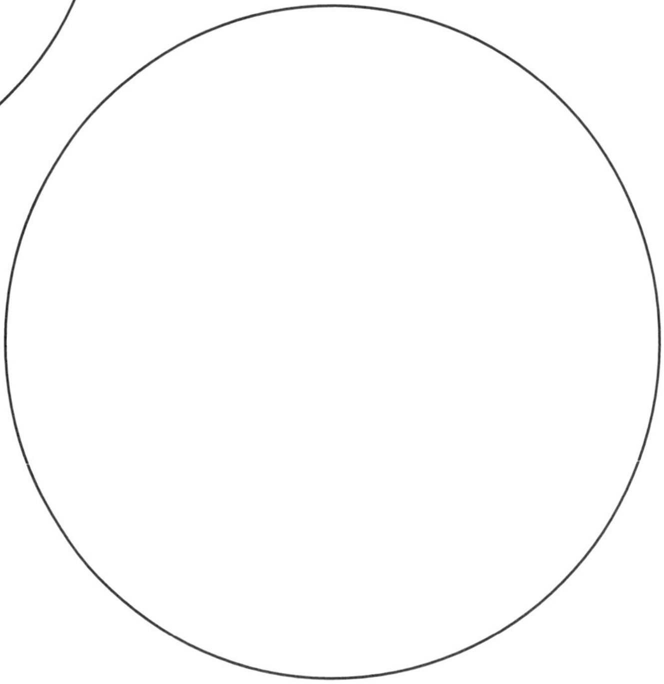

____ sixths $\frac{__}{6}$

____ of ____ equal parts

$\frac{__}{3}$ is the same size as ___

- **Mystery Fraction Puzzle**
  You show me with sixths.
  I am the same size as one half.
  What fraction am I?

 - **Skill: Showing fractions**

Name: _____

Rectangles

Fraction Pieces

Use: 1 set of Fraction Builder® pieces and crayons

• Find the fraction pieces. Cover each shaded part. Color to match. Write the missing numbers.

A.

eight eighths   ___ of ___ equal parts   ___

B.

_____ fifths   ___ of ___ equal parts   ___

C.

_____ tenths   ___ of ___ equal parts   ___

• **Explore Some More**
Color three fourths of the robots.

139

Are They the Same?

Name: _____

Fraction Pieces

Use: 1 set of Fraction Builder® pieces and crayons

- Trace and color to show pieces.
  Write the missing numbers.

A. Find pieces to match the shaded space.

one fourth   ___ of ___ equal parts   ___

- Now find different pieces that cover the same space.

B.

_____   ___ of ___ equal parts   ___

C.

_____   ___ of ___ equal parts   ___

- **Explore Some More**
  Color one fourth of the birds.

140   © Ideal School Supply • A Division of Instructional Fair Group, Inc. • Doing Basic Math with Manipulatives, Grades 1-3 - **Skill: Showing fractions**

Name: _____

Comparing Pieces

Fraction Pieces

Use: 1 set of Fraction Builder® pieces and crayons

- Find the pieces. Trace and color to show the pieces. Write the missing numbers.

A.

[ ]

one half   ___ of ___ equal parts   ___

B. Use pieces to show a fraction that is less than one half.

[ ]

_____   ___ of ___ equal parts   ___ < $\frac{1}{2}$

C. Use pieces to show a fraction that is greater than one half.

[ ]

_____   ___ of ___ equal parts   ___ > $\frac{1}{2}$

- **Mystery Fraction Puzzle**
  You show me with twelfths.
  I am greater than $\frac{2}{3}$ and less than $\frac{10}{12}$.
  What fraction am I?

Name: _____

Which One Is Greater?

Fraction Pieces

Use: 1 set of Fraction Builder® pieces and crayons

- Trace pieces and color to show each fraction.
  Then see which fraction is greater.
  Write the missing numbers.

A.

one sixth   ___ of ___ equal parts   ___

B.

one fourth   ___ of ___ equal parts   ___

C. Which fraction is greater?   ___ > ___

- **Explore Some More**

  Color more than $\frac{1}{6}$ but fewer than $\frac{4}{6}$ of the mice.
  Use twelfths to check.

Name: _____

Putting Pieces Together

Fraction Pieces

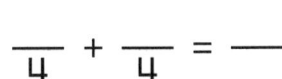

Use: 1 set of Fraction Builder® pieces and crayons

- Trace pieces and color to show your fractions. Write the missing numbers.

A. Cover the shaded part with fourths. How many? $\frac{}{4}$

Now add $\frac{1}{4}$. How much in all? $\frac{}{4}$ $\frac{}{4} + \frac{}{4} = \frac{}{}$

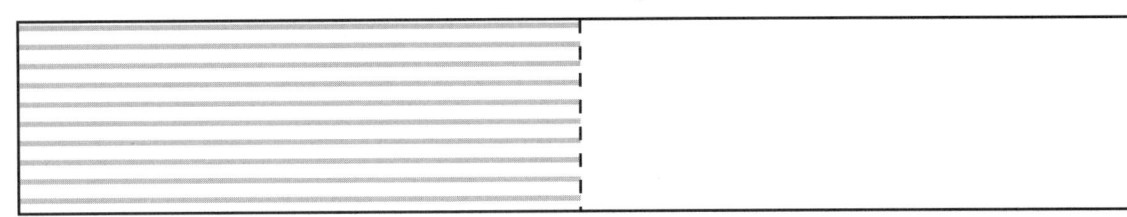

B. Cover the shaded part with fifths. How many? $\frac{}{5}$

Now add $\frac{3}{5}$. How much in all? $\frac{}{5}$ $\frac{}{5} + \frac{}{5} = \frac{}{}$

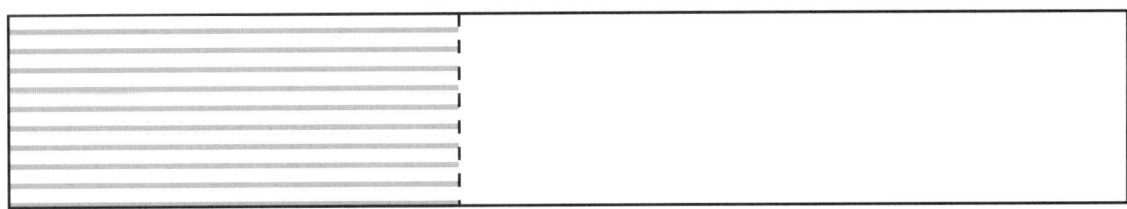

C. Cover the shaded part with tenths. How many? $\frac{}{10}$

Now add $\frac{5}{10}$. How much in all? $\frac{}{10}$ $\frac{}{10} + \frac{}{10} = \frac{}{}$

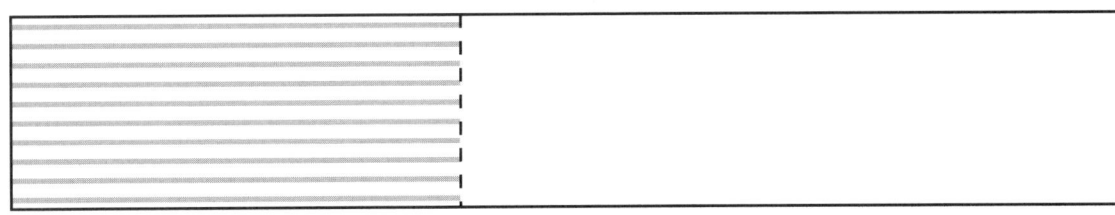

- **Mystery Fractions Puzzle**
  We are two fractions made of fourths.
  Together we equal $\frac{3}{4}$. What fractions are we?

Taking Pieces Away

Name: _____

Fraction Pieces

Use: 1 set of Fraction Builder® pieces and crayons

- Trace and color to show what's left.
  Write the missing numbers.

A. Put $\frac{7}{8}$ on the whole. Then take away $\frac{3}{8}$.

How much is left? $\frac{}{8}$ $\frac{}{8} - \frac{}{8} = \frac{}{}$

B. Put $\frac{8}{10}$ on the whole. Then take away $\frac{5}{10}$.

How much is left? $\frac{}{10}$ $\frac{}{10} - \frac{}{10} = \frac{}{}$

C. Put $\frac{9}{12}$ on the whole. Then take away $\frac{3}{12}$.

How much is left? $\frac{}{12}$ $\frac{}{12} - \frac{}{12} = \frac{}{}$

- **Mystery Fraction Puzzle**
  You show me with eighths. If you take away $\frac{4}{8}$ from me, $\frac{2}{8}$ is left. What fraction am I?

Attribute Blocks

Attribute Blocks help children develop these concepts and skills:

Patterns and Algebra
- Sort and classify by attribute differences
- Identify and extend difference patterns

Data Analysis and Statistics
- Sort, classify, and organize by attributes

Geometry
- Recognize geometric shapes

Problem Solving
- Use logical reasoning to solve matrix puzzles
- Use logical reasoning to solve Venn diagram puzzles

What Are Attribute Blocks?

Attribute Blocks are a set of plastic blocks that have four easily recognized attributes: color, shape, size, and thickness. There are three colors (red, blue, yellow), five shapes (circle, square, triangle, rectangle, hexagon), two sizes (large, small), and two kinds of thickness (thick, thin). While each block is unique, it shares one or more attributes with every other block in the set. There are 60 blocks altogether. Children may begin with a subset of 30 thin blocks or 30 thick blocks, which is more manageable than the full set.

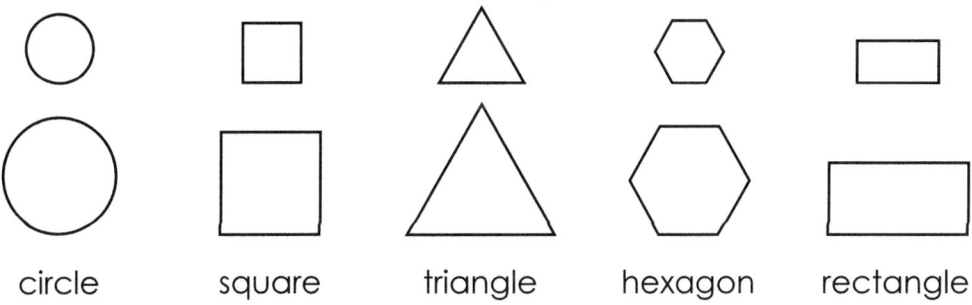

© Ideal School Supply • A Division of Instructional Fair Group, Inc. • Doing Basic Math with Manipulatives, Grades 1-3

Why Use Attribute Blocks?

We are bombarded with information in our daily lives, and this seems to be increasing with every year. We sort out important information to pay attention to. Attributes are properties of objects, and on a daily basis we choose attributes to focus on. The Attribute Blocks are a carefully designed set of blocks with attributes easily defined and identified. Children learn to pay attention to particular attributes of the blocks. In this way they are learning to sort, classify, and organize by attributes. They are also learning some of the language of sorting: How are things alike? How are they different?

Exploring Math With Attribute Blocks

Following are descriptions of 12 explorations that children can do with the Attribute Blocks, and the concepts and skills they will be developing. Reproducible masters for the explorations are given on pages 149-160. Most of the explorations end with extra challenging puzzles to extend the learning.

The children use a subset of 30 thick or 30 thin blocks for explorations 1-6. These blocks have the attributes of color, shape, and size.

1 Sort by color, shape, and size
The children sort the blocks by color, then by shape, and then by size. They count the blocks in the groups after each sorting.

2 Identify blocks that are alike in two ways
The children find blocks that are alike in two ways: size and color. They count the blocks in each group.

3 Identify blocks that are different in one way
The children begin with the large blue triangle and look for blocks that are different in one way from it. They put the blocks they find into an organized list by attribute difference.

4 Identify blocks that are different in two ways
The children begin with the large red circle and look for blocks that are different in two ways from it. They put the blocks they find into an organized list by combinations of two differences.

5 Identify blocks that are different in three ways
The children begin with the small yellow hexagon and look for blocks that are different in three ways from it. There is only one combination possible for three differences.

6 Recognize and extend patterns
   The children make a train of five blocks. Then they look at how each block in the train is different from the block next to it. They look for a pattern in the differences, and then extend the pattern by adding the sixth, seventh, and eighth blocks.

The children use all 60 blocks for explorations 7-12. These blocks have the attributes of color, shape, size, and thickness.

7 Identify one and two attribute differences
   The children begin with the large yellow thick square and look for all the blocks that are different in one way from it. Then they look for blocks that are different in two ways from it.

8 Identify three and four attribute differences
   The children begin with the small blue thick rectangle and look for all the blocks that are different in three ways from it. Then they look for blocks that are different in four ways from it.

9 Identify one, two, and three attribute differences
   The children begin with two blocks, leaving a space between them. They look for blocks that fit in the middle that are different in one way from each of the blocks. Then they find blocks to fit in the middle that are different in two ways from each of the blocks.

10 Identify a pattern in the number of differences
   The children make a line of blocks. Then they look for the number of differences between each block and the block next to it. They find a pattern in the number of differences and then extend the pattern.

11 Use logical reasoning to solve a matrix puzzle
   The children solve a 3-by-3 matrix puzzle. They look at the blocks shown in the puzzle to find the rule for the columns and the rule for the rows. They find blocks that fit the rules and put them in the empty squares.

12 Use logical reasoning to solve a Venn diagram puzzle
   The children solve a Venn diagram puzzle. They look at the blocks in each part of the overlapping circles to discover the rule for each circle. Then they find other blocks that belong in each part of the circles, including the overlapping part. You may wish to review the parts of the circles in a Venn diagram, emphasizing that the overlapping part belongs to both circles. The blocks that belong there fit both rules.

Organizing for Attribute Blocks Explorations

Attribute Blocks explorations can be used effectively with the whole class. Have children work in groups of two sharing materials. Each pair should have a set of 60 Attribute Blocks. Each student in the pair can use 30 of the blocks for the first six explorations. Then they can share the materials and work together on the next six explorations. Working in pairs will encourage children to discuss their thinking and develop problem-solving skills.

Attribute Blocks explorations can also be used effectively in centers. Each student or pair of students should have 60 Attribute Blocks. Package each set of blocks separately in a plastic bag or container. This will help children check to be sure the set is complete.

Introducing Attribute Blocks

Let the children begin by just exploring the Attribute Blocks. They can build with them, put them in groups, or make colorful arrangements. When the children are ready, ask them questions about the blocks:

> What can you tell me about the blocks?
> What colors are the blocks?
> How many different shapes do you see?
> Are the blocks all the same size?
> Are some blocks thicker than others?
> How are the blocks alike?
> Can you find two blocks that are exactly alike?

Let the children take turns choosing a block and telling everyone about their block. Let them practice using the words to describe how the blocks are alike and how they are different.

Introduce the names of the shapes, and show the children the symbols they will be using to record the blocks.

Recording Symbols

Y = large yellow
B = large blue
R = large red
y = small yellow

b = small blue
r = small red
Tk = thick
tn = thin

⬭ B/Tk = large blue thick circle

⬡ r/tn = small red thin hexagon

You may want to remind children that a square is a rectangle, but that the name rectangle will only be used for the rectangular Attribute Blocks that are not square.

Name: _____

Colors, Shapes, and Sizes

Attribute Blocks

1

Use: 30 thick or 30 thin Attribute Blocks

A. How many different colors are there? _____
Put all the blocks that are the same color together.
How many are there of each color?

red _____   yellow _____   blue _____

B. How many different shapes can you find? _____
Put all the blocks that are the same shape together.
How many are there of each shape?

squares _____   circles _____   rectangles _____

triangles _____   hexagons _____

C. How many different sizes are there? _____
Put all the blocks that are the same size together.
How many are there of each size?

large _____   small _____

© Ideal School Supply • A Division of Instructional Fair Group, Inc. • Doing Basic Math with Manipulatives, Grades 1-3 - **Skill:** Sorting

149

How Are They Alike?

Name: _____

Attribute Blocks
2

Use: 30 thick or 30 thin Attribute Blocks

A. Look for blocks that are large and yellow.
How many blocks are alike in these 2 ways? _____

Look for blocks that are small and yellow.
How many blocks are alike in these 2 ways? _____

B. Look for blocks that are large and red.
How many blocks are alike in these 2 ways? _____

Look for blocks that are small and red.
How many blocks are alike in these 2 ways? _____

C. Look for blocks that are large and blue.
How many blocks are alike in these 2 ways? _____

Look for blocks that are small and blue.
How many blocks are alike in these 2 ways? _____

• **Mystery Blocks Puzzle**
We are not large.
We are not red or blue.
What blocks are we?

Different in One Way

Name: _____

Attribute Blocks
3

Use: 30 thick or 30 thin Attribute Blocks

• Take this block:

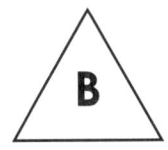

large blue triangle

B = large blue	**b** = small blue
Y = large yellow	**y** = small yellow
R = large red	**r** = small red

• Look for blocks that are different in 1 way from this block. A block may be a different color, different shape, or different size.

• Show your blocks in the table.

Different color	Different shape	Different size

• **Mystery Block Puzzle**
I am different in 1 way from the ◁B▷.
I am a different shape.
I have no straight sides.
What block am I?

© Ideal School Supply • A Division of Instructional Fair Group, Inc. • Doing Basic Math with Manipulatives, Grades 1-3 - **Skill: Classifying**

Different in Two Ways

Name: _____

Attribute Blocks
4

Use: 30 thick or 30 thin Attribute Blocks

- Take this block:

large red circle

B = large blue	**b** = small blue
Y = large yellow	**y** = small yellow
R = large red	**r** = small red

- Look for blocks that are different in 2 ways from this block. A block may be a different color and shape, a different shape and size, or a different size and color.

- Show your blocks in the table.

Different color and shape	Different shape and size	Different size and color

- **Mystery Block Puzzle**
  I am different in 2 ways from (R).
  I am the same shape.
  I am not blue.
  What block am I?

152 © Ideal School Supply • A Division of Instructional Fair Group, Inc. • Doing Basic Math with Manipulatives, Grades 1-3 - **Skill:** Classifying

Different in Three Ways

Name: _____

Attribute Blocks
5

Use: 30 thick or 30 thin Attribute Blocks

- Take this block:

  small yellow hexagon

B = large blue	**b** = small blue
Y = large yellow	**y** = small yellow
R = large red	**r** = small red

- Look for blocks that are different in 3 ways from this block. A block must be a different color, a different shape, and a different size.

- Show your blocks.

> Different color, shape, and size

- **Mystery Block Puzzle**
  I am different in 3 ways from .
  I am not red.
  I have 4 sides.
  I am not a square.
  What block am I?

Trains

Name: _____

Attribute Blocks

Use: 30 thick or 30 thin Attribute Blocks

B = large blue	b = small blue
Y = large yellow	y = small yellow
R = large red	r = small red

- Make a block train like this one:

 ___  ___  ___ ___

- What is the difference between the 1st and 2nd blocks? _____

  Between the 2nd and 3rd blocks? _____

  Between the 3rd and 4th blocks? _____

  Between the 4th and 5th blocks? _____

- What is the pattern? _____

- Add more blocks to the train.
  Your blocks have to fit the pattern.
  Draw your blocks:

  6th   7th   8th

- **Extra Challenge**
  Make your own block train. Use a pattern.
  Let someone find your pattern.

More Ways to be Different

Name: _____

Attribute Blocks

7

Use: 60 Attribute Blocks

- Look at all the blocks.
  They can be different in 4 ways:
  color, shape, size, and thickness.

  Tk = thick
  tn = thin

- Take this block:

  large yellow thick square

A. Look for blocks that are different in 1 way from the 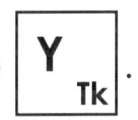.
Draw your blocks.

B. Look for blocks that are different in 2 ways from the 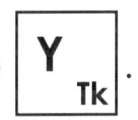.
Draw your blocks.

- **Mystery Block Puzzle**
  I am different in 2 ways from the 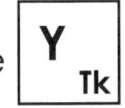.
  I am not yellow or red.
  I am a different size.
  What block am I?

Looking for Differences

Attribute Blocks
8

Name: _____

Use: 60 Attribute Blocks

- Take this block: | b Tk |

    small blue thick rectangle

    | **Tk** = thick |
    | **tn** = thin |

A. Look for blocks that are different in 3 ways from the | b Tk |.
Draw your blocks.

B. Look for blocks that are different in 4 ways from the | b Tk |.
Draw your blocks.

- **Mystery Block Puzzle**
    I am different in 4 ways from the .
    I am not blue.
    I have more than 4 sides.
    What block am I?

In the Middle

Name: _____

Attribute Blocks

Use: 60 Attribute Blocks

A. Take these blocks. Leave a space between them:

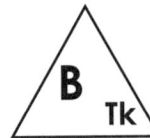   

large blue thick triangle   large red thick circle

What block could fit in the middle that is different in 1 way from each of the blocks? Draw the blocks you find.

B. Take these blocks. Leave a space between them:

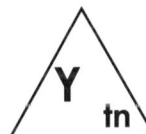   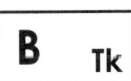

large yellow thin triangle   large blue thick rectangle

What block could fit in the middle that is different in 2 ways from each of the blocks? Draw the blocks you find.

- **Mystery Block Puzzle**
  I am different in 3 ways from these blocks:
  I am thick.
  I am not yellow or blue.
  What block am I?

© Ideal School Supply • A Division of Instructional Fair Group, Inc. • Doing Basic Math with Manipulatives, Grades 1-3 - **Skill:** Classifying

Patterns

Name: _____

Attribute Blocks

10

Use: 60 Attribute Blocks

A. Make this line of blocks:

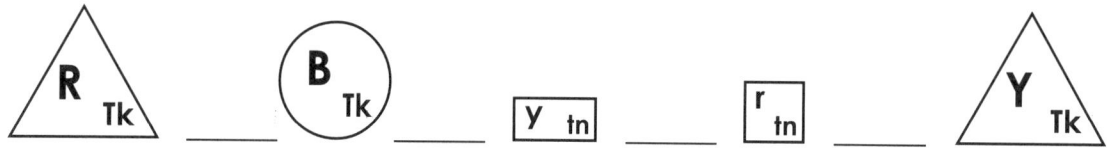

Find the number of differences between each pair of blocks. Write the number between each pair. Look for a pattern. What is it?

_____

B. Add blocks to the line. Continue the pattern. Draw your blocks.

- **Extra Challenge**
  Make your own pattern puzzle.
  Make a line of blocks that shows a number pattern.
  Let someone solve your puzzle.

A Square Puzzle

Name: _____

Attribute Blocks

Use: 60 Attribute Blocks

- In this puzzle, the rows have a rule and the columns have a rule. A rule tells how many ways each block is different from the blocks next to it. Find both rules.
Hint: Look for the number of differences.
Put blocks in the empty squares. Draw your blocks.

	⟨r, tn⟩	
B Tk (rectangle)	⟨B Tk⟩ (hexagon)	

- **Extra Challenge**
Make up new rules for the puzzle.
Put blocks in the squares to fit your rules.
Let someone solve your puzzle.

A Circle Puzzle

Name: _____

Attribute Blocks

Use: 60 Attribute Blocks, yarn

- Make 2 overlapping circles with yarn.

- Take the blocks shown in each circle. Put the blocks in the yarn circles. Find the rule for each circle. Find the missing blocks for each part of the circles. Blocks that fit both rules go in the space where the circles overlap. Write the rules. Draw your blocks.

A. Rule _____   **B.** Rule _____

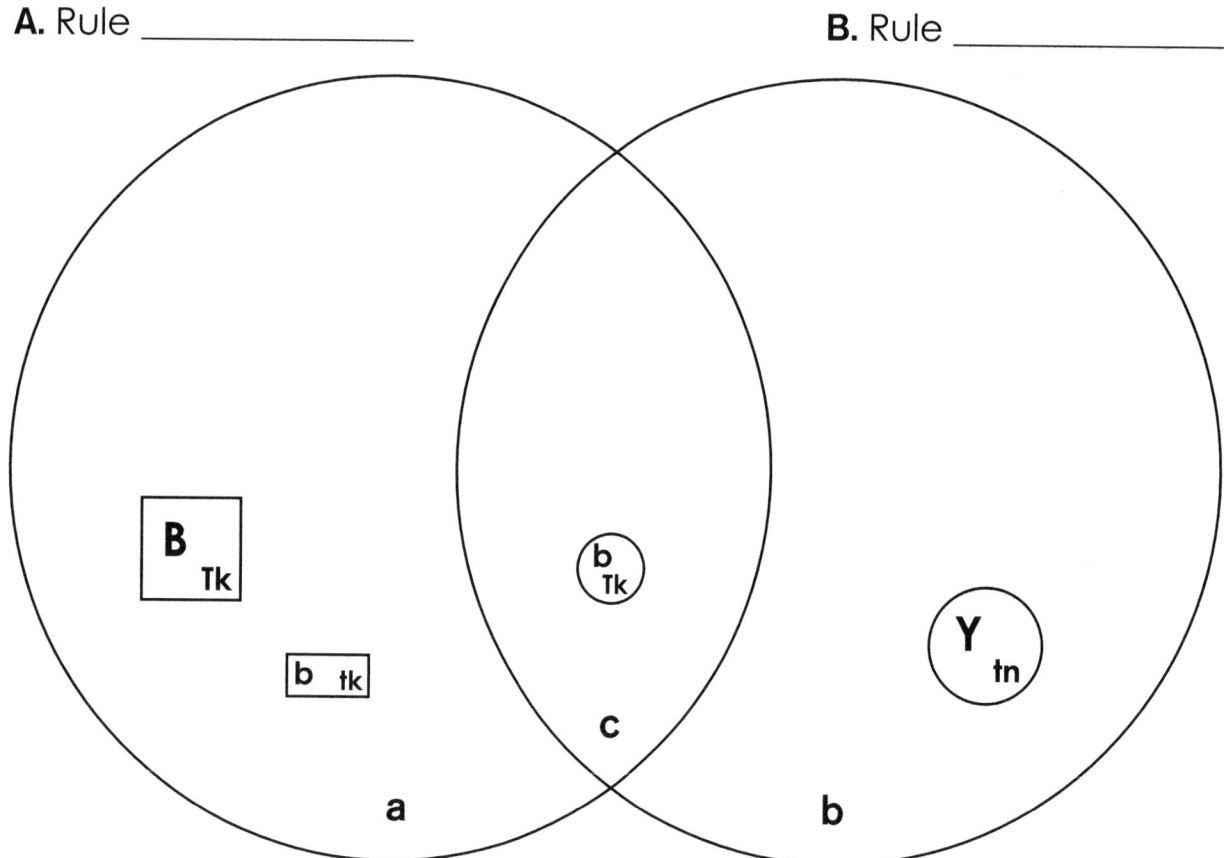

- **Extra Challenge**
  Think of new rules for the circles.
  Put a few blocks in each part of the circles.
  Let someone find your rules and the missing blocks.

Pattern Blocks

Pattern Blocks help children develop these concepts and skills:

Patterns and Algebra Thinking
- Identify and extend repeating and growing number patterns
- Sort and classify shapes by their attributes

Geometry and Spatial Sense
- Recognize geometric shapes
- Put shapes together to make other shapes
- Count sides and corners of geometric shapes; explore the relationship between sides and corners
- Cover a shape using the most blocks and the fewest blocks
- Change shapes to other shapes
- Explore mirror symmetry
- Make congruent shapes

Measurement
- Measure perimeter, using nonstandard units

Fractions
- Show halves, thirds, sixths, and fourths of a whole shape

Problem Solving
- Use logical reasoning to solve Venn diagram problems

What Are Pattern Blocks?

Pattern Blocks are colorful blocks that fit together to create a variety of shapes and patterns. There are 6 different kinds of blocks in a set: green triangles, orange squares, yellow hexagons, red trapezoids, blue rhombuses, and tan rhombuses. A basic set of Pattern Blocks consists of 100 blocks, some of each shape. The blocks are available in wood and in plastic.

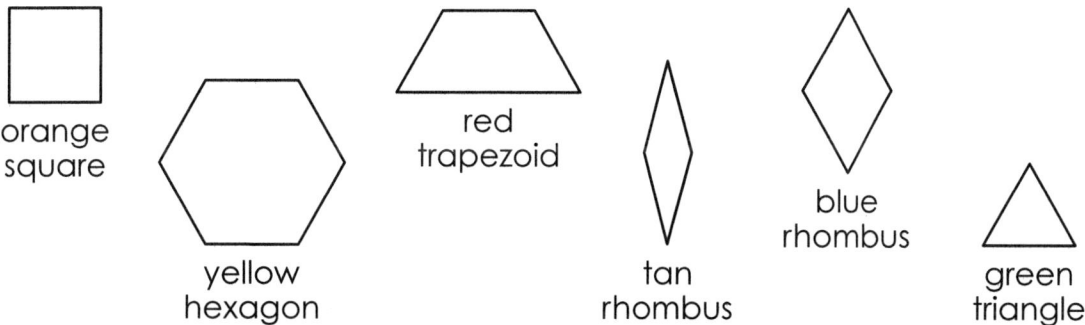

Why Use Pattern Blocks?

These colorful blocks invite exploration. As the children explore, they will learn about the properties of geometric shapes, such as the number of sides, length of sides, number of angles or corners, and length of perimeter. The mathematical relationships between the blocks are easy for children to discover. For example, they will find that the length of the sides of all the shapes are the same except for one side of the trapezoid, which is twice this length. Using the blocks allows the children to compare polygons to see how they are alike and different, and the many ways in which shapes can be subdivided and combined to make other shapes.

Exploring Math With Pattern Blocks

Following are descriptions of 12 explorations that children can do with Pattern Blocks, and the concepts and skills they will be developing. Reproducible masters for the explorations are given on pages 165-176. Many of the explorations end with an extra challenging puzzle to extend the learning.

1 Identify and extend a pattern
The children match blocks to the shapes shown. Then they look for a pattern and find the block that comes next.

2 Use shapes to cover another shape in different ways
The children use the blocks to cover a shape in two different ways. They record the blocks they used for each way.

3 Cover a shape using the most blocks and the fewest blocks
The children explore covering a shape with different numbers of blocks. They find the most blocks that will cover it and the fewest blocks that will cover it. They do this for two different shapes.

4 Count sides and corners of geometric shapes
The children cover shapes with blocks, and count the sides and corners of the shape. They do this on 3-sided, 4-sided, and 6-sided shapes.

5 Put shapes together to make other shapes with 4 or 6 sides
The children begin with a given group of blocks. They use these blocks to make two different shapes, one with 4 sides and one with 6 sides. They start with another group of blocks and make two different shapes that each have 4 sides.

6 Explore mirror (line) symmetry
The children cover a shape on one side of a dotted line, then flip the blocks over the line to make the mirror image of the shape. If a small mirror is available, have students put the mirror on the dotted line to see what the whole shape will look like.

7 Sort shapes by their attributes
The children look at the shapes in the first circle and decide if there are Pattern Blocks that fit the rule: Shapes that have 3 sides. They look at the shapes in the second circle and find the rule (Shapes that have 4 sides). Then they find Pattern Blocks that fit the rule.

8 Make twin (congruent) shapes
The children begin with a given group of blocks. They use some of the blocks to cover a shape and they use the rest of the blocks to make a twin shape. You may want to tell the children that another word for twin shapes is congruent shapes.

9 Measure perimeter, using nonstandard units
The children begin by measuring the perimeter of each of the Pattern Blocks, using a side of the green triangle as 1 unit of length. Then they put blocks together to make a shape that has a perimeter of 10 units.

10 Identify and extend a number pattern
The children use 4 blocks to make a bird. They make more birds, finding the total number of blocks needed for 1, 2, and 3 birds. Using a table, they look for a pattern that can help them find the blocks needed for 10 birds. They should see that each time they add 4 blocks, or that 4 times the number of birds gives the total number of blocks.

11 Show fractions
Using the yellow hexagon as the whole, the children first find 2 equal pieces to cover the whole (red trapezoids). They look for 3 equal pieces (blue rhombuses) and then 6 equal pieces (green triangles). With the equal pieces, they show one half, two thirds, and three sixths of the whole.

12 Identify and extend a growing pattern; use algebra thinking
The children make a rocket with 1 puff of smoke, then 2 puffs of smoke, and then 3 puffs of smoke. They record in a table, then look for a pattern in the numbers recorded. They use the pattern to predict how many blocks will be needed for a rocket with a larger number of puffs. Some students may need help finding this pattern. The algebraic expression for this pattern is $B = 2n + 3$, where n equals the number of puffs.

Organizing for Pattern Blocks Explorations

Pattern Blocks explorations can be used effectively with the whole class. Have students work in pairs sharing materials. Each pair should have 100 blocks. Working in pairs will encourage children to discuss their thinking and develop problem-solving skills.

Pattern Blocks explorations can also be used effectively in centers. Each student or pair of students should have 100 blocks. Package each set of blocks separately in a plastic bag or container.

Introducing Pattern Blocks

Let the children begin by just exploring the Pattern Blocks. They can make pictures or patterns, or build with them. When the students are ready, begin by having them describe the different shapes. Use these questions:

What shapes are the blocks?
What color is each shape?
How are the shapes alike?
How are the shapes different?
Can you cover one block with some of the other blocks?

Then have the children take the hexagon. Encourage them to find as many ways as they can to cover the hexagon with the other blocks. Have the students share all the different ways of covering the hexagon with other blocks.

Patterns

Name: _____

Pattern Blocks

Use: Pattern Blocks

- Match the shapes.
  What block comes next?
  Trace to show the block.

A.

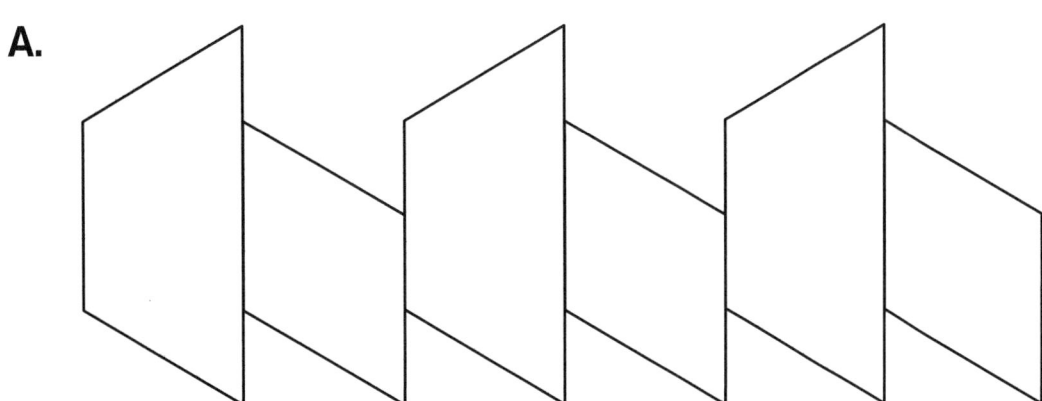

B.

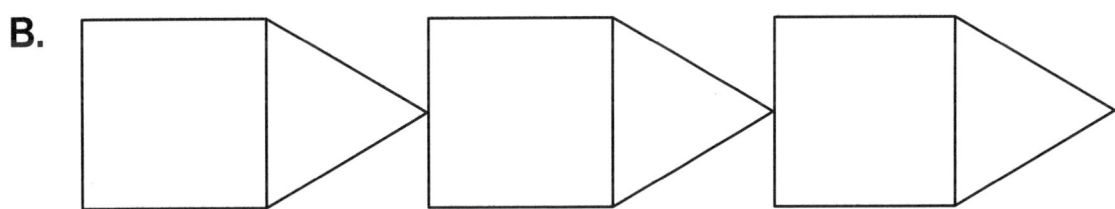

- **Extra Challenge**
  Make your own pattern with the blocks.

Different Ways

Name: _____

Use: Pattern Blocks

- Cover the shape in two different ways.
  Show how many blocks you used for each way.

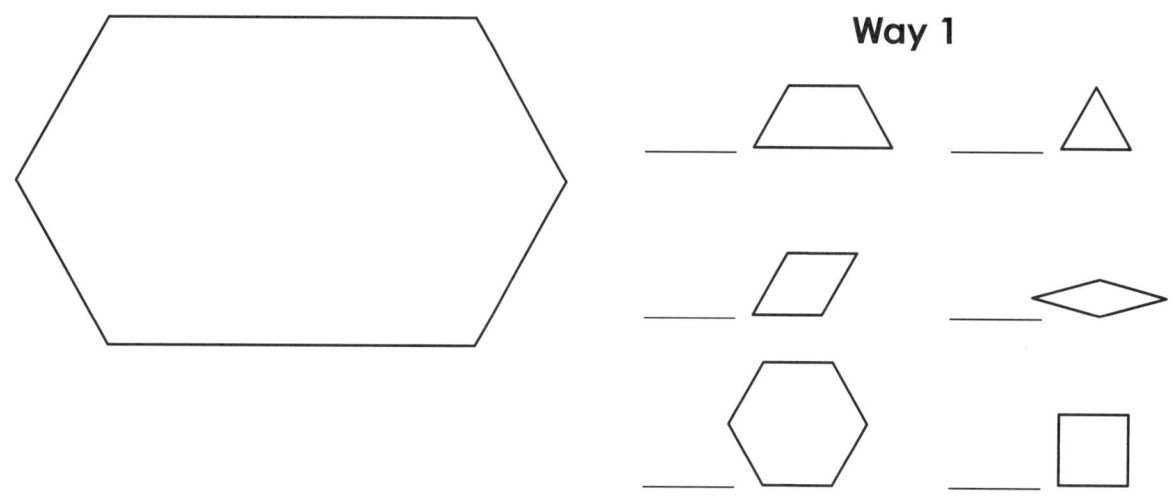

Way 1

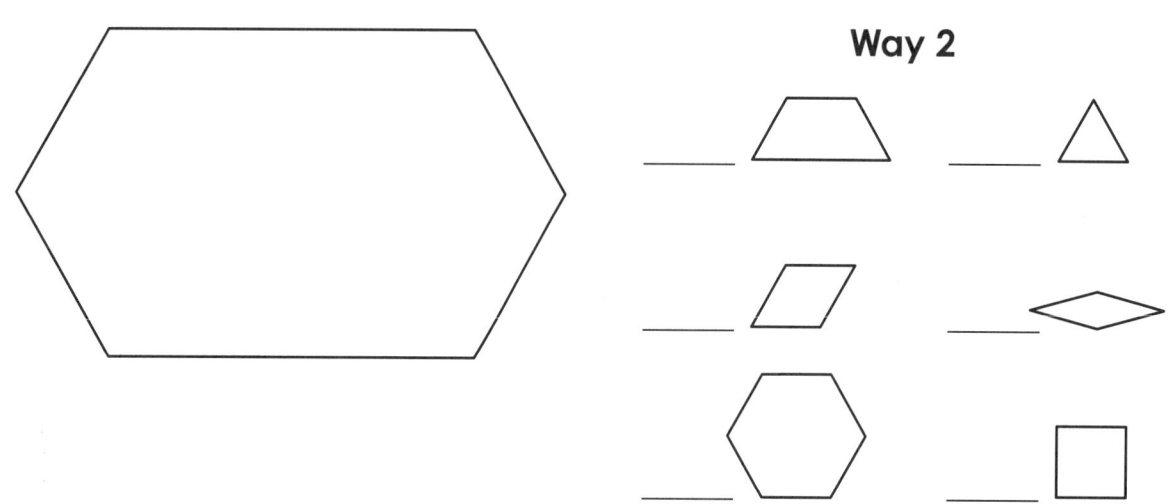

Way 2

- **Mystery Pattern Blocks Puzzle**
  You can cover me with 2 green triangles.
  What block am I?

Name: _____

The Most and the Fewest

Pattern Blocks

Use: Pattern Blocks

- Cover each shape.
  What is the most blocks you can use?
  What is the fewest blocks you can use?

A.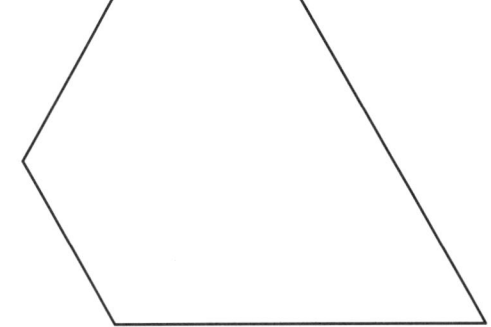

most blocks _____

fewest blocks _____

B.

most blocks _____

fewest blocks _____

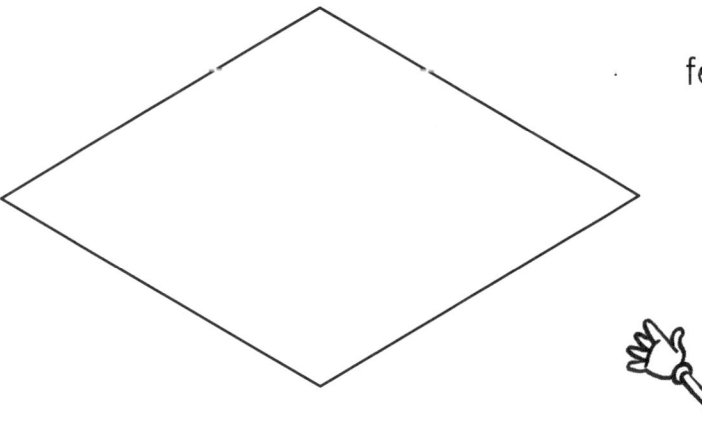

- **Mystery Pattern Blocks Puzzle**
  You can cover me with 6 blocks.
  You can cover me with 2 blocks.
  What block am I?

© Ideal School Supply • A Division of Instructional Fair Group, Inc. • Doing Basic Math with Manipulatives, Grades 1-3 - **Skill:** Geometry

Name: _____

How Many Sides and Corners?

Pattern Blocks

4

Use: Pattern Blocks

- Cover each shape with blocks. Count the sides and corners.

A.

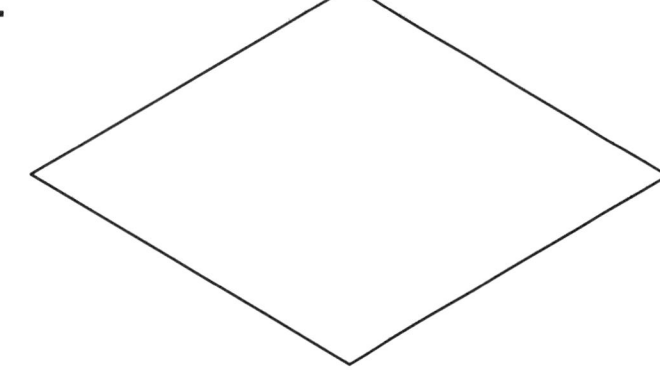

sides ____

corners ____

B.

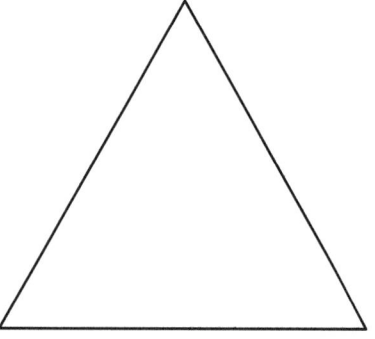

sides ____

corners ____

C.

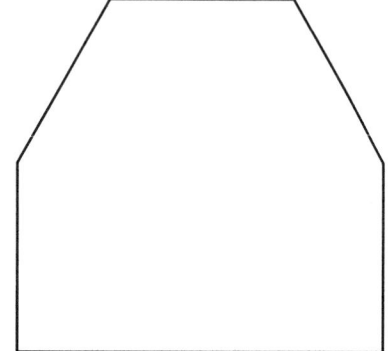

sides ____

corners ____

- **Extra Challenge**
  Make a shape that has 5 sides.
  How many corners do you think it will have?

Count the Sides

Use: Pattern Blocks

A. Take 2 ⏢ 2 ◇

Use all the blocks for each shape.
Make a shape that has 4 sides.
Make a shape that has 6 sides.
Trace your shapes.

B. Take 3 △ 1 ⏢ 1 ⬡

Use all the blocks for each shape.
Make 2 different shapes that have 4 sides.

- **Mystery Pattern Blocks Puzzle**
  We are 2 blocks.
  We are twin shapes.
  You can put us together to make a shape that has more than 6 sides.
  What blocks are we?

Flip the Blocks Over

Name: _____

Pattern Blocks

6

Use: Pattern Blocks

- Cover each shape with blocks.
  Flip the blocks over the dotted line.
  Trace to finish the picture.

A.

B.

- **Explore Some More**
  Make your own shape with blocks.
  Flip the blocks over a dotted line.
  Trace to show your whole picture.

In the Circles

Name: _____

Pattern Blocks

Use: Pattern Blocks

A. Look at the rule for this circle. Do any Pattern Blocks belong in this circle?

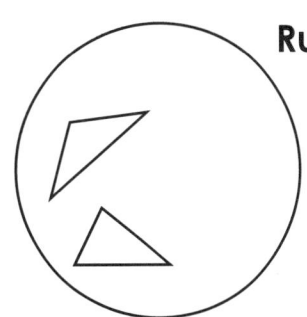

Rule: Shapes must have 3 sides

B. Look at the shapes in this circle. Find the rule. Look for Pattern Blocks that fit the rule. Show them in the circle.

Rule: _____

- **Extra Challenge**
  Use the blocks.
  Make more shapes that belong in the circles.

Twins

Use: Pattern Blocks

- Take

- Cover the shape with blocks.
  Use the leftover blocks to
  make a twin parallelogram.
  Twin shapes are exactly alike.
  Trace the blocks in your shapes.

- **Extra Challenge**
  Use the same blocks.
  Make a different pair of twin
  shapes that have 4 sides.

Name: _____

How Many Units Long?

Pattern Blocks

Use: Pattern Blocks

- Use one side of the triangle as 1 unit of length.

1 unit long

- **Perimeter** is the distance around the outside of a shape.

A. How many units long is the perimeter of each Pattern Block?

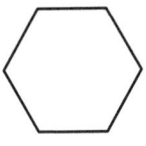

perimeter ____ units long

perimeter ____ units long

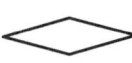

perimeter ____ units long

perimeter ____ units long

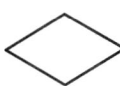

perimeter ____ units long

perimeter ____ units long

B. Make a shape that has a perimeter 10 units long.

- **Extra Challenge**
Make 2 different shapes that each have a perimeter 12 units long.

© Ideal School Supply • A Division of Instructional Fair Group, Inc. • Doing Basic Math with Manipulatives, Grades 1-3 - Skill: Measurement

Birds

Name: _____

Use: Pattern Blocks

A. Use blocks to make birds.

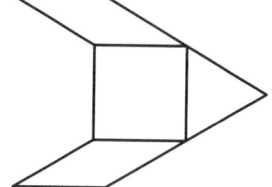

How many blocks do you need for 1 bird? _____

How many blocks do you need for 2 birds? _____

How many blocks do you need for 3 birds? _____

B. How many blocks do you need to make 10 birds? _____

Use a table to help you find out.

Birds	Blocks
1	4

- **Extra Challenge**
  How many blocks would you need for 20 birds?

Name: _____

Parts of a Whole

Use: Pattern Blocks

- Use the ⬡ as one whole.

A. Find 2 equal pieces to cover the whole.
Show $\frac{1}{2}$ of the whole, or 1 out of 2 equal pieces.

B. Find 3 equal pieces to cover the whole.
Show $\frac{2}{3}$ of the whole, or 2 out of 3 equal pieces.

C. Find 6 equal pieces to cover the whole.
Show $\frac{3}{6}$ of the whole, or 3 out of 6 equal pieces.

- **Mystery Pattern Blocks Puzzle**
Put 4 orange squares together to make a larger square.
How many squares show $\frac{3}{4}$ of the whole square?

Rockets

Name: _____

Pattern Blocks

Use: Pattern Blocks

12

A. Use blocks to make the rocket with 1 puff of smoke.

How many blocks for the rocket with 1 puff of smoke? ____

How many blocks for the rocket with 2 puffs of smoke? ____

How many blocks for the rocket with 3 puffs of smoke? ____

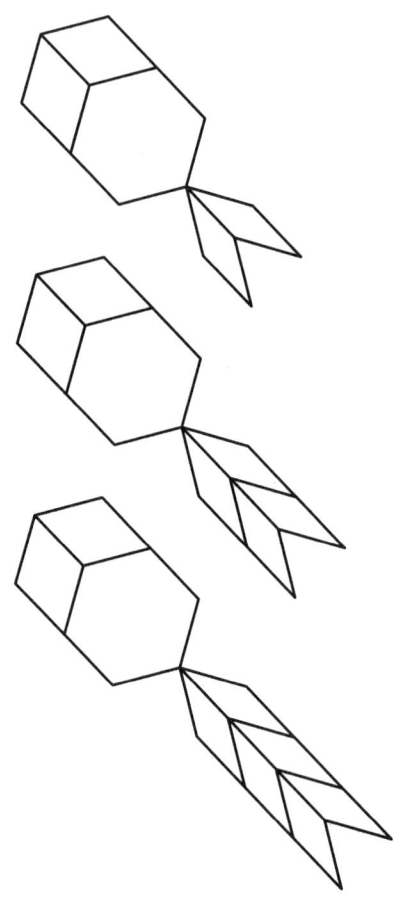

B. How many blocks for a rocket with 10 puffs of smoke? ____

Use a table to help you find out.

Puffs of smoke on rocket	Number of blocks

- **Extra Challenge**
  How many blocks for a rocket with 20 puffs of smoke?

Tangrams

Tangrams help children develop these concepts and skills:

Geometry and Spatial Sense
- Match shapes to their outlines
- Combine shapes to make other shapes
- Recognize congruent shapes
- Count sides and corners of geometric shapes; explore the relationship between them
- Recognize sides of shapes that have the same length
- Recognize right angles
- Explore line symmetry using a mirror
- Explore congruent and similar shapes

Measurement
- Measure length, using nonstandard units
- Measure area, using nonstandard units

Problem Solving
- Use spatial and logical reasoning to solve problems

What Are Tangrams?

A Chinese legend tells the story of a teacher who had a very special tile. One day he dropped his tile on a stone floor and it broke into seven pieces. He spent the rest of his life trying to put the tile back together again. We do know that the tangram is a very old Chinese puzzle. The Chinese name is ch'i ch'iao t'u, which means "ingenious seven-piece plan." A tangram puzzle is made up of seven pieces: 2 large triangles, 1 medium triangle, 2 small triangles, 1 square, and 1 parallelogram.

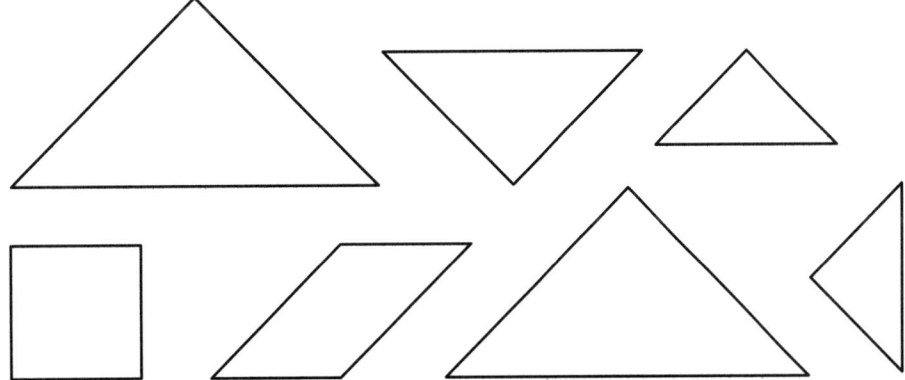

Why Use Tangrams?

This appealing puzzle can be a powerful tool for introducing children to basic concepts of geometry and for helping them develop their spatial sense. When exploring with pieces, children become familiar with a wide variety of geometric shapes and their characteristics, and they discover relationships between the shapes.

Exploring Math With Tangrams

Following are descriptions of 12 explorations that children can do with the tangrams, and the concepts and skills they will be developing. Reproducible masters for the explorations are given on pages 181-192. Children can trace around the pieces and color to show their work. Many of these explorations end with an extra challenging puzzle to extend the learning.

1 Match shapes to their outlines
The children use all the pieces of one set of tangrams to cover the pictures. They match each piece to its outline.

2 Match shapes; combine shapes to make other shapes
The children put the pieces together to make different shapes. The outline of each piece is shown, so that it is easy for children to match the pieces and make the larger shape.

3 Combine shapes to make other shapes
Children use all the pieces of one set. The interior outlines are not shown, so the children need to try different ways of combining the pieces to make them fit the shapes. This helps the children learn to visualize shapes and turn them around in their minds.

4 Recognize twin (congruent) shapes
The children cover two congruent shapes with pieces. They cover each shape with different pieces. The congruent shapes are called twin shapes in the exploration. You may want to tell the children that the mathematical word congruent can also be used for twin shapes.

5 Count the sides and corners (angles) of shapes
The children use given pieces to make a shape that has 4 sides. They count the corners. Then they use the same pieces to make a different shape that has 4 sides. Again, they count the corners. In this exploration, the children will begin to see that the number of sides is the same as the number of corners in shapes.

6 Recognize sides of shapes that have the same length
The children look for a piece that has all sides the same length as the leg of the small triangle. Then they look for a piece that has 2 sides the same length as a leg of the medium triangle.

7 Recognize right angles
The children make shapes that have right angles. They learn about the characteristics of a square, and then make other shapes that have right angles.

8 Explore line symmetry, using a mirror
The children use given pieces to make a shape. Then they use a mirror on the sides and on the dotted line of symmetry in the middle to look for different shapes.

9 Explore congruent and similar shapes
The children first make twin shapes that are exactly alike. Then they make the same shape (triangle) but in a larger size.

10 Show fractions: one half, one fourth, three fourths
The children first cover a square with 2 pieces that are exactly alike, then take away $\frac{1}{2}$, leaving $\frac{1}{2}$. Then they cover the large triangle with 4 pieces that are the same. They take away $\frac{1}{4}$, leaving pieces that show $\frac{3}{4}$.

11 Measure area, using nonstandard units
The students use the small triangle as 1 unit of area. They measure the area of different shapes by covering them with pieces from 2 sets of tangrams.

12 Measure area, using nonstandard units
The students use the medium triangle as 1 unit of area. They measure the area of 2 shapes by covering them with pieces from 2 sets of tangrams.

Organizing for Tangram Explorations

Tangram explorations can be used effectively with the whole class. Have students work in groups of four sharing materials. Have the students work in pairs within each group. Provide 4 sets of tangrams for a group, 2 sets for each pair of students working together. Working in pairs will encourage children to discuss their thinking and develop problem-solving skills together.

Tangram explorations can also be used effectively in centers. Each student or pair of students should have 2 sets of tangrams. It is helpful if the sets are different colors. Package each set of tangram pieces separately in a plastic bag. This makes it easy for students to know that they have all 7 pieces.

Introducing Tangrams

Let the children begin by just exploring the tangram pieces–putting them together, taking them apart, finding out about their shapes. Then discuss the tangrams, using some of these questions:

> Look at the pieces and think about how they are alike.
> Think about how they are different.
> How are they alike? How are they different?
> How many pieces have 3 sides? How many have 4 sides?
> How many different shapes are there?

Have the children try covering a piece with other pieces. Have them start with the square, and cover it with other tangram pieces. Then have them try to cover the parallelogram with other tangram pieces. Have them try covering the medium triangle and the large triangle.

Show the children the symbols that are used to record the sizes of the tangram triangles:

small   medium   large

Tangram Pictures

Name: _____

Tangrams
1

Use: 1 set of tangram pieces

- Cover the tangram pictures.
  Use all your pieces.

- **Explore Some More**
  Make your own tangram pictures.

Tangram Shapes

Name: _____

Tangrams

Use: 1 set of tangram pieces

- Cover the tangram shapes. Use all your pieces.

A.

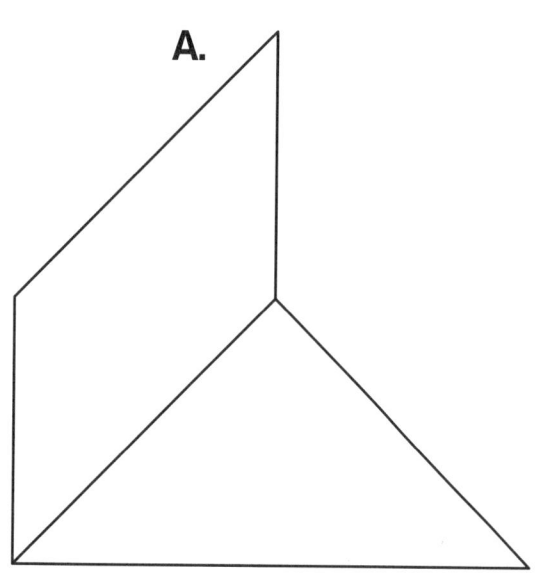

B.

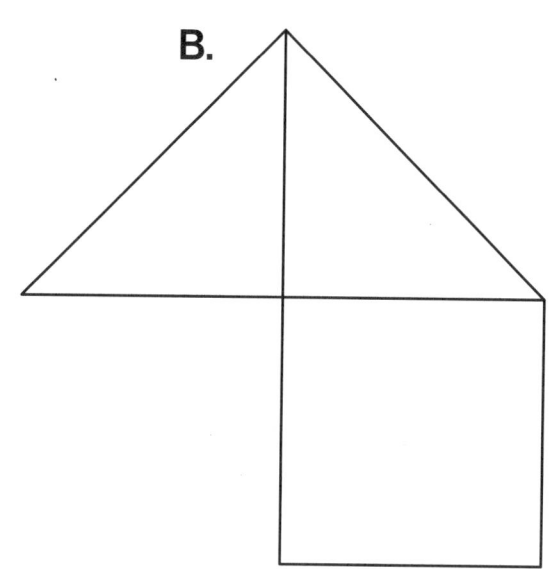

C.

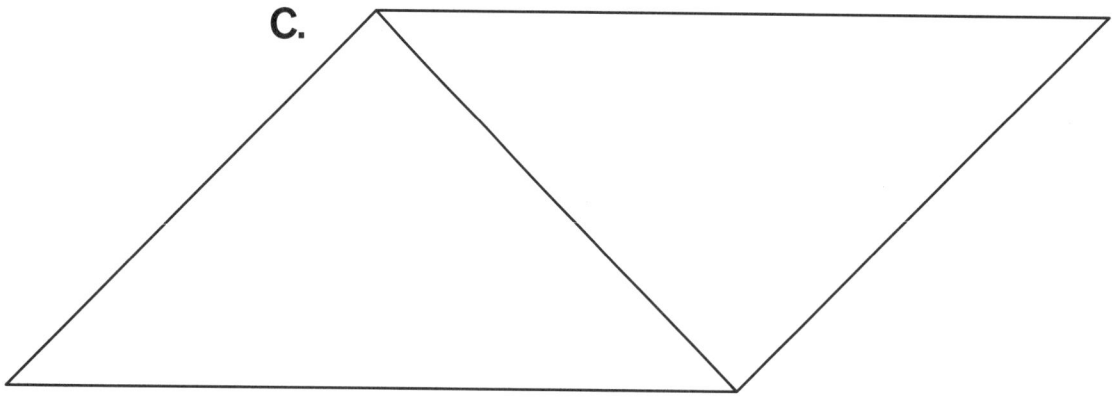

- **Mystery Tangram Puzzle**
  I have fewer than 4 sides.
  There is only 1 piece my size.
  What tangram piece am I?

Name: _____

More Tangram Shapes

Tangrams
3

Use: 1 set of tangram pieces

- Cover each shape with tangram pieces. Trace your pieces.

A.

B.
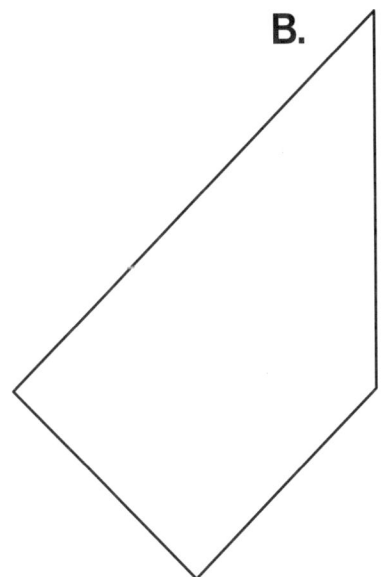

C.
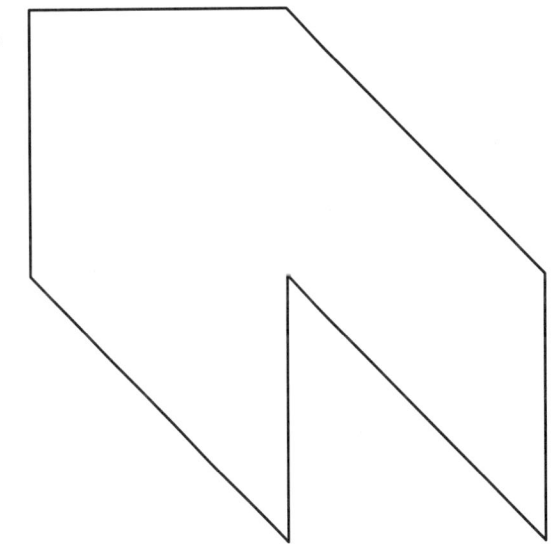

- **Mystery Tangram Puzzle**
  I have more than 3 sides.
  I have **no** square corners like this: └┘
  What tangram piece am I?

Making the Same Shapes

Name: _____

Tangrams

Use: 1 set of tangram pieces

- Cover the first shape. Then cover the twin shape with different pieces. **Twin shapes** are exactly alike.

A.

B.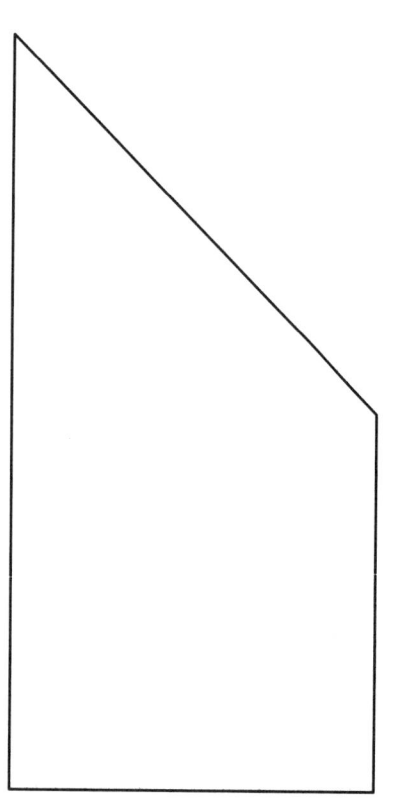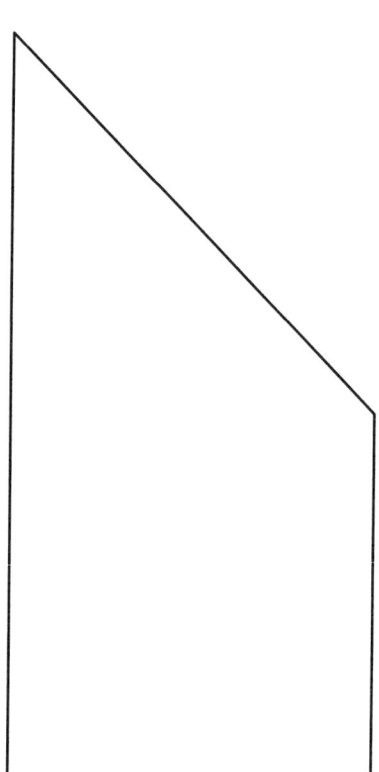

- **Mystery Tangram Puzzle**
  We are twin shapes.
  A square and 2 small triangles will cover each of us.
  What tangram pieces are we?

Name: _____

Sides and Corners

Tangrams

Use: 1 set of tangram pieces

- Take these tangram pieces:

A. Cover the shape. Count the sides and the corners.

How many sides? _____

How many corners? _____

B. Use the same pieces.
Make a different shape that has 4 sides.

Count the corners. How many? _____

- **Extra Challenge**
Use the same pieces to make a shape that has 3 sides. How many corners do you think it will have?

Name: _____

Do the Sides Match?

Tangrams
6

Use: 1 set of tangram pieces

A.

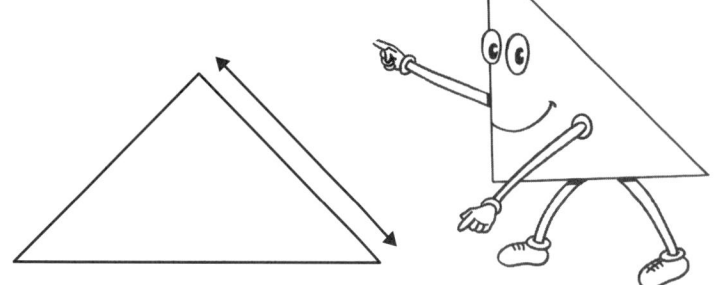

Cover the shape. Can you find a different piece whose sides are all this long?
Trace your piece.

B.

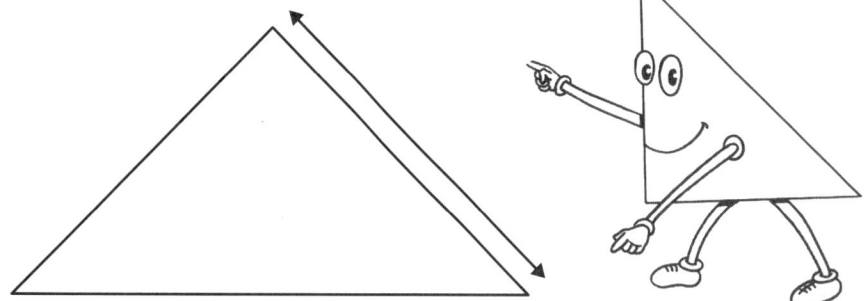

Cover the shape. Can you find a different piece with 2 sides that are this long?
Trace your piece.

• **Mystery Tangram Puzzle**

I have a side that is twice as long as this side:

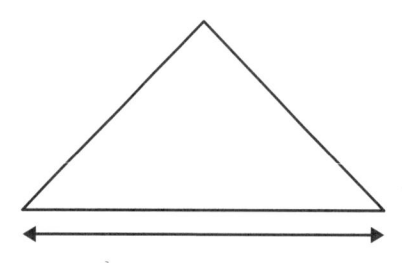

What tangram piece am I?

Make it Right!

Name: _____

Tangrams
7

Use: 1 set of tangram pieces

- All 4 corners of a square look like this:

- Each corner is a **right angle**.

A. Make 3 different squares with the tangram pieces. Trace your squares.

B. Use these pieces:

Make a shape that has 4 right angles.

- **Extra Challenge**
  Take away 1 piece from the last shape you made, to make a shape that has only 2 right angles.

Name: _____

What Do You See?

Tangrams
8

Use: 1 set of tangram pieces and a small mirror

- Take these pieces:

A. Make this shape.

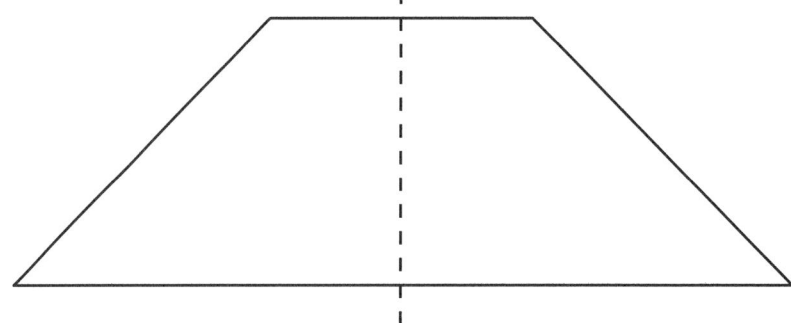

Put the mirror on the dotted line. What do you see?
Put the mirror on different sides of the shape. What do you see?
Move the mirror around. What kinds of shapes do you see?

B. Make this shape.

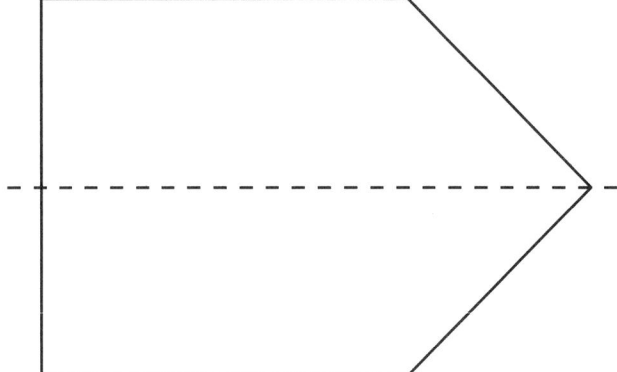

Use your mirror to look for other shapes.

- **Extra Challenge**
  Put the mirror on each tangram piece.
  What shapes do you see?

Are They the Same Shape?

Name: _____

Tangrams
9

Use: 2 sets of tangram pieces

A. Cover the shape. Then use other pieces to make a twin shape.
Twin shapes are exactly alike.
Trace your pieces.

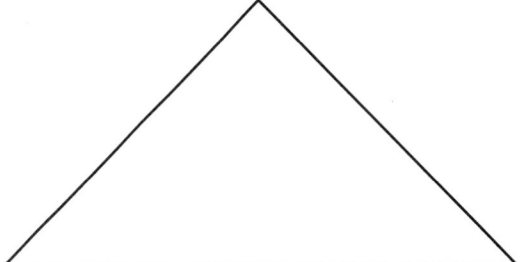

B. Now find pieces to make a larger triangle.
Trace your pieces.

- **Mystery Tangram Puzzle**
  We are 3 tangram pieces.
  Six of our sides are the same length.
  Together we make a twin shape for a large triangle.
  What tangram pieces are we?

Equal Parts

Tangrams

10

Use: 2 sets of tangram pieces

A. Cover the square with 2 pieces that are exactly alike.

Take away 1 piece.
This is 1 of 2 equal parts, or $\frac{1}{2}$.
Color $\frac{1}{2}$ of the square.
What fraction does the other piece show?

B. Cover the large triangle with 4 pieces that are exactly alike.

Take away 1 piece. This is 1 of 4 equal pieces or $\frac{1}{4}$.
Color $\frac{1}{4}$ of the triangle. What fraction do the rest of the pieces show?

- **Mystery Tangram Puzzle**
  We are part of 4 equal pieces
  that cover the large triangle.
  We show a fraction that is equal to $\frac{1}{2}$.
  What tangram pieces are we?

How Many Small Triangles?

Tangrams 11

Use: 2 sets of tangram pieces

- Use the small triangle as 1 unit of **area**.

1 unit of area

- Cover each shape with triangles.
  How many units of area does each shape have?

A.

____ units of area

B.

____ units of area

C.

____ units of area

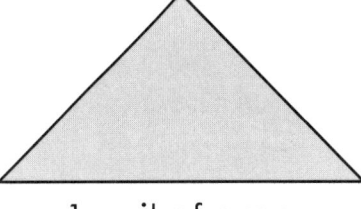

- **Extra Challenge**
  Make a shape that has 3 units of area.

How Many Medium Triangles? Tangrams

Use: 2 sets of tangram pieces

- Use the medium triangle as 1 unit of area.

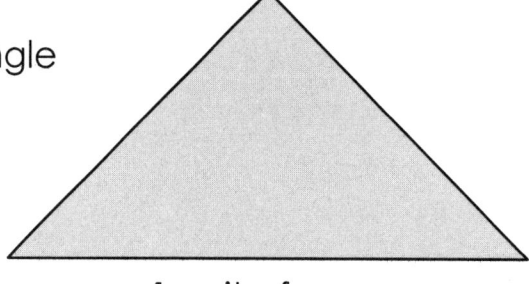

1 unit of area

- How many units of area does each shape have?

A.

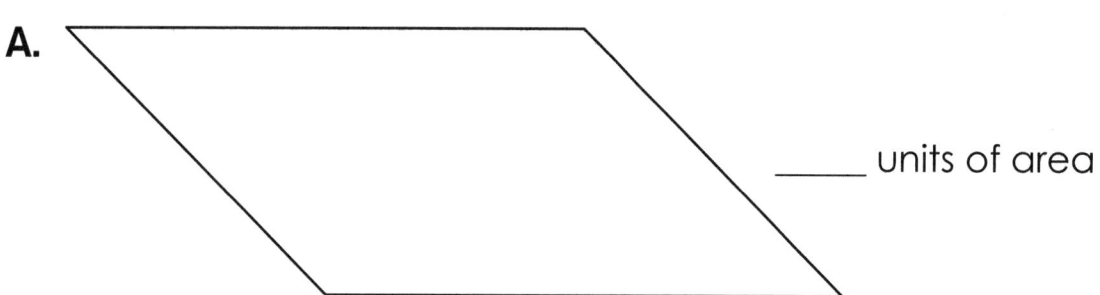

____ units of area

B.

____ units of area

- **Extra Challenge**
  Make a shape that has 6 units of area.

Geoboards

Geoboards help children develop these concepts and skills:

Geometry
- Recognize and describe geometric shapes
- Construct and draw geometric shapes
- Describe attributes of geometric shapes
- Count sides and corners of geometric shapes
- Combine and subdivide shapes to make other shapes
- Recognize congruent and similar shapes
- Explore line symmetry and turn symmetry
- Recognize right angles

Measurement
- Measure length and height of rectangles, using nonstandard units
- Measure sides, perimeter, and area of shapes, using nonstandard units

Patterns
- Identify, describe, and extend geometric patterns

Numbers
- Show one half of different shapes

Problem Solving
- Use visualization and spatial reasoning to solve problems

What Are Geoboards?

Geoboards are boards that have arrays of pins on them. The 5-by-5 pin geoboard used for the explorations in this book has 25 pins, forming 16 square units of area. (There is also an 11-by-11 pin geoboard that has 121 pins, forming 100 square units of area.)

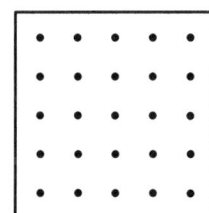

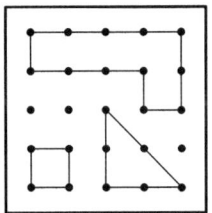

Various-sized rubber bands are used to construct two-dimensional shapes on the geoboard pins.

Why Use Geoboards?

The geoboard is an excellent model for children to use to explore geometry in an informal way. The geoboard is comfortable to use because children can so easily "erase" incorrect solutions and construct new ones.

Children find it easy to construct geometric shapes on the pins of a geoboard. The pins help them identify the sides and corners (angles) of shapes, and provide visual clues for measuring. They can measure the length of sides, perimeter, and area of shapes by counting units of length between pins and square units of area bounded by four pins.

When children explore with rubber bands on geoboards, they discover the attributes of polygons. They discover how polygons are alike and different, and the almost limitless ways in which they can be subdivided and combined to make other shapes.

Exploring Math With Geoboards

Following are descriptions of 12 explorations that children can do with the geoboard, and the concepts and skills they will be developing. Reproducible masters for the explorations are given on pages 197-208. Many of the explorations end with an extra challenging puzzle to extend the learning.

1 Copy geometric shapes
The children copy geometric shapes from dot arrays on paper to corresponding pins on their geoboards. The shapes are combined in a way that forms pictures.

2 Count sides of geometric shapes
The children make geometric shapes (polygons) on their geoboards and count the sides of each shape.

3 Count sides and corners of geometric shapes
The children make polygons on their geoboards, and count the sides and corners of the shapes. (You may want to tell the children that a mathematical word for corner is vertex, and the word for corners is vertices.) In this exploration, children will begin to see that the number of sides and number of corners is the same in a polygon.

4 Subdivide geometric shapes to make other shapes
The children make polygons on their geoboards, and connect pins on the boundary of each shape to subdivide it into other shapes.

5 Subdivide geometric shapes to make twin (congruent) shapes
Examples are shown of a hexagon divided into twin shapes. The children make polygons on their geoboards, and connect pins to subdivide each shape into two twin shapes. (You may want to tell the children that the mathematical word for twin is congruent.)

6 Show one half of a shape
Examples are given of 1 square unit of area and $\frac{1}{2}$ square unit of area. The children begin by making a rectangle that has 4 square units of area, then dividing it in half and counting the square units of area in one half. The children go on to make larger rectangles, divide them in half, and count the square units of area in each half.

7 Explore flips and line symmetry
The children begin by folding a square of paper so that one half fits exactly onto the other half. An illustration shows that the fold line can be called a line of symmetry. Then the children find three more ways to fold the square so that one half fits exactly onto the other, and they draw the lines of symmetry they find. The children go on to make shapes on their geoboard, mentally flip the shapes over lines of symmetry, then add the flipped shapes to the shapes on the geoboard to make a whole shape.

8 Explore turns and turn symmetry
The children begin by putting a piece of tape on the top left corner of their geoboard. They make a shape on their geoboard, turn it clockwise one-quarter turn, then compare it with the illustration given. They keep turning the geoboard and draw the shape after each turn. Then they make a triangle on the geoboard, turn it three quarter turns, and draw the triangle in on the dot array after each turn. The children then look at the whole shape (square) made by their turning triangles.

9 Measure length, height, and square units of area in rectangles, using nonstandard units
Examples are given of the unit of length and square unit of area the children will use. The children begin by making rectangles on their geoboards, then counting to find the length and height and square units of area for each rectangle. They go on to make rectangles with given heights and lengths, then count the square units of area.

10 Measure length of perimeter and square units of area in shapes, using nonstandard units
Examples are given of the unit of length, square unit of area, and the perimeter of a shape. The children begin by making shapes on their geoboard, and counting to find the length of the perimeter and the square units of area in each shape. They go on to make shapes with given perimeters, then count the square units of area.

11 Recognize right angles in polygons
Examples are given of right angles. The children make polygons on their geoboard and count the right angles in each one.

12 Identify and extend patterns in growing squares
The children make a series of four squares, with sides 1, 2, 3, and 4 units long. They count the square units of area in the squares, and keep track of the measurements in a table. Then they look for patterns in the ways the squares grow. Children may describe the pattern in many different ways. Some may find visual patterns in the drawings, while others may discover number patterns in the table. They are challenged to extend the pattern to find the length of sides and the square units of area in the seventh square in the series.

Organizing for Geoboard Explorations

Geoboard explorations can be used effectively with the whole class, with small groups, and in learning centers. Each child will need a geoboard and rubber bands in various sizes. Have the students work in pairs. This will encourage them to discuss their thinking and share problem-solving strategies.

Package each geoboard separately with a small plastic bag of rubber bands, including a few each of small, medium, and large sizes.

There is a reproducible master for geoboard dot arrays on page xvi.

Introducing the Geoboard

Let the children begin by just exploring with rubber bands on the geoboard. (Some teachers find it useful to call the rubber bands "geobands," which seems to give them special importance in the minds of children.) They can make many kinds of shapes with the rubber bands. When the children are ready, ask them questions about the geoboard:

What can you tell me about the geoboard?
How many pins are there in the top row?
How many rows of pins are there?
How many pins are there in all?

Draw a large 5-by-5 array of dots on a board, or display the array on an overhead projector. Point to dots, and let the children find the corresponding pins on their geoboards. Then draw a shape on the dots, and let the children copy the shape on their geoboards. Encourage pairs of children to work as partners: one child making a shape on a geoboard, then the other child copying it.

Name: _____

Shapes in Pictures

Geoboards
1

Use: a geoboard and rubber bands

A. Copy the shapes on your geoboard.

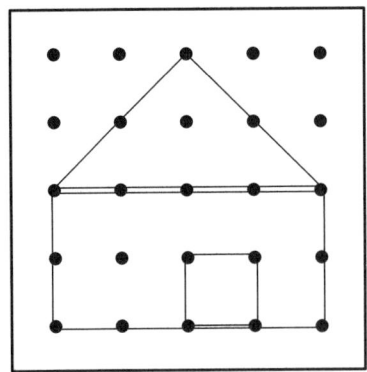 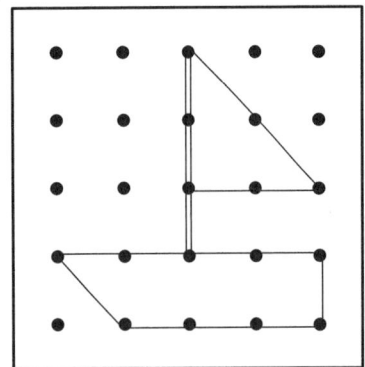

B. Copy the shapes on your geoboard.

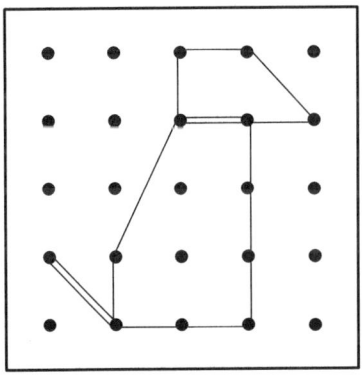 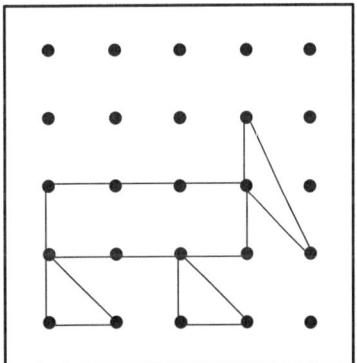

• **Explore Some More**
Make more shapes on your geoboard.

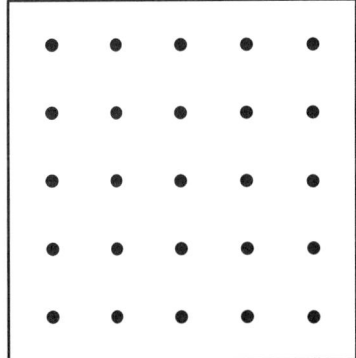

© Ideal School Supply • A Division of Instructional Fair Group, Inc. • Doing Basic Math with Manipulatives, Grades 1-3 - **Skill: Geometry**

Name: _____

Shapes and Sides

Geoboards

2

Use: a geoboard and rubber bands

A. Copy each shape on your geoboard. Count the sides.

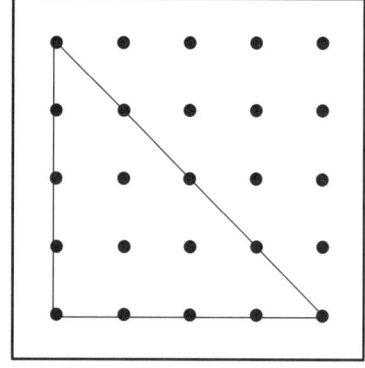 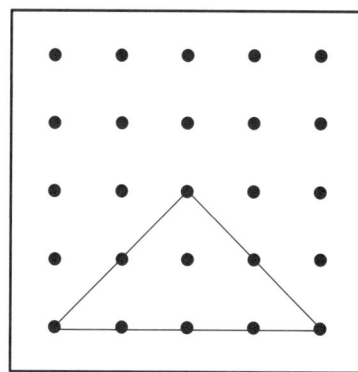

sides __3__   sides _____

B. Make each shape on your geoboard. Count the sides.

   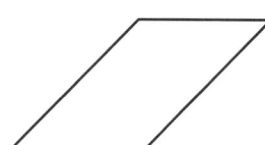

sides _____   sides _____

- **Extra Challenge**
  If you connect the pins shown, how many sides do you think the shape will have?

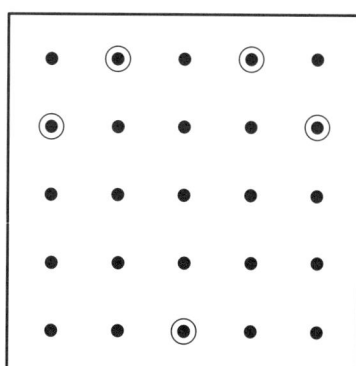

198 © Ideal School Supply • A Division of Instructional Fair Group, Inc. • Doing Basic Math with Manipulatives, Grades 1-3 - **Skill: Geometry**

Name: _____

Sides and Corners

Geoboards
3

Use: a geoboard and rubber bands

A. Copy each shape on your geoboard.
Count the sides. Count the corners.

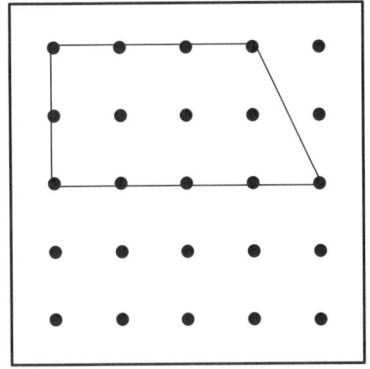 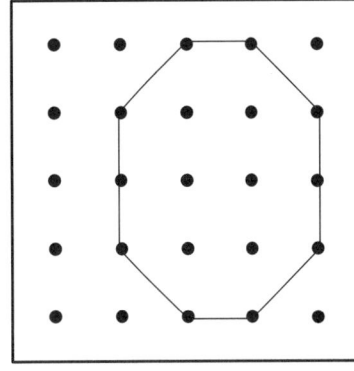

sides ____ corners __4__   sides ____ corners ____

B. Make each shape on your geoboard.
Count the sides. Count the corners.

 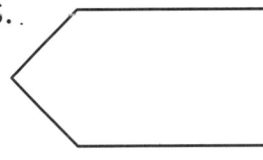

sides ____ corners ____   sides ____ corners ____

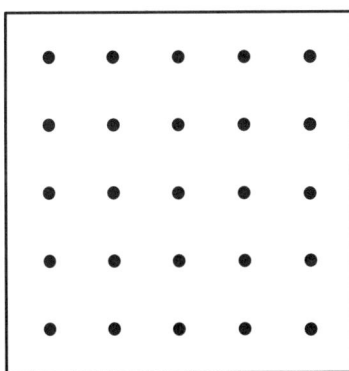

- **Extra Challenge**
  On your geoboard, make a shape that has 6 corners. How many sides do you think it will have?

199

Shapes Inside Shapes

Name: _____

Geoboards

4

Use: a geoboard and rubber bands

A. Copy each shape on your geoboard.
Then connect the two pins shown.
What new shapes are inside? Draw them.

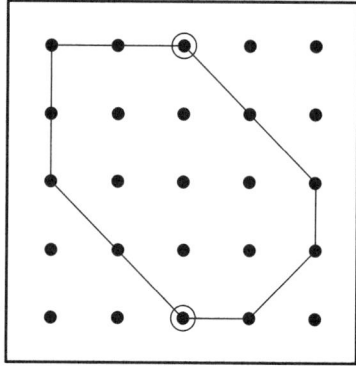 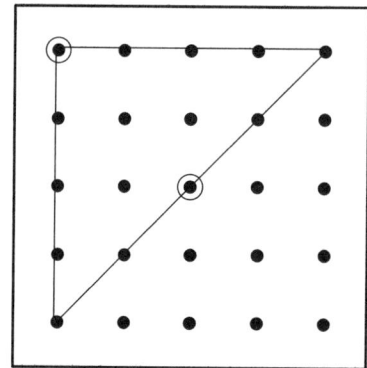

B. Copy each shape on your geoboard.
Choose two pins in each shape. Connect the pins.
Draw the new shapes inside.

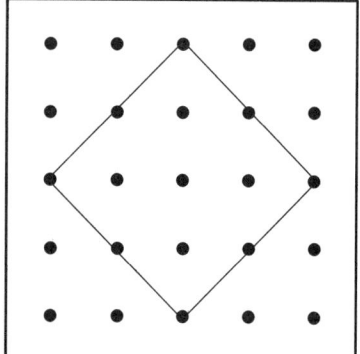 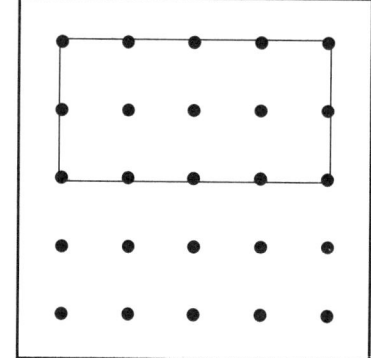

- **Extra Challenge**
  On your geoboard, make a shape that has 6 sides. Can you connect pins to make two shapes inside that have 5 sides?

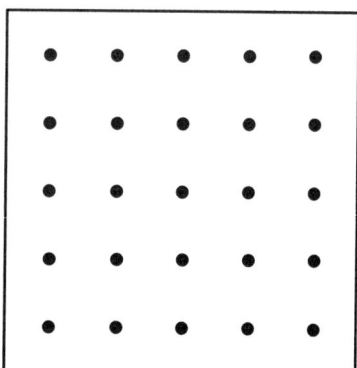

Name: _____

Twin Shapes Inside

Geoboards

5

Use: a geoboard and rubber bands

twin shapes

A. Copy each shape on your geoboard. Then connect two pins to make twin shapes inside. **Twin shapes** are the same size and the same shape. Draw the shapes.

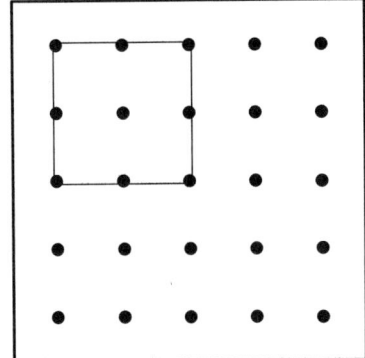 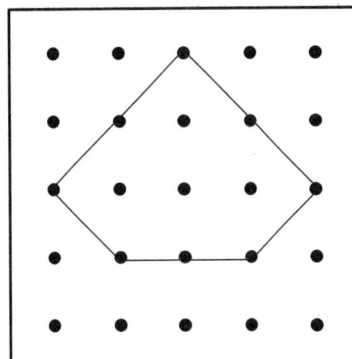

B. Copy this shape on your geoboard. Find two ways to connect two pins to make twin shapes inside. Draw the ways.

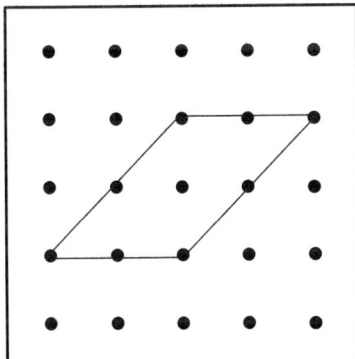 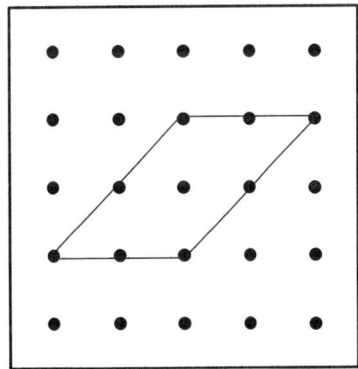

- **Explore Some More**
  Make a new shape on your geoboard.
  Connect 2 pins to make twin shapes inside.

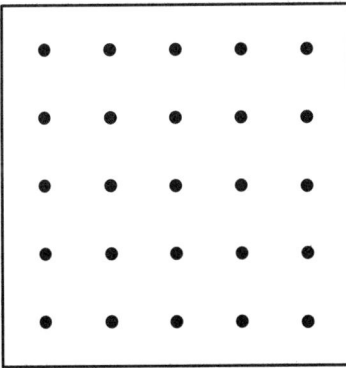

Half the Space

Name: _____

Geoboards

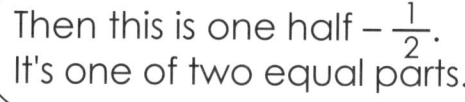

Use: a geoboard and rubber bands

This is one square of space.

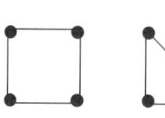

Then this is one half – $\frac{1}{2}$. It's one of two equal parts.

A. Make this shape on your geoboard. How many squares of space are there in it? _____

With another rubber band, divide the shape into two equal parts. How many squares of space are there in each half? _____

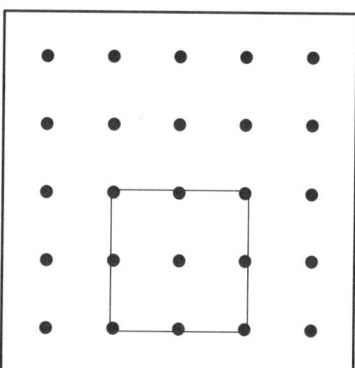

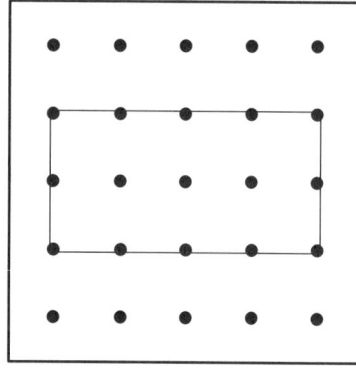

B. Make this shape on your geoboard. How many squares of space are there in it? _____

Divide the shape into two equal parts. How many squares of space are there in each half? _____

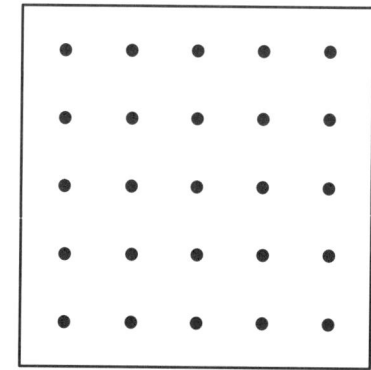

• **Extra Challenge**
Make a shape that has 16 squares of space. Divide the shape in half. How many squares of space in one half?

Name: _____

Flip the Shapes

Geoboards

7

Use: a geoboard, rubber bands, and a square of paper

A. Fold the square of paper in half so that one half fits onto the other half exactly.

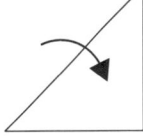

The line of the fold is called a **line of symmetry**.

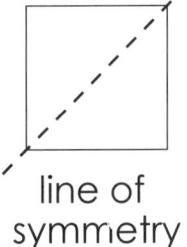
line of symmetry

Find three more ways to fold the square so that one half fits exactly on top of the other half. Draw the lines of symmetry.

B. Make each shape on your geoboard. In your mind, flip it over the dotted line. Then make it on the geoboard. Draw the shapes.

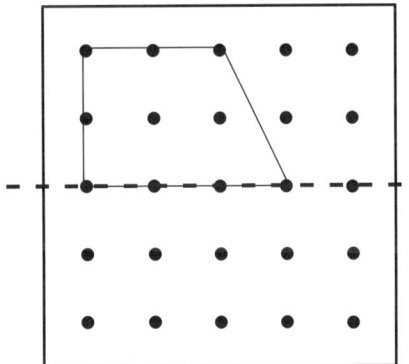   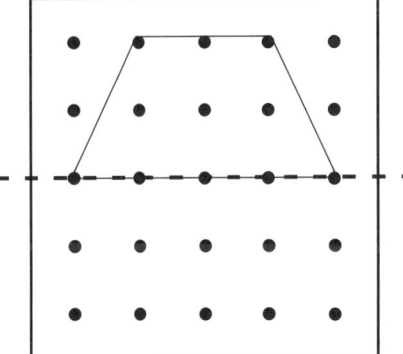

- **Extra Challenge**
  Look at the 6-sided hexagon you made in part B. Can you find more lines of symmetry in it?

Name: _____

Turn the Shapes

Geoboards
8

Use: a geoboard, rubber bands, and a small piece of tape

• Put the piece of tape on the top left corner of your geoboard.

A. Copy the shape on your geoboard. Then turn the geoboard clockwise until the tape is in each place shown. Draw the shape after each turn.

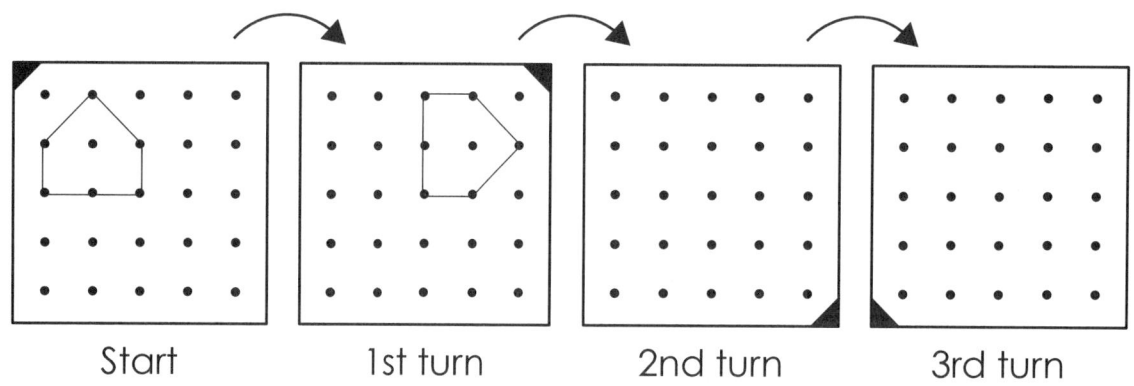

Start   1st turn   2nd turn   3rd turn

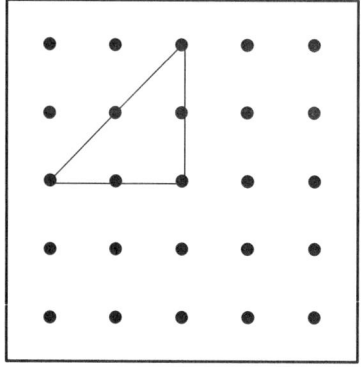

B. Copy the shape on your geoboard. Turn the geoboard three times. Draw the shape after each turn.

What new shape did you make?

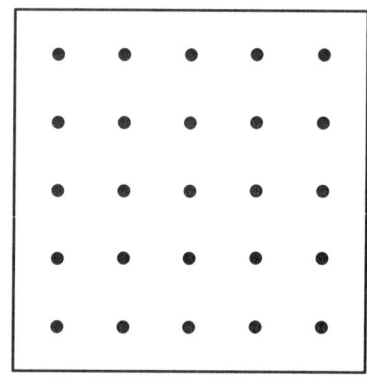

• **Explore Some More**
Make a shape on your geoboard. Turn the geoboard three times. Draw the shape each time.

204   © Ideal School Supply • A Division of Instructional Fair Group, Inc. • Doing Basic Math with Manipulatives, Grades 1–3 - **Skill: Geometry**

Rectangle Roundup

Name: _____

Geoboards

Use: a geoboard and rubber bands

This square is 1 unit high and 1 unit long. It has 1 square unit of area inside the rubber band.

A. Make each rectangle on your geoboard.
How high is it? How long is it?
How many square units of area?

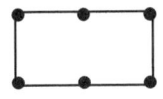

____ units high
____ units long
____ square units of area

____ units high
____ units long
____ square units of area

B. Make each rectangle on your geoboard.
Count the squares. Draw the rectangle.

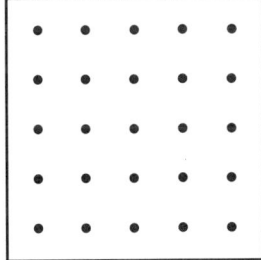

2 units high
3 units long
____ square units of area

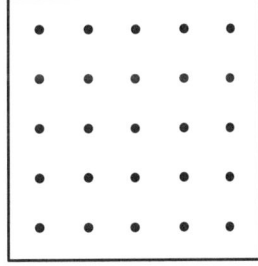

3 units high
3 units long
____ square units of area

- **Mystery Shape Puzzle**
  I am a rectangle.
  I am 2 units high.
  I have 8 square units of area.
  What do I look like?

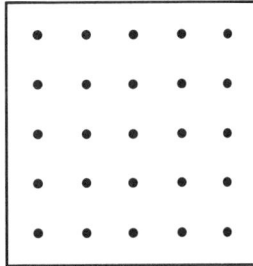

Inside and Outside

Name: _____

Geoboards
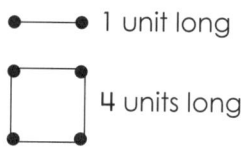

Use: a geoboard and rubber bands

- The perimeter of this square is 4 units long. **Perimeter** is the distance around the outside of a shape.

A. Make each shape on your geoboard.
How long is the perimeter?
How many square units of area in the shape?

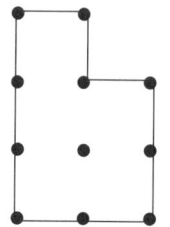

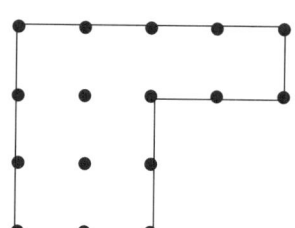

perimeter ____ units long
____ square units of area

perimeter ____ units long
____ square units of area

B. Make the shape on your geoboard. Draw it.
Count the square units of area in it.

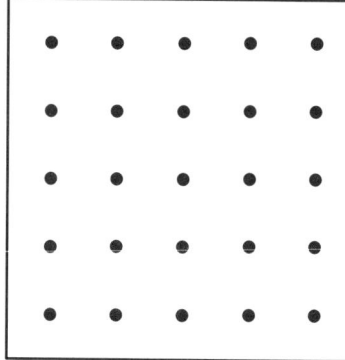

perimeter 12 units long
____ square units of area

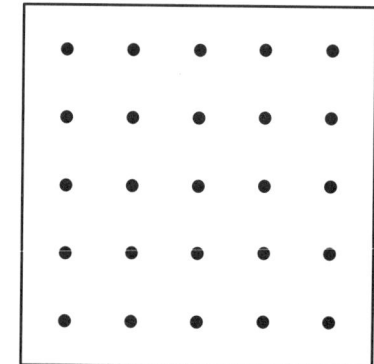

- **Mystery Shape Puzzle**
I am a rectangle.
My perimeter is 10 units long.
What do I look like?

Right Angles

Name: _____

Geoboards

Use: a geoboard and rubber bands

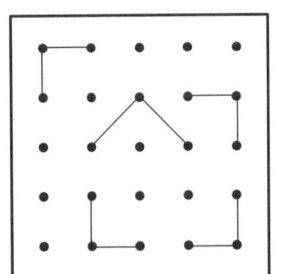 right angles

These are all **right angles**. Right angles look like square corners.

A. Make each rectangle on your geoboard.
How many right angles are there in each rectangle?

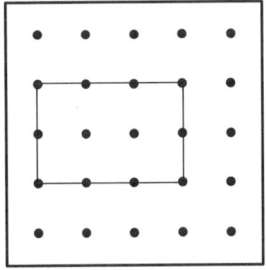

____ right angles

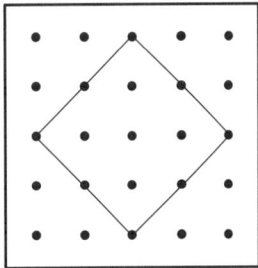

____ right angles

B. Make each shape on your geoboard.
How many right angles are there in each shape?

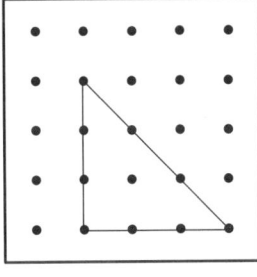

____ right angles

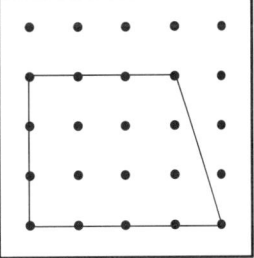

____ right angles

- **Extra Challenge**
  Make one of these shapes on your geoboard.
  - A pentagon with 5 sides and 3 right angles
  - A hexagon with 6 sides and 2 right angles

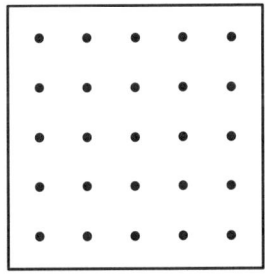

Growing Squares

Name: _____

Geoboards

12

Use: a geoboard and rubber bands

- Make each square on your geoboard.
  How long are the sides?
  How many square units of area in it?
  Keep track in the table.
  Look for a pattern in how the squares grow.
  Make the next larger square.

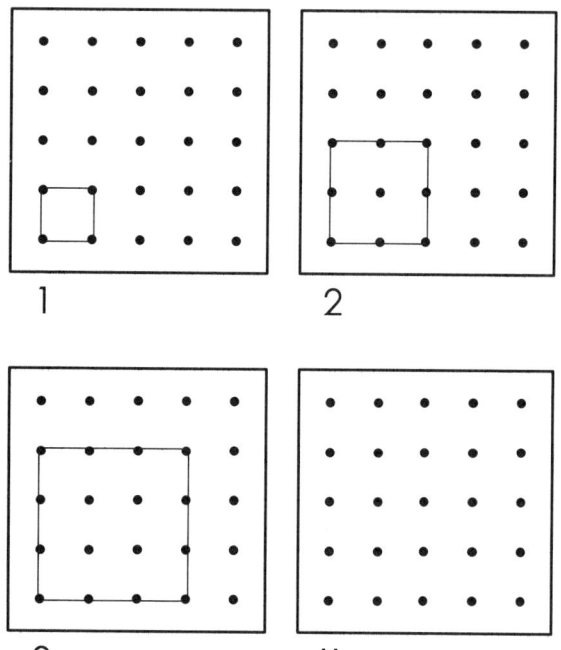

Square	Sides Units long	Area Square units
1	1	1

- What pattern did you find?

- **Extra Challenge**
  If you could make a square with sides 7 units long,
  how many square units of area would it have?
  How do you know?

3-D Shapes

3-D Shapes help children develop these concepts and skills:

Geometry and Spatial Sense
- Recognize two- and three-dimensional geometric shapes
- Identify 3-D shapes that roll and stack
- Count faces, edges, and corners of 3-D shapes
- Identify shapes of faces on 3-D shapes
- Sort and classify shapes by their attributes
- Recognize congruent shapes
- Identify jackets (nets) of 3-D shapes
- Recognize geometric shapes in the world

Measurement
- Measure length and area, using nonstandard units

Problem Solving
- Use visualization and spatial reasoning to solve problems
- Use logical reasoning to solve problems

What Are 3-D Shapes?

The set of 3-D shapes includes 10 plastic three-dimensional shapes, also known as geometric solids and space shapes. Each 3-D shape is unique, but shares attributes with other shapes.

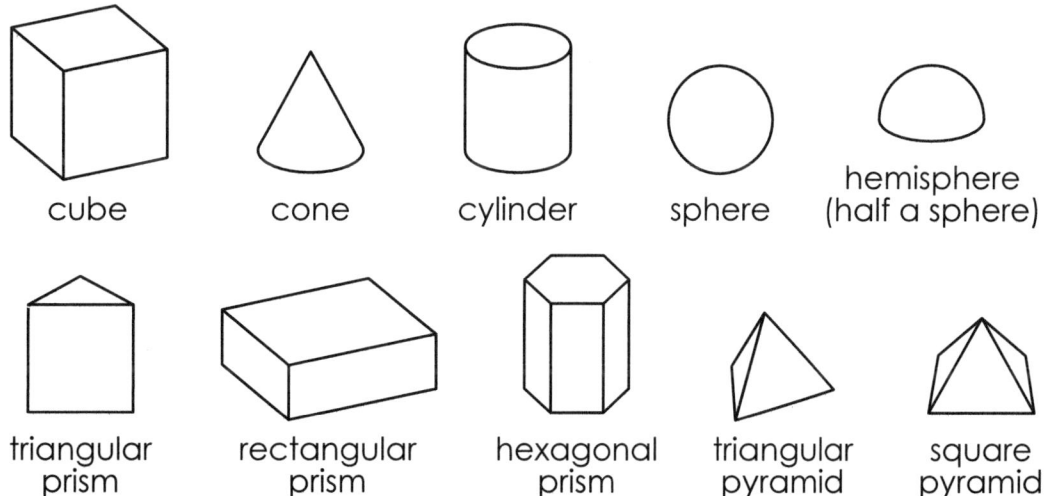

Why Use 3-D Shapes?

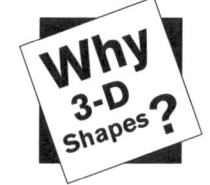

3-D Shapes are excellent models for children to use to explore three-dimensional geometry in an informal way. These small versions of geometric solids are attractive and easy for young children to hold in their hands. Students can learn to recognize attributes of the solids, such as the shapes of faces, the numbers of faces and corners and edges, and the flat and curved surfaces. Students can compare the solids to find how they are alike and different. They can sort and classify the shapes in many ways according to their attributes.

As children become familiar with the 3-D Shapes, they will begin to find similar geometric shapes in objects all around them. They will see the shapes in cans, cereal boxes, ice cream cones, balls, and in buildings and other structures. They will begin to recognize that the same shape may look different when viewed from various perspectives.

Exploring Math With 3-D Shapes

Following are descriptions of 12 explorations that children can do with the 3-D Shapes, and the concepts and skills they will be developing. Reproducible masters for the explorations are given on pages 213-224. Many of the explorations end with extra challenging puzzles to extend the learning.

1. **Find which 3-D shapes roll and which ones stack**
   The children try rolling each of the 3-D shapes, and write R on the picture of the shape if it rolls. Then the children try stacking each of the 3-D shapes, and write S on the pictures of those which stack. This exploration introduces the children to the flat and curved surfaces of the 3-D shapes.

2. **Count faces on 3-D shapes**
   An illustration introduces the concept of flat faces on 3-D shapes. The children count the faces on each 3-D shape. Children may need help in marking faces as they count them, so that they don't miss a face or count one more than once.

3. **Identify shapes of faces: circle, triangle, and square**
   The children begin by finding all 3-D shapes that have circle-shaped faces. Then they find all 3-D shapes that have triangle-shaped faces and square faces.

4 Identify shapes of faces: hexagon and rectangles
The children begin by finding all 3-D shapes that have hexagon-shaped faces. Then they find all 3-D shapes that have faces that are rectangles. Children often hold the misconception that squares are not rectangles. So as they do this exploration, you may want to talk about squares being special rectangles that have sides that are all the same length.

5 Sort 3-D shapes according to their attributes
The children begin with all ten 3-D shapes, then sort them out as they read through a series of clues. They eliminate 3-D shapes that do not fit the clues, until they can identify the remaining shape.

6 Sort 3-D shapes by the shapes of their faces
The children find the 3-D shapes that belong in a circle for triangle-shaped faces. Then they find the 3-D shapes that belong in a circle for square faces. Finally they find the 3-D shapes that belong in both circles, in the space where the circles overlap.

7 Count edges on 3-D shapes
An illustration introduces the children to the concept of edges on 3-D shapes. The children count the edges on each shape.

8 Identify jackets (nets) of 3-D shapes
An illustration of a "jacket" introduces the children informally to covering surface area on 3-D shapes. The children look at the jacket and predict which 3-D shape it fits. Then they check by tracing the jacket on a sheet of paper, cutting it out, folding it, and fitting it around the shape.

9 Identify jackets (nets) of 3-D shapes
Two jackets are shown, and the children predict which 3-D shapes the jackets fit. They check by tracing the jackets, cutting them out, folding them, and fitting them around the shapes.

10 Count corners on 3-D shapes
An illustration introduces the children to the concept of corners on 3-D shapes. The children identify and count the corners on each shape.

11 Use attribute clues to identify 3-D shapes
The children use clues about faces, edges, corners, and other attributes to identify four 3-D shapes.

12 Sort 3-D shapes according to their attributes
The children begin with all ten 3-D shapes, then sort them out as they read a series of clues. They eliminate 3-D shapes that do not fit the clues, until they can identify the remaining shape.

Organizing for 3-D Shapes Explorations

3-D Shapes explorations can be used effectively with the whole class, with small groups, and in learning centers. Have the children work in pairs, sharing materials. Working as partners will encourage students to discuss their thinking and share problem-solving strategies. Each pair should have a set of the ten 3-D Shapes. Package each set separately in a plastic bag or container. This will help children check to be sure the set is complete.

Introducing the 3-D Shapes

Let the children begin by just exploring and playing with the 3-D shapes. They can stack them in towers or sort them into groups. When the children are ready, ask them questions about the shapes:

> What can you tell me about the 3-D shapes?
> How many different shapes do you see?
> Can you find two shapes that are alike in some way?
>   How are they alike?
> Sort your shapes into two groups. How are the shapes alike in
>   each group?
> Do any of these shapes look like shapes you've seen before?

You can introduce the mathematical names of the shapes, or let the children use their own descriptive names until they become more familiar with the pieces.

Children will also enjoy playing a Mystery Shape Game with the 3-D shapes. Put a complete set of the shapes where the children can see them. Put another set of 3-D shapes into a paper bag. Let the children take turns feeling one of the shapes in the bag, describing it, pointing it out in the displayed set, then taking it out of the bag to check. The children can play this game before they begin the explorations and at any time during the explorations.

Name: _____

Can You Roll It? Can You Stack It?

Use: the 3-D shapes

A. Which 3-D shapes can you roll?
Write R on their pictures.

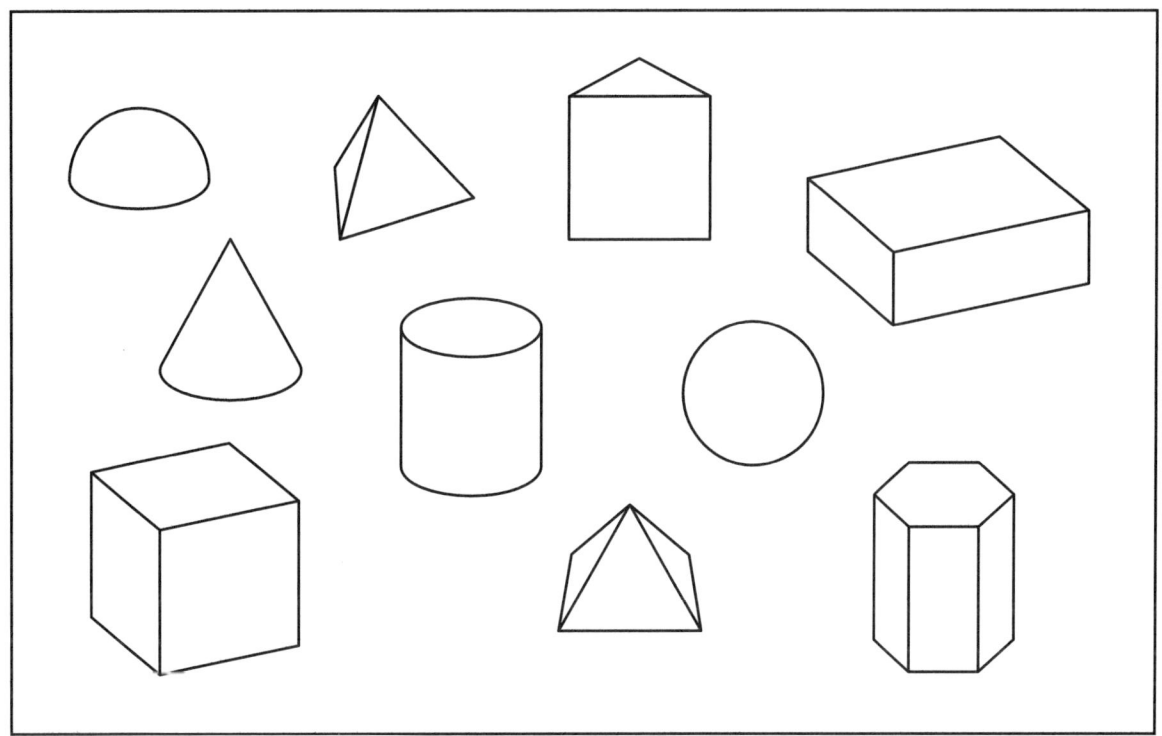

B. Which 3-D shapes can you stack?
Write S on their pictures above.

- **Mystery Shape Puzzle**
  You can roll me and stack me.
  I look like a drum.
  What 3-D shape am I?

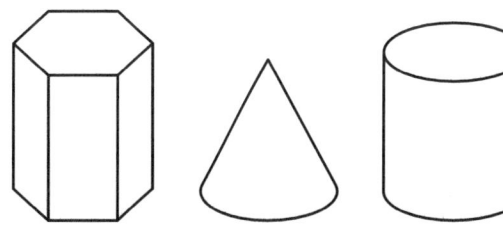

How Many Faces?

Name: _____

3-D Shapes

Use: the 3-D shapes

A flat shape on a 3-D shape is called a **face**. The cube has 6 faces.

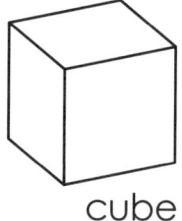

cube

- How many faces does each 3-D shape have? Write the number.

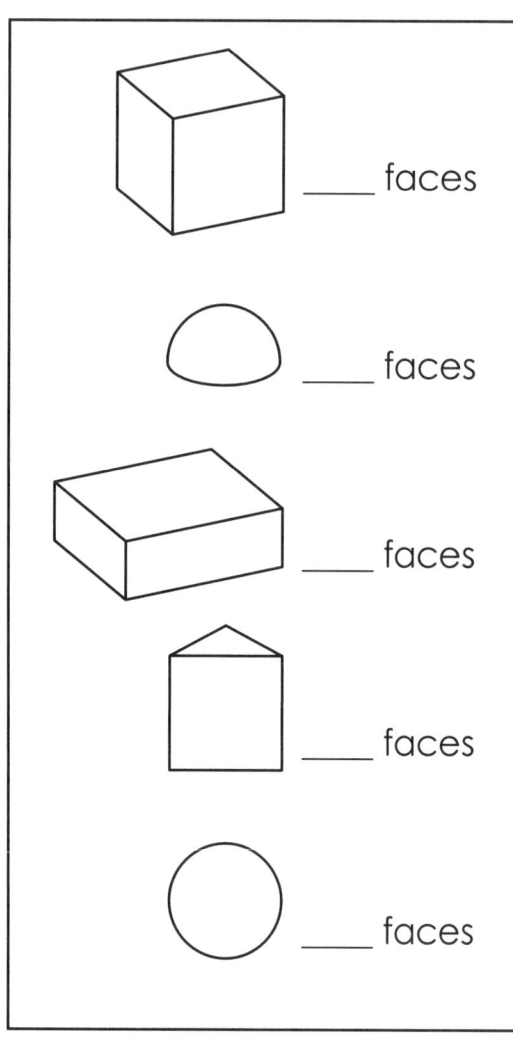

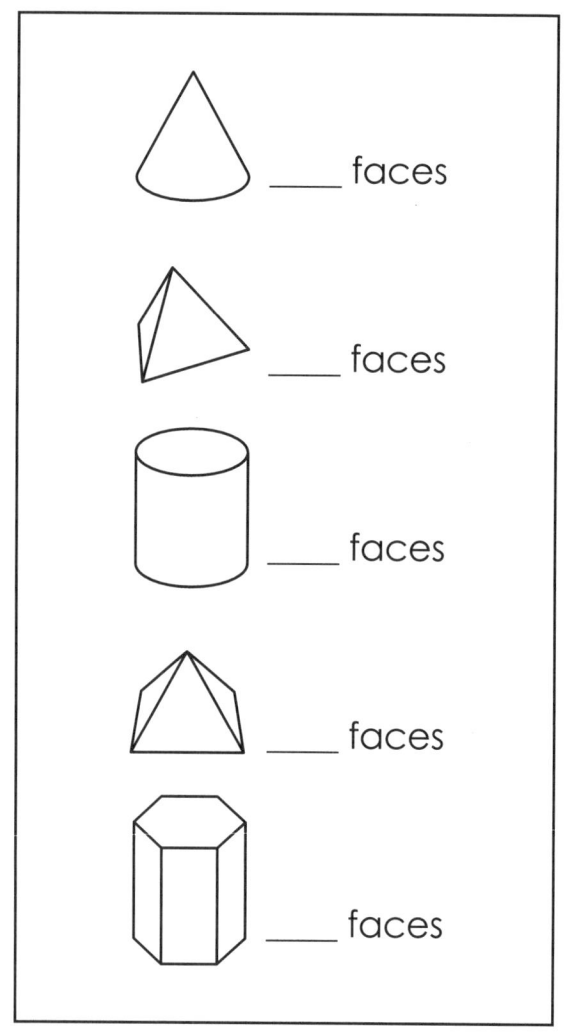

- **Mystery Shapes Puzzle**
  We each have one flat face. If you put us together, we look like an ice cream cone. Which two 3-D shapes are we?

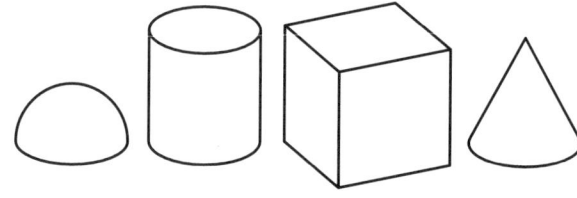

214 © Ideal School Supply • A Division of Instructional Fair Group, Inc. • Doing Basic Math with Manipulatives, Grades 1-3 - **Skill:** Geometry

Name: _____

What Shapes Are Our Faces?

3-D Shapes
3

Use: the 3-D shapes

A. Which 3-D shapes have faces that match this flat shape? Mark each shape.

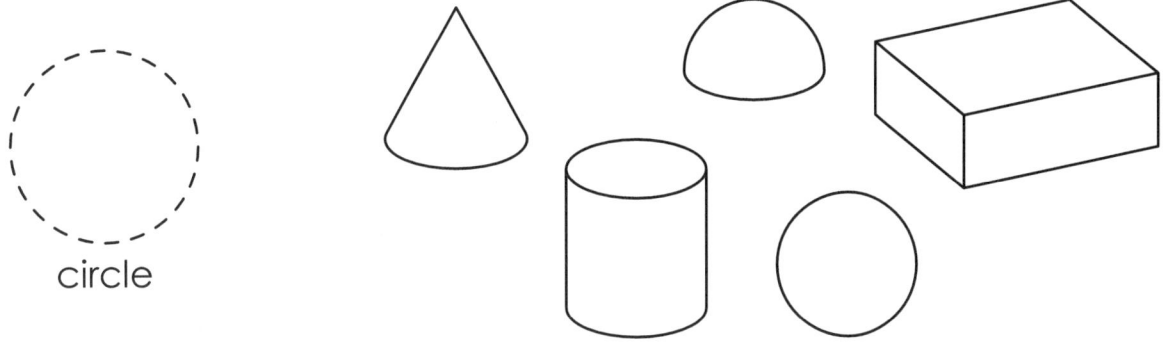

circle

B. Which 3-D shapes have faces that match these flat shapes? Mark each shape. Mark it twice if it matches both flat shapes.

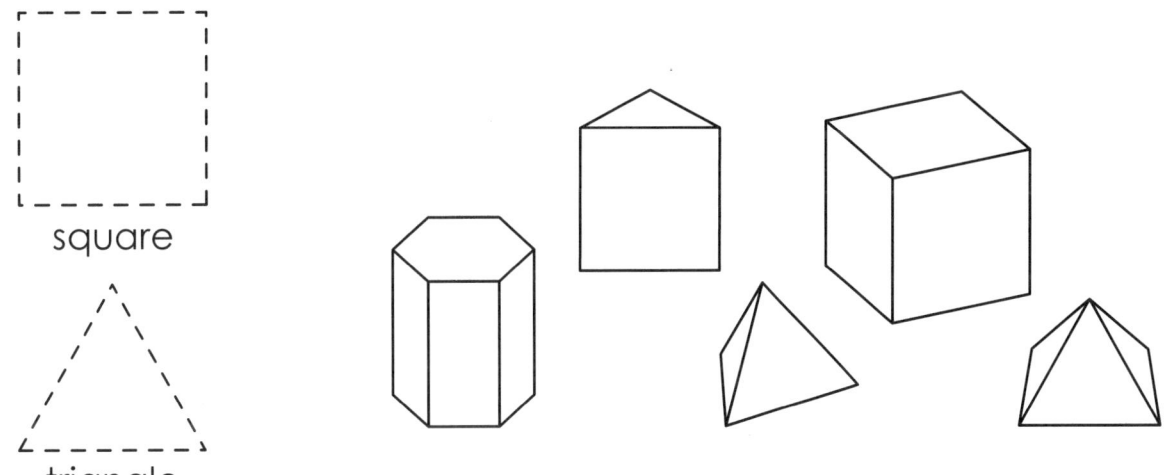

square

triangle

- **Explore Some More**
  Choose a 3-D shape. Draw around the flat shapes of its faces. Let a friend find your mystery 3-D shape.

Name: _____

Shapes of Faces

3-D Shapes

Use: the 3-D shapes

A. Which 3-D shapes have faces that match this flat shape? Mark each shape.

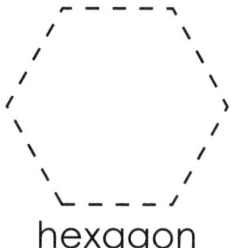
hexagon

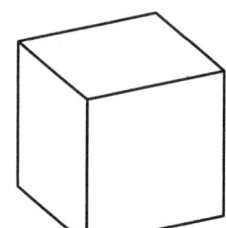
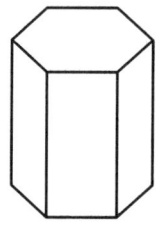

B. Which 3-D shapes have faces that match these flat shapes? Mark each shape.

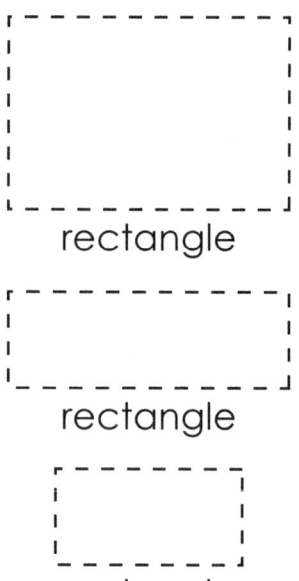
rectangle

rectangle

rectangle

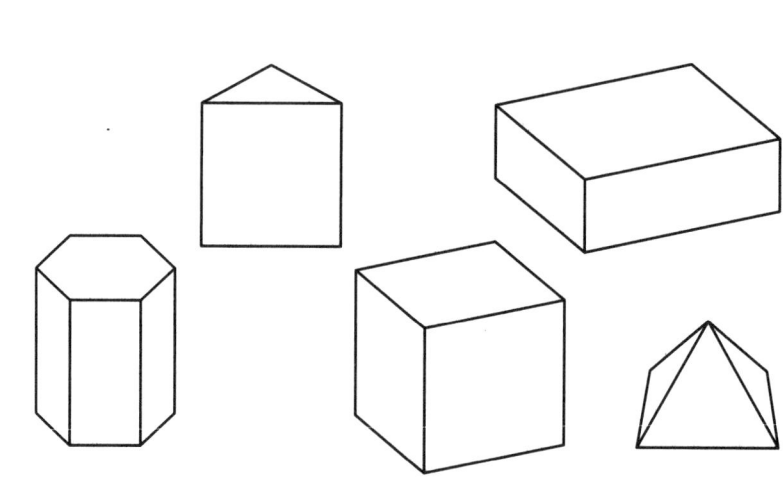

- **Mystery Shape Puzzle**
  I have 2 faces of one shape.
  I have 3 faces of another shape.
  Which 3-D shape am I?

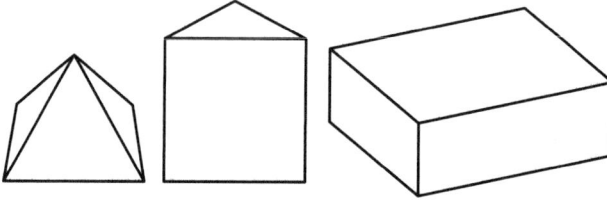

216

Name: _____

Follow the Clues

3-D Shapes
5

Use: the 3-D shapes

- Follow the clues. Cross out all the 3-D shapes that do not fit. Find the 3-D shape that is left.

CLUES

- It has more than one face.

- You can't roll it.
  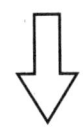
- It has an even number of faces.
  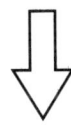
- All of its faces are rectangles.

- The rectangles are not squares.

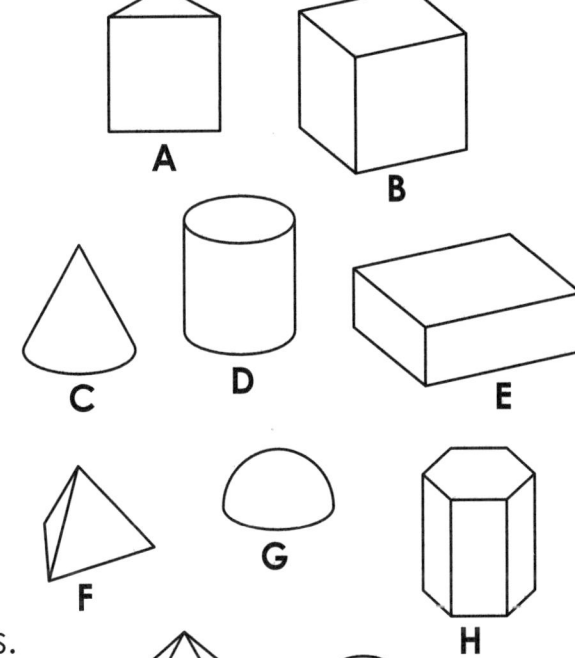

Which 3-D shape is left? _____

- **Extra Challenge**
  If the last clue said the rectangles were squares, which 3-D shape would be left?

© Ideal School Supply • A Division of Instructional Fair Group, Inc. • Doing Basic Math with Manipulatives, Grades 1-3 - **Skill: Sorting**

Rules for Circles

Name: _____

3-D Shapes

Use: the 3-D shapes

- Look at the rule for each circle. Put 3-D shapes in the circles where they belong. If a 3-D shape belongs in both circles, put it in the space where the circles overlap.

Rule: ☐ face   **Rule:** △ face

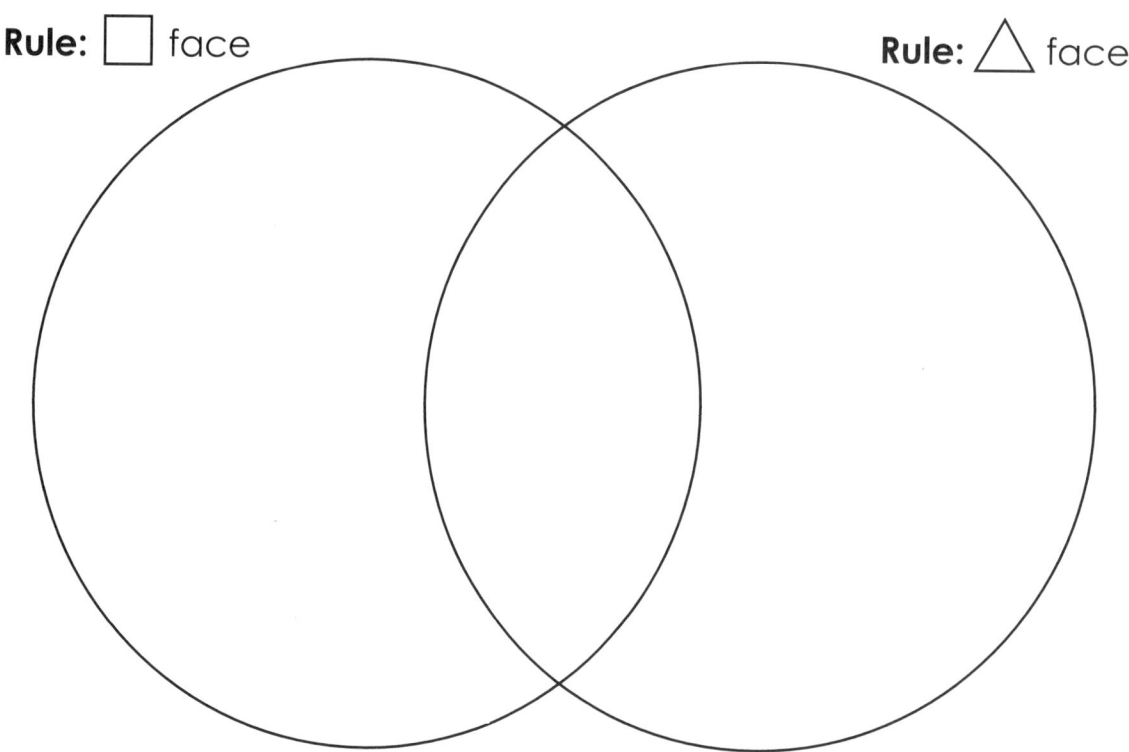

- Which 3-D shapes did you put in the circles? Write their letters in the parts of the circles.

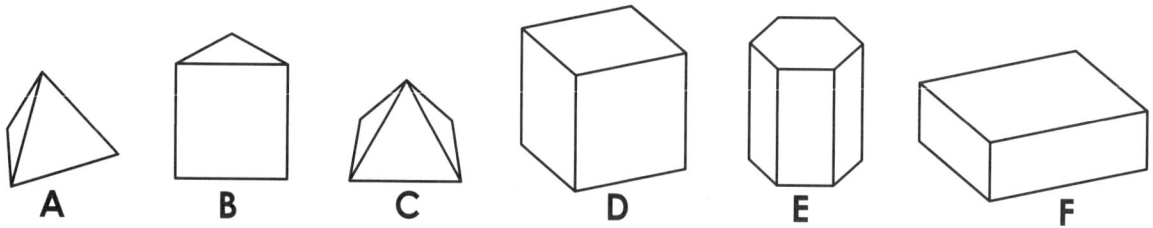

A   B   C   D   E   F

- **Mystery Shape Puzzle**
  All of my faces have 4 sides. My edges are not all the same length. Which 3-D shape am I?

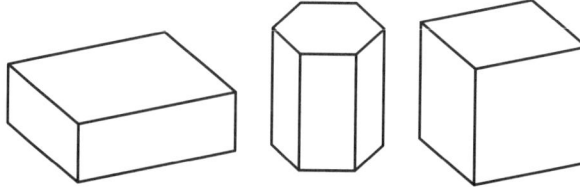

Edges

Name: _____

3-D Shapes

Use: the 3-D shapes

An **edge** is made where 2 faces come together. The rectangular prism has 12 edges.

rectangular prism

- How many edges does each 3-D shape have? Write the number.

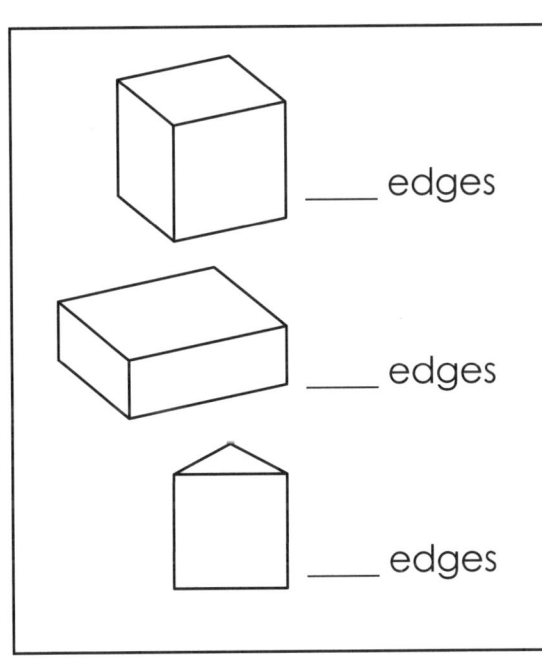

___ edges

___ edges

___ edges

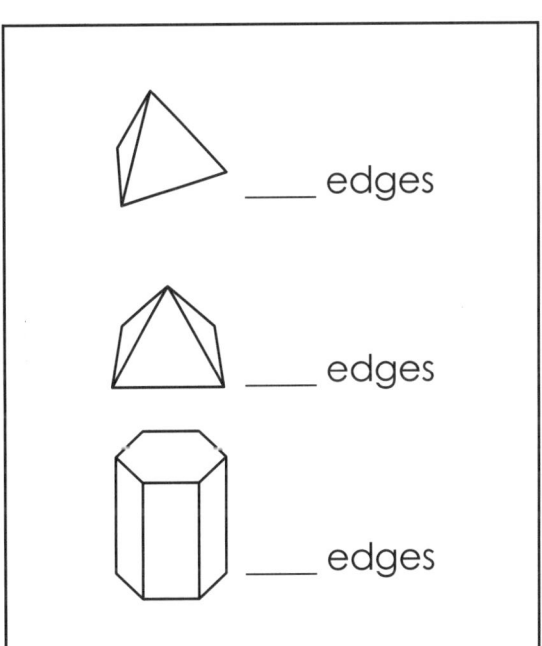

___ edges

___ edges

___ edges

- **Mystery Shapes Puzzle**
  We have twice as many edges as faces. Which 3-D shapes are we?

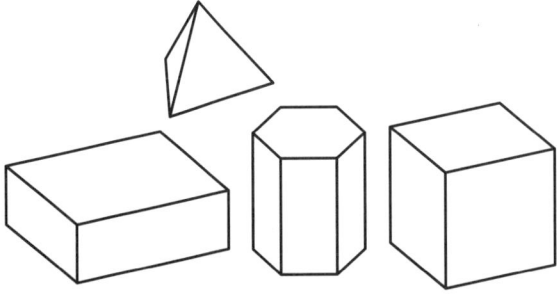

Name: _____

Whose Jacket Is It?

3-D Shapes

Use: the 3-D shapes, a sheet of paper, and scissors

- This is a jacket for a 3-D shape. If you could cut it out and fold it on the dotted lines, it would cover the whole 3-D shape.

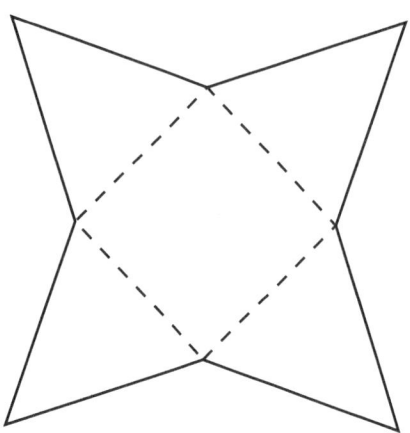

- What 3-D shape do you think this jacket fits? _____

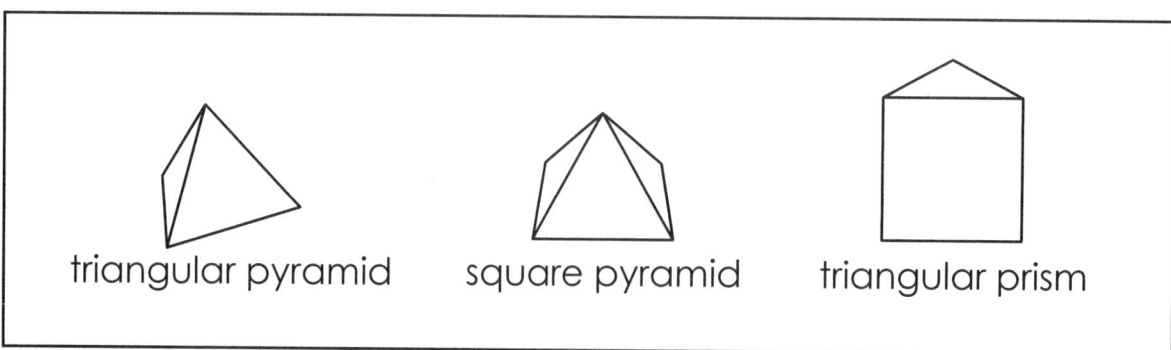

triangular pyramid   square pyramid   triangular prism

- **Check Your Answer**
  Put a sheet of paper over the jacket. Trace the outside of the shape and the dotted lines. Cut out the jacket and fold it on the dotted lines. Does it fit?

Name: _____

More Jackets

3-D Shapes
9

Use: the 3-D shapes, a sheet of paper, and scissors

- Find the 3-D shapes that the jackets fit.

A.

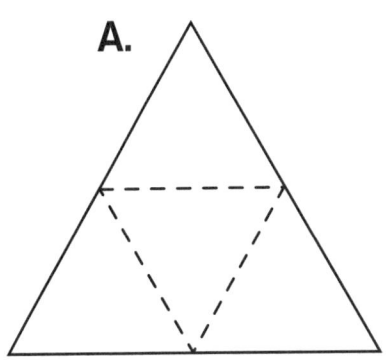

Which 3-D shape do you think this jacket fits? _____

B.

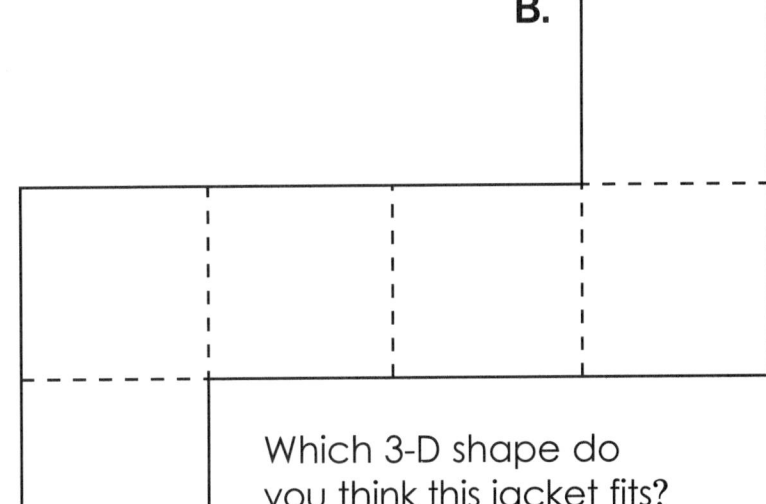

Which 3-D shape do you think this jacket fits? _____

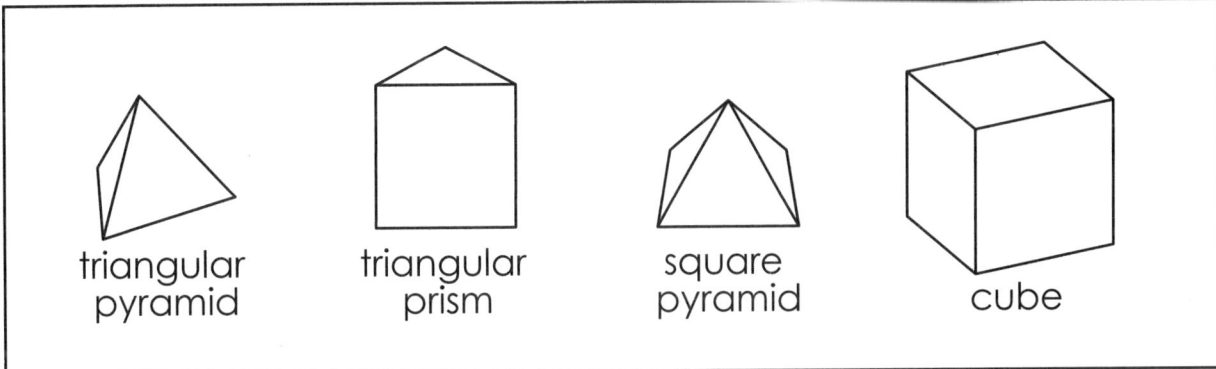

triangular pyramid   triangular prism   square pyramid   cube

- **Check Your Answers**
    Put a sheet of paper over the jackets. Trace the outside of each shape and the dotted lines. Cut out the jackets and fold them on the dotted lines. Do they fit?

Corners

Name: _____

3-D Shapes

Use: the 3-D shapes

- A **corner** is made where edges come together. The square pyramid has 5 corners.

square pyramid

- How many corners does each 3-D shape have? Write the number.

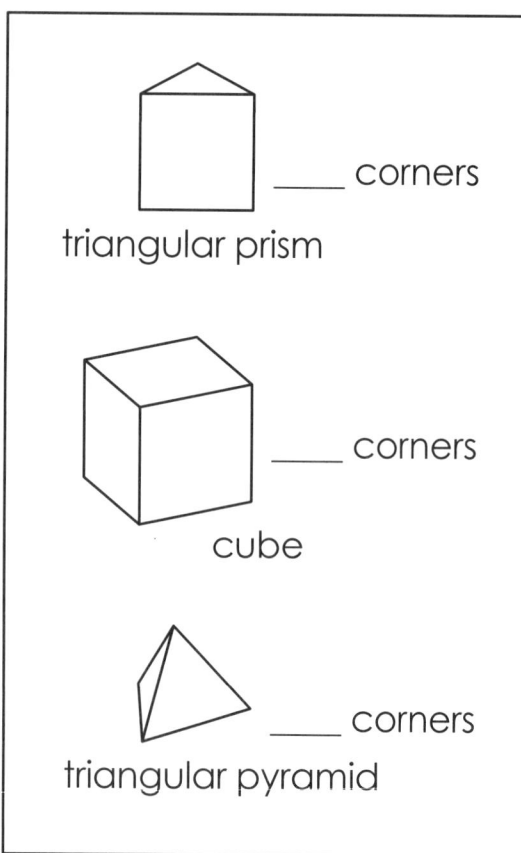

___ corners
triangular prism

___ corners
cube

___ corners
triangular pyramid

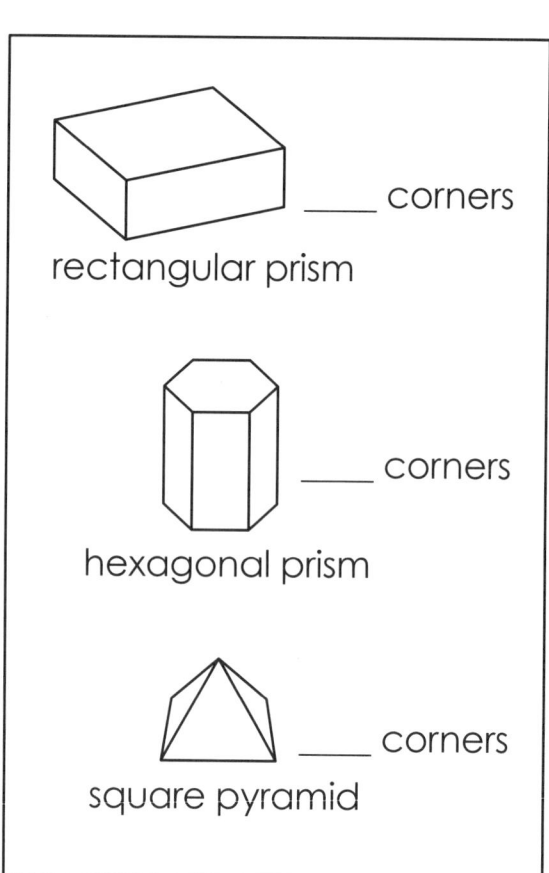

___ corners
rectangular prism

___ corners
hexagonal prism

___ corners
square pyramid

- **Mystery Shape Puzzle**
  I have the same number of corners as faces.
  I have 3 more edges than corners.
  Which 3-D shape am I?

Mystery Shape Puzzles

Name: _____

3-D Shapes

Use: the 3-D shapes

A. My top and bottom faces are the same shape.
I have no corners.
Which 3-D shape am I?

_____

B. I have 1 flat face.
You can roll me.
I roll like this:

Which 3-D shape am I?

_____

C. I have 8 corners.
I have twice as many edges as faces.
The sides of my faces are all the same length.
Which 3-D shape am I?

_____

D. We both have 2 shapes of faces.
One of those shapes has 3 sides.
The other shape has 4 sides.
Which 3-D shapes are we?

_____
_____

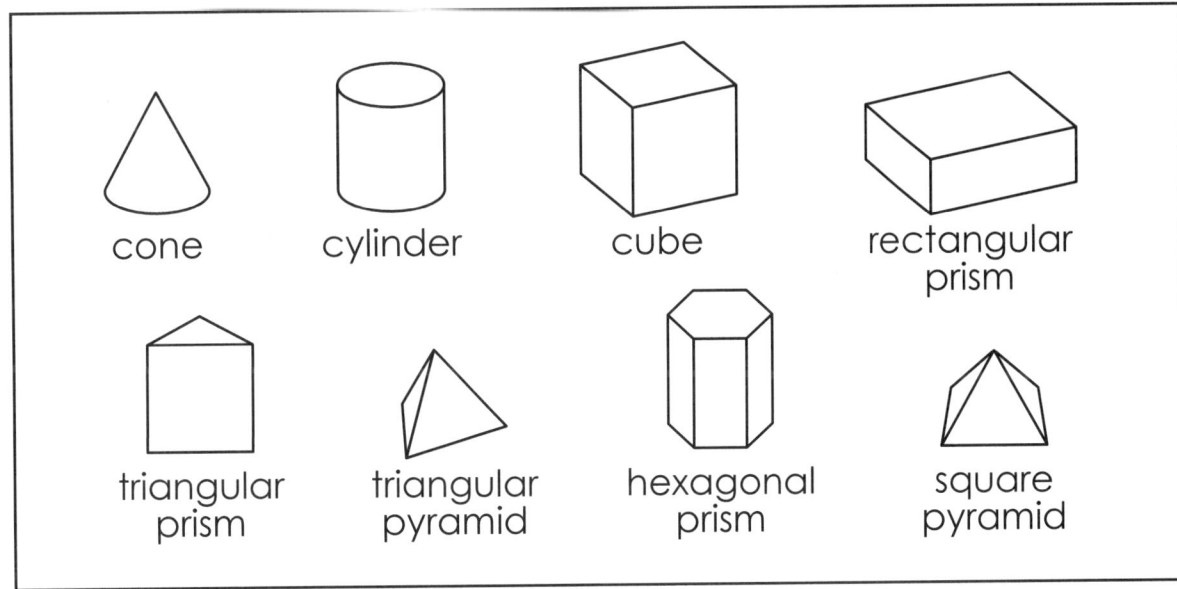

- **Extra Challenge**
Write clues about a 3-D shape.
Let someone solve your mystery puzzle.

Follow the Clues

3-D Shapes

Use: the 3-D shapes

- Follow the clues. Cross out all the 3-D shapes that do not fit. Find the 3-D shape that is left.

CLUES

- It has an even number of corners.

- Its faces are not all the same shape and size.

- It has an even number of faces.

- Some of its faces have 6 sides.

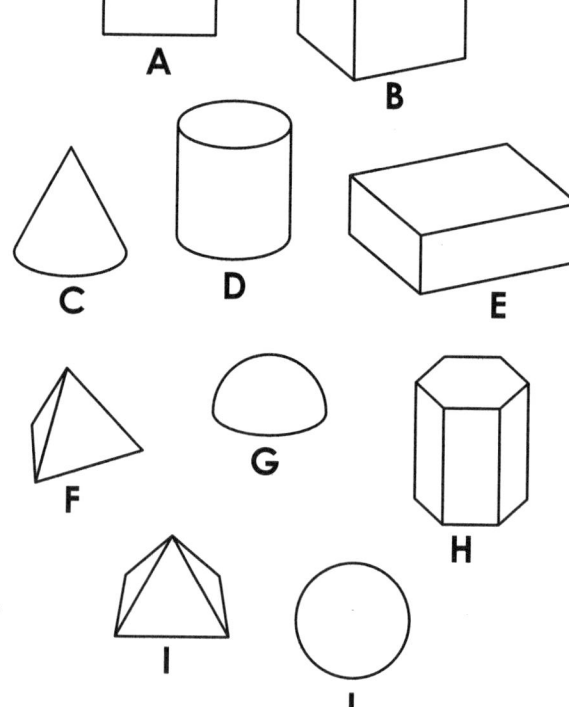

Which 3-D shape is left? _____

- **Extra Challenge**
  If the last clue said that none of its faces had 6 sides, which 3-D shape would be left?